The
BIG
BOOK
of
Amaro

The

BIG
BOOK

of

Amaro

THE COUNTRYMAN PRESS

A Division of

W. W. Norton & Company

Independent Publishers

Since 1923

MATTEO ZED

Originally published in Italian as *Il Grande Libro Dell'Amaro Italiano*
Translation by Kosmos srl 2020
Texts and images: Matteo Zed (unless otherwise indicated below)
Editorial realization: Plan.ed srl (Rome)
Editorial collaboration: Daniela Dioguardi
www.giunti.it

All images belong to the author except on the pages listed below:
Andrea Savelli: XI, 8, 72, 194, 201, 202, 204, 206, 208, 211, 212, 215,
216, 218, 221, 223, 224, 227, 228, 233, 234, 237, 238, 239, 241
Alberto Blasetti: II, 3, 4–5, 7, 13, 23, 24, 27, 35, 36, 39, 40, 41, 47
(all), 49, 50, 52, 56, 59, 60, 62, 64, 67, 69, 75, 188
Shutterstock: AKaiser: flourishes and borders, throughout; Milanchikov Sergey: 18;
jorisvo: 22; pisitpong2017: 48; cuttlefish84: 53; wasanajai: 55
Alamy/IPA: 6, 16, 17 (both), 21, 22, 30
Getty Images: 10, 44
Archivio Giunti/Bernardo Ticli: 37
Daniele Pace: 197

For information about permission to reproduce selections from this book, write to
Permissions, The Countryman Press, 500 Fifth Avenue, New York, NY 10110

For information about special discounts for bulk purchases, please contact
W. W. Norton Special Sales at specialsales@wwnorton.com or 800-233-4830

Manufacturing by Toppan Leefung Pte. Ltd.
Book design by Raphael Geroni
Production manager: Devon Zahn

Library of Congress Cataloging-in-Publication Data

Names: Zed, Matteo, author.
Title: The big book of amaro / Matteo Zed.
Other titles: Grande libro dell'amaro italiano. English
Description: New York : The Countryman Press, a Division of W. W. Norton
& Company, [2021] | Translation of: Grande libro dell'amaro italiano. | Includes
bibliographical references and index.
Identifiers: LCCN 2021011038 | ISBN 9781682686515 (hardcover) |
ISBN 9781682686522 (epub)
Subjects: LCSH: Herbal liqueurs—Italy—History. | Herbs.
Classification: LCC TP573.I8 Z43 2021 | DDC 663/.550945—dc23
LC record available at https://lccn.loc.gov/2021011038

The Countryman Press
www.countrymanpress.com

A division of W. W. Norton & Company, Inc.
500 Fifth Avenue, New York, NY 10110
www.wwnorton.com

10 9 8 7 6 5 4 3 2 1

Like every good Italian, I have another great love in my life,
other than amaro: my mother, Argia. I dedicate this book to her.
She sacrificed her life for her family and, without her support,
I would not be the person I am today.

CONTENTS

BOTANICALS ✦ 33

HOW TO DRINK AN AMARO ✦ 71

LABELS ✦ 77

RECIPES ✦ 199

PREFACE

W E CAN IMAGINE THEM THERE, IN SALERNO, NEXT TO THE botanical garden flooded by sun, pounding herbs and roots in a mortar for the patients of the first medical school in Europe. We can see the great queen Catherine de' Medici giving the French court a taste of the rosolio that came from her Italy (and woe to those who didn't like it). And then the alchemists who had given up making gold, the apothecaries of the monasteries in their stunningly scented rooms, the pharmacists who reinvented themselves as liquorists so as not to force patients to go to the doctor for a prescription each time they needed an *ammazzacaffè* (literally a "coffee killer"). The story of Italian amaro is theirs. A story interwoven in the thousand territories of the country: Every little village has its amaro, every after-dinner has its flavor. The link with medicine matters; amaro must help digestion above all. But even at those tables where there is little to digest, liquor made in the kitchen from the herbs gathered around the house is one of the few luxuries within reach of many. Then, about half a century ago, tastes changed. All over the world, in fact.

Young people preferred smoking their herbs, consumption of liquor dropped dramatically, and the venerable Scottish distilleries as well as the provincial or regional liquor stores began closing. In the crisis of the 1970s only vodka remained, cheap (then) and not very tasty (even today): a suitable active ingredient to mix with lemonade, or to be tossed down in shots by Clint Eastwood types. Iced, so it doesn't burn your guts. Not right away, at least.

The fact is, the destruction left few desirable options: the usual friars whose amari sat in their showcases for years; bitter Campari, which, on the contrary, has no medical history but was created for pleasure; the monumental

Fernet-Branca; and the sweet Averna, Montenegro, Lucano, and Strega. Those who didn't close simply got by, not even hoping to get out of the province where they were born.

In the end, Italians forgot about their amari, which were the most numerous and varied in the world. The great wine countries have no tradition of mixing and if a country has amari, there are even fewer thoughts about cocktails. But that's how, customarily, amari pale in the background without even nurturing a tradition of mixing.

For the turning point, we need the intervention of those who have that tradition: the Americans and the British. They too were facing a drop in consumption, and even their distilleries began to slow down. Rye whiskey came close to extinction: Eddie Russell of Wild Turkey said that one or two days of distillation per year were enough to meet demand.

But then people like Dale DeGroff, Salvatore Calabrese, Toby Cecchini, Dick Bradsell, Audrey Saunders, Sasha Petraske, Gaz Regan and Jim Meehan, Tony Conigliaro, Ago Perrone, and Dario Comini began working, some earlier than others. And this changed the world: They, along with many others, are the men and women of the "renaissance of drinking." They opened bars where young people wanted to go, they broke the monopoly of fancy drinks in five-star hotels, places where ancient know-how had been protected and preserved but not introduced into the wider world. At least, not in the world of mass consumption. The bartenders on the other side of the ocean, or at least the English Channel, understood the value of amaro as a source of taste available to those who wanted to experiment. And they put intuition into practice. The spritz, even if the *New York Times* doesn't like it anymore, was the great vehicle: Bars modify it by "spritzing" prosecco together with other flavors. Campari and Fernet grew. If you see an amaro at the bottlers, it is likely that there is also some vermouth.

A couple of Italian relatives, one being spirits and the other being wine, become the trade secret of any Italian bartender who wants to work in the world. They are their curriculum vitae and their added value, their letter of introduction and the giant from whose shoulders they see into the distance. Vodka and gin are more versatile, rum more suitable for easy and thirst-quenching drinks. The biodiversity of the thousand new brands of amaro in Italy, crossed with the thousand different techniques and preparations, will never leave a bartender without cues. In a world where a bottle of vodka can cost $50 or even twice as much, you can put your amaro friends on the counter with half of half. And if you're looking for a profile for your new bar, take a walk on the amaro side: There, among grandfather's recipes, spectacular bottles, and spices you've never heard of, you may discover something special. For that I am grateful to Matteo Zed. With great humility and determination, he has built something with his own hands. The first Amaro bar in Brooklyn, the Il Marchese amaro bar in Rome, the first in Europe, the *Amaro Obsession* website, this book . . . Matteo, in his own way, is an evangelist and a prophet. Let's hope he can be one in his own country. For himself, but also for all of us. He's already converted me.

— *Marco Cremonesi*

INTRODUCTION

E ACH ONE OF US IN THIS WORLD HAS OUR OWN OBSESSIONS. There are those who collect butterflies and those who aim to own a monumental home video library. There are those who would spend entire days watching trains pass by or admiring airplanes landing on airport runways.

And then there are those like me who are obsessed with the magical, immense world of amari. I've been passionate about amaro for a lifetime, from the moment when I was very young and I chose to stand behind a bar counter, at $15 a day, to help a friend. Already famous in the 1980s, these spirits are experiencing a moment of authentic renaissance that sees them used not only as a digestive remedy but also as an exclusive ingredient in mixing and cooking.

In America, for example, talking about amaro today is like talking about gin. And it was precisely in the United States, where I had the opportunity to work, that I received the input to make this ancient yet modern family of Italian spirits "mine" in order to make it accessible to everyone. I am providing correct information but, above all, shining a spotlight on brands that are now appearing on the market, with excellent results, alongside historic brands. Observing American people approaching amari with such passion and curiosity has encouraged me to do my utmost to ensure that they are once again appreciated

in Italy where, on the wave of a millenary tradition, the category has now flourished in terms of production.

And this is how I became an ambassador at home of what has been recorded at an international level as true amaro-mania.

The Amaro Universe holds so much information, and so many stories and adventures that it is impossible to fully tell them in the pages of this book.

In general, when we speak of amaro, we are referring to the collective class of spirits with a prevalent bitter taste—obtained from herbs, roots, barks, berries, fruits, leaves, and flowers—produced in Italy and traditionally served as an after-meal digestif. Amari are created by macerating the vegetable components just mentioned in a neutral spirit or wine, which is then often sweetened, most often with sugar syrup. Most of the blends obtained are then left to rest for a more or less long period of time, with frequent aging in wood, to help balance the aromatic peaks and to achieve greater complexity.

Common bitter agents used to produce

amaro include cinchona bark, gentian root, angelica and dandelion flowers and roots, along with other herbs and spices such as cardamom, chamomile, rhubarb, mint, orange peel, fennel, artichoke, licorice, eucalyptus, juniper, ginger, thistle, cloves, aniseed, saffron, and sage.

The bitter content can range from sweet and syrupy to bitter and dry, with a range of flavors from citrusy to floral, from vegetal to woody, and from aromatic and herbaceous to invigorating and medicinal.

Typically never less than 15 percent alcohol by volume, amari represent the most impressive family of spirits you can find on the market today. However, the use of herb-based spirit mixtures and bitter-aromatic roots dates back thousands of years. The Greeks and Romans used botanicals in wine for curative purposes. But the true

origins of amaro, as we know it today, can be traced back to the medieval friars and monks in abbeys and monasteries throughout Italy, who, enriched by contacts with Arab alchemy—favored by the Medical School of Salerno—deepened the art of distillation and the unique properties of botanical products then used to create regenerating and medicinal tonics and elixirs.

Certainly, a great push toward diversification of ingredients and flavors came with Europeans' progressive discovery of new lands, which increased the import of sugar from the Americas and herbs and spices never before known by great powers such as the Republic of Venice and imposing commercial enterprises such as the West and East India Companies.

Subsequently, the French Revolution that broke out in 1789 and the start of anticlerical movements in Italy forced many monasteries to stop the production of amari, which gradually became more and more the prerogative of secular society. In the wake of these changes from the 19th century onward, many courageous individuals, endowed with a remarkable entrepreneurial spirit, decided to turn the knowledge of a few into a pleasure for all, leading to industrial liquor production.

After World War II, amari went from being an aid prescribed by doctors and sold by pharmacists to products purchased for pleasure, when not made at home. Of course, our attraction to amaro, as natural as it may seem, is not natural at all: Not everyone knows that human beings are born with a genetic predisposition to avoid bitterness. Years of evolution have forced us to treat anything bitter as a potential toxin, so when the brain perceives bitterness it sets the digestive system in motion, activating saliva and gastric juices in an attempt to expel what has just been ingested.

This cycle, however, also explains why we feel a sense of relief when sipping an amaro after a heavy meal.

In this regard, one of my favorite descriptions of the impact of a glass of amaro on the body comes from the coauthor of *The Modern Gentleman: A Guide to Essential Manners, Savvy and Vice*, Jason Tesauro, who summarized it for the *New York Times*: "After a decadent meal, amaro is like Harvey Keitel in *Pulp Fiction*. It's the cleaner who erases any evidence of your exaggeration and transgression with food." As we get older, however, we learn that not all bitter things are poisonous

and we end up enjoying coffee, beer, or gin and tonics, until we become passionate about them. And certainly, in Italy, we are facilitated in this change of perception by a food heritage that embraces many bitter foods and drinks to which we are accustomed since childhood, unlike the United States, where palates are more accustomed to sweet tastes.

In my personal vision, amaro is the bad boy who is asked to stay in school after class: sweet, sour, and salty at the same time. It is the perfect path to get to the umami of taste. In the last 10 years, love for amaro has crossed the European borders to reach new and more dynamic territories, most of all the United States, followed by South America and Australia: "The new peoples of amaro" have learned to appreciate our beloved drink, but they also have been able to give it new life and splendor by starting up local productions with a strong "territorial connotation." In the world of international beverages, meanwhile, amaro is the basis of increasingly popular cocktails, while in restaurant kitchens it has become a cool and classy ingredient that is used in refined recipes or as an "additional touch" to give character to a dish.

This book will help you understand and get better acquainted with a friend you have always had at home, but never really knew, and which is much more than a digestif at the end of a meal. You will rediscover amaro as a star attraction on the table, an incomparable expression of tradition and territory but also of transformation and new ideas. Because just speaking about amaro is never enough!

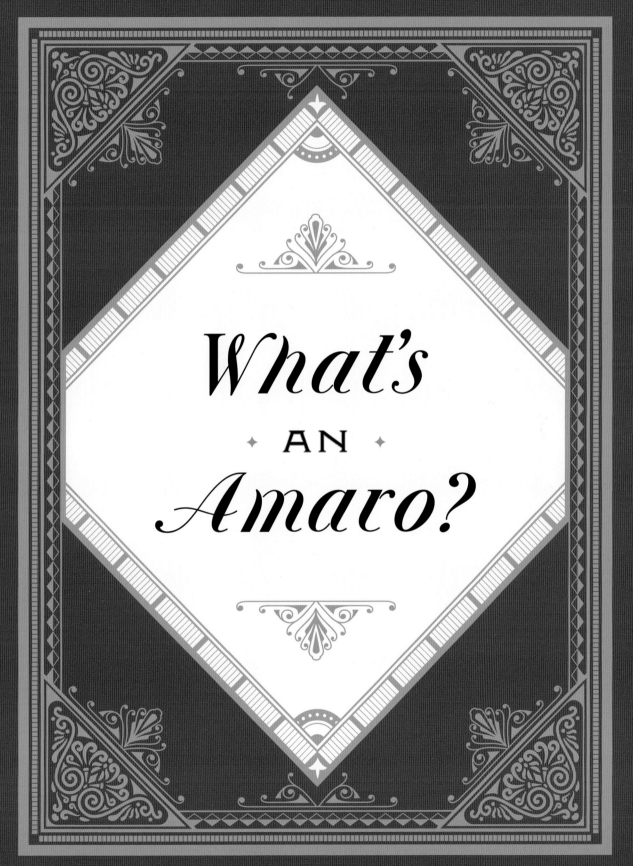

What's
✦ an ✦
Amaro?

Too often, when I talk about amaro during my workshops or simply when having a conversation with a colleague, I hear this question, "What is an amaro?"

The most incredible thing is that most of the time the people who ask it are Italians, a people who have always been surrounded by amari. Since childhood, from north to south of the *bel paese*—the beautiful country—we Italians see them peeping out from the shelves of the neighborhood bars, in TV advertisements, or simply on the table with relatives and friends as the seal of a cheerful and Pantagruelian meal. On the other hand, our professional drinkers at home are becoming more and more adept at enjoying the pleasures of international beverages from London and New York City, deepening their knowledge of spirits such as gin, tequila, vodka, or mescal that are produced in other parts of the world, without paying much attention to Italian liquors. But back to our question: **"What is an amaro?"**

I will try to explain it here, starting from the definition given in the *Manuale del Barman* ([Barman's Manual] Giunti 2016):

> *The category of bitters, and liquors that reflect an exquisitely Italian habit, is relevant and consists of a large number of products with different alcohol and sugar content, but the composition of the recipe includes the prevalence of substances rich in bitter-type aromas such as artichoke leaves, rhizomes of rhubarb and cinchona bark. The vast constellation of amari differs in intensity of bitter flavor.*

As far as legislation, the most up-to-date reference is found in EU Regulation 2019/787 of the European Parliament and Council of April 17, 2019. In particular, point 30(a) of Annex I, dedicated to bitter or bitter-tasting spirit drinks, which reads: "A bitter-tasting spirit drink or *bitter* is a spirit drink with a predominantly bitter taste, obtained by flavoring ethyl alcohol of agricultural origin, distillate of agricultural origin or both, with flavoring substances, flavoring preparations or both."

This text informs us of the possibility of creating amari through **"flavoring,"** the use of natural essences or those produced by chemical synthesis. The standard makes no distinction between the two. The use of synthetic aromatic principles actually allows a substantial cut in production time, which is particularly advantageous for companies that sell a large number of bottles. But it should not be forgotten that some of the major producers of amaro still infuse real herbs into quality alcohol, inside huge steel extractors. From a didactic point of view, the Amaro Universe can be very interesting to explore, given the growth and complexity of the category. For example, a producer has a vast range of botanicals to choose from, as well as the number, type, and place of origin to create the product they want.

Therefore, amaro is one of the few platforms where passionate producers can express themselves as they wish, manifesting the unique qualities of their regions.

*Amaro is a spirit that demands the
consumer becomes intimately familiar
with production methods*

The Main Extraction Methods

A M A R O, in my opinion, is a spirit that not only encourages but explicitly asks its consumer to become intimately familiar with its methods of production, as well as with the irrepressible history of each producer. It is well known that the creation of an amaro is first and foremost achieved through the selection of botanicals—roots, bark, berries, leaves, flowers, and fruits—that contribute to creating the aromatic bouquet of the drink. Considering that the origins of amaro are lost in the mists of time, what we know for sure is that the methods of extracting the flavors and active principles of the herbs that make up the blends, as well as their dosages, have often been collected in veritable recipe books kept in jealous custody from generation to generation. The first holders of this knowledge were the medieval monks, wise plant experts, who were able—through specific methods—to isolate the beneficial principles for human health, resulting in elixirs and healing tinctures often considered "miraculous." As you can well imagine, every botanical has unique characteristics of structure and needs specialized extraction techniques to get their active ingredients. We are going to delve into the most ancient methods used by medieval apothecaries, and we will investigate the most modern methods, which I like to describe as "borderline science fiction."

Traditional Extraction Methods

MACERATION

MACERATION is the most common extraction method and is carried out at room temperature. It consists of immersing the botanical product in a solvent liquid (for example, water or ethyl alcohol). The mixture is contained in a hermetically sealed container for a time that varies according to the substances involved. Each botanical component—fresh or dried—is cleaned and chopped up in advance so as to increase the extractive surface area as much as possible, without the risk of pulverization, which would result in the loss of the active ingredients. After extraction, the macerated product is filtered and the solid residues are pressed. In the case of amaro, maceration of the plant material always takes place in a hydroalcoholic solution and, in some cases, can last up to 40 days.

PERCOLATION

PERCOLATION is an extraction technique that is also carried out at room temperature. In this case, the solvent slowly passes through the botanical components—suitably shredded—from top to bottom, inside a special instrument called a percolator. Pressing and filtration complete the process. As with maceration, the solvent liquid is represented by a hydroalcoholic mixture of water and alcohol at different volumes in order to extract the best possible active ingredients, colors, and flavors from the botanicals.

DIGESTION

DIGESTION is a method similar to maceration. The main difference is that the solvent and the plant parts are heated to between 95°F and 150°F (35–65°C) in order to enhance the extractive action of the solvent.

INFUSION

WITH INFUSION, the solvent is extracted from boiling water, which is poured over the chopped-up medicinal plant (drug)[1] to allow the active ingredients to be extrapolated. The infusion time will vary depending on whether the producer wants to obtain a therapeutic or aromatic infusion. At the end of the operation, the extraction liquid is subjected to appropriate filtration. The infusion can also be made in alcohol.

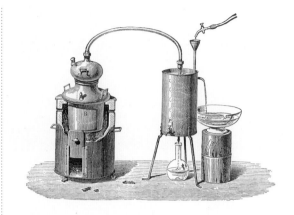

DECOCTION

IN DECOCTION, the botanical material is boiled with the solvent for at least 30 minutes. The resulting liquid is then properly filtered.

This technique is useful for particularly solid plant sources such as roots and barks that are in any case poor in thermolabile active ingredients.

DISTILLATION

DISTILLATION consists of a process based on the variation of two important extraction parameters: pressure and temperature. The key instrument here is the distiller, which consists of three main parts. In the first part is the containment chamber of the botanical mixture and the solvent that, once heated to evaporation, carries the active ingredients. The second part consists of a low-temperature condensation area where the extracted substances pass from a gaseous state to a liquid state. The third and last part is the container that collects the fluid extract, which is called a distillate. There are different types of distillation. These include:

- DISTILLATION IN A WATER VAPOR STREAM, IN WHICH THE SOLVENT CONSISTS OF WATER

- LOW-PRESSURE DISTILLATION, USED TO EXTRACT EXTREMELY THERMOLABILE ACTIVE INGREDIENTS

---

1. drug: In pharmacology, any natural, vegetal, or animal product containing one or more active ingredients (alkaloids, glycosides, essential oils, bitter, purgative, aromatic substances, etc.), and which, appropriately prepared and stored, finds therapeutic or experimental indications that are the subject of pharmacognosy studies. (*Treccani Dictionary*)

Innovative Extraction Methods

COUNTERCURRENT EXTRACTION

COUNTERCURRENT extraction is a technique normally used to extract fats from drugs (medicinal substances) of an oleaginous (oily) nature.

ULTRASOUND EXTRACTION

ULTRASOUND extraction operates through the mechanical action of ultrasounds (mechanical sound waves with frequencies above 20 kHz) on plant walls. This process, which takes place without the use of chemical products, involves a liquid solvent that allows the waves to propagate, permitting the complete extraction of the active ingredients while keeping the molecules of the plant source intact. Extraction times are also greatly reduced.

NAVIGLIO PRINCIPLE

RECENTLY, in the international *Journal of Food Science*, a paper was published on research conducted by an interdisciplinary group headed by professors Daniele Naviglio, Andrea Formato, and Monica Gallo at the prestigious University of Naples Federico II. The article introduced a new method of solid-liquid extraction from cyclic pressurization based on the innovative Naviglio Principle. Among the most evident results of this technique are the reduction of the extraction time and the preservation of the composition of the substances contained in the botanicals due to the absence of thermal stress at the expense of thermolabile costs and active ingredients. The Naviglio Extractor works at room or subenvironment temperature and guarantees consistent results, essentially because of the forced mechanical action of the extracting liquid on the plant material..

Amaro Classifications

MARO CAN BE CLASSIFIED ACCORDING TO DIFFERENT CRITERIA such as, for example, sugar content. In this respect, amari containing a percentage of **added sugar** are defined as **amari liqueurs**; whereas **true amari** are considered to be those obtained from the infusion of botanicals into ethyl alcohol, with a percentage of sugar less than 70 g/l. Among these latter, the most significant example is that of **fernet.** I love fernet and its bitter, dry, balsamic flavor; I think it fully reflects the durability and originality of Old World amari.

The genesis of the name is still uncertain: According to some, fernet pays homage to the Swedish doctor and herbalist of the same name who lived between the 18th and 19th centuries, and who is said to have been a collaborator of the Italian entrepreneur Bernardino Branca. The idea of launching fernet as a medicinal drink (and as a market class) in 1845 is attributed to Branca.

Other sources believe that the name derives from the Milanese dialect. The term *fer net*, which means "clean iron," references the brightness of the metal plate used in ancient times to extract the active ingredients of spices and medicinal plants, or the brilliant patina created by the *Aloe ferox* sap that covered the equipment (now on display in the Branca Museum in Milan). When you think of fernet, however, undoubtedly the first image that comes to mind is a bottle of Fernet-Branca. However, the number of fernet brands in Italy are many, and they are largely unknown to most people. In reality, there is no clear definition of the category. Basically, we

know that fernet possesses a higher volume of alcohol as compared to a classic amaro, a more overbearing taste, and a darker, almost black color. The botanicals that compose the mixture of a fernet certainly vary according to the choices made by the manufacturer, but there are still some fixed components, which include aloe, myrrh, saffron, chamomile, rhubarb, and mint.

Depending on the aromatic characteristics, amari may be considered:

- **VERY, VERY BITTER**
- **VERY BITTER**
- **AROMATIC**
- **MEDIUM AROMATIC**
- **VERY AROMATIC**

If taken before or after meals, amari can be an effective **aperitif** (appetite stimulant) or a good digestive aid.

As far as organoleptic characteristics are concerned, I prefer to classify each amaro using my own personal classification:

CITRUSY: draws its character from the essential oils present in the peel of citrus fruits such as oranges, lemons, chinotti, mandarins, and limes.

ALPINE: produced with alpine herbs and botanicals, with an intense taste.

BALSAMIC: made from balsamic herbs such as peppermint, glacial mint, or eucalyptus.

REVITALIZING: rich in herbs with restorative properties for the human body. Mentholated flavor, like fernet or similar.

HERBACEOUS: predominantly curative and with aromatic herbs; often light in color, often greenish, and characterized by an intense vegetal aroma.

FLORAL: very rare in the amaro world, generally made with flowers from the high mountains.

LIGHT: soft taste and light color.

MEDICINAL: very bitter and not very drinkable.

MEDIUM: balanced, with an even taste.

ROOTY: created with the help of roots and barks that prevail in the botanical blend. Very dark in color; normally bitter or very bitter; pleasant and intense on the palate.

EARTHY: made with tubers and wild fungi such as mushrooms. The most beloved characteristic, and rare in Italy, is the truffle-scented amaro.

VEGETAL: with a strong presence of vegetal scents derived from artichoke, thistle, arugula, chicory, and horseradish.

The Amaro Macrocosm

At this point we should be able to adequately answer the previous question: "What's an amaro?" Unfortunately, it is not yet easy to give a detailed and precise definition, because other categories of spirits in the amaro macrocosm—which share many characteristics with amaro even if they do not identify with it—should be considered:

1. Aperitifs and Bitters

2. Vermouths and Americanos

3. Chinato Wines and Cinchona Elixirs

APERITIFS AND BITTERS

In the collective imagination, aperitifs and bitters, two bitter liquors typical of the *Aperitivo Italiano*, are considered strangers to the amaro world but are instead close relatives. Among the elements that distinguish these "appetizing" drinks from an amaro are, for example, *the color*, which is normally between orange and red (even if there are transparent and even green amari on the market), *the time of consumption* (both are usually consumed in the period before dinner), and the *alcohol content* (which is lower). Aperitifs and bitters are also rarely drunk neat—they are more often mixed with soda or sparkling wines. Despite this, the botanicals and methods of extraction of flavors are practically the same used for amaro.

MANY amari are produced with a wine base, such as Cardamaro di Tosti, Elisir Novasalus di Cappelletti, and Rossoamaro al Nero d'Avola. The family of fortified and aromatic wines, even if they have a modest alcohol content, can be considered to be part of the amaro macrocosm. The extraction of flavors in this case takes place by maceration of botanicals or by adding flavors and colorants, while the alcoholic fortification is obtained by adding a neutral spirit to the wine, for example brandy. Vermouth and Americanos fall into the fortified and aromatized wines group. Originally from the alpine areas of Piedmont (in the past, as far as Haute-Savoie in France), vermouth—developed by the distiller Benedetto Carpano in 1786—is one of the historical ingredients most used in the blending of old-style and new-style drinks. The name derives from the German word *Wermut*, or "wormwood," because this bitter aromatic ingredient is indispensable in the production of vermouth. Chamomile, cinnamon, marjoram, and citrus peel are also found in the botanical mix. The quantity of sugar used changes according to the type of production (sweet, dry, and extra dry), and that of alcohol can vary from a minimum of 14.5% vol. to a maximum of 22% vol. In this context, to speak of Americano does not mean an allusion to the classic Italian cocktail, even less so to an espresso with hot water, but to a category of fortified and aromatized wines that owes its name to the Italian expression *amaricante*. The addition of gentian in the recipe means that an Americano can be distinguished from a vermouth. The most important and well-known global brands are Cocchi Americano Bianco, Cocchi Americano Rosa, Americano Cappelletti, and Americano Contratto.

FINALLY, it is worth mentioning Barolo Chinato, one of the first experiments carried out by Benedetto Carpano in his workshop in Turin, which he produced by fortifying and flavoring one of the most beloved wines of the Langhe: Barolo. The wine, made from Nebbiolo grapes, is used for the maceration of ingredients such as ginger, rhubarb, citrus peel, and cloves. The botanical reference is still cinchona bark, with its unmistakable flavor. The cinchona elixir (or Elixir di China), which is obtained by infusion in alcohol of the bark of *Cinchona calisaya*, was invented between the 18th and 19th centuries as a cure in the fight against malaria. With the eradication of the disease in Europe, the drink began to be used as a tonic and digestive aid, and then came to be used as a liquor, consumed more purely for pleasure. In the traditional formula, in addition to cinchona bark, there must also be bitter orange peel.

CINCHONA CALISAYA

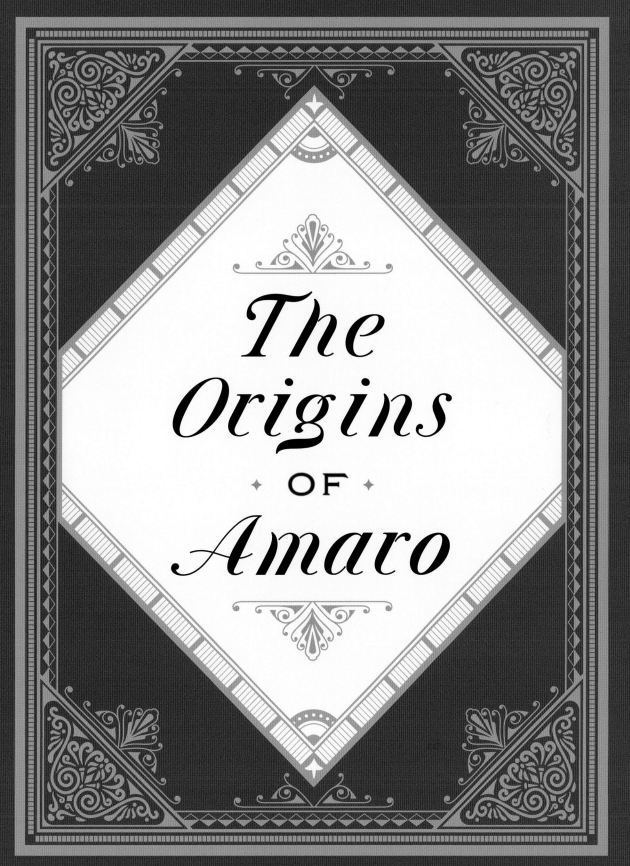

The Origins
OF
Amaro

T HE RELATIONSHIP BETWEEN HUMANS AND ALCOHOL DATES BACK to ancient times. In fact, according to the "drunken monkey" hypothesis, developed by Robert Dudley, a biologist at the University of California, Berkeley, primates and hominids have long been able to digest ethanol. The gene by which the human body is able to metabolize ethyl alcohol is ADH4, which would have appeared more than 10 million years ago. It benefited the ancestral hominids by offering them the possibility of feeding on fermenting fruit that fell from trees. However, it is widely believed that the oldest alcoholic beverage in the world was mead, obtained from the fermentation of honey, and discovered by pure chance by African hunter-gatherers about 20,000 years ago. In any case, with the passage of time and the refinement of the technique, humans learned to produce alcohol themselves. Spirits subsequently played a leading role in medicine, social life, and the culture of many ancient civilizations.

Medieval Alchemy and the Contribution of Arab Culture

T HE art of distillation and the practice of herbalism are the basis of the birth of liquors in general and amari in particular. In this regard, a crucial role can be attributed to medieval alchemy. (The word *alchemy* is of uncertain etymology; it could be derived from the Arabic *al-kīmiyā,'* or "art of the philosopher's stone," or from the Greek *chyméia*, indicating "the art of bonding metals," from *chéo*, "to pour, to melt.") The greatest experts in distillation practiced alchemy. Among

them was the Greek-speaking Zosimus of Panopolis, who between the end of the third century and the beginning of the fourth century A.D. had already described the equipment for distillation with a detailed representation. But it was the Arab alchemists who were the true holders of the knowledge necessary for the production of the first herb-based alcoholic infusions for curative purposes. Between the seventh and eighth centuries A.D., Islamic culture was decisive for the cultural

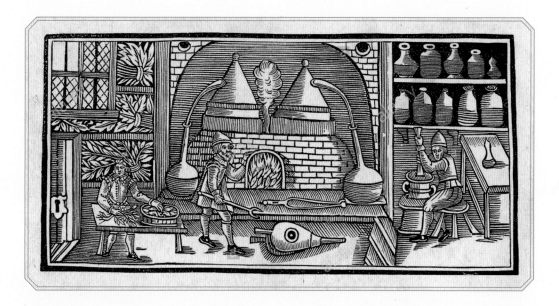

awakening of the West, which had been paralyzed by the decadence of the Roman Empire and exhausted by barbarian invasions. In fact, in the city of Alexandria, under Arab domination, alchemical science began to develop, which significantly influenced the development of the pharmaceutical arts. In the therapeutic prescriptions of common use were drugs (medicinals) such as galangal, sandalwood, nutmeg, cloves, bergamot, and zedoary.

But the most significant turning point was the use of essential oils distilled by botanists. Egyptian alchemy, still permeated by a magical and mysterious aura, was then transformed, with the fundamental contribution of Islamic experts, into practical chemistry that saw the installation of actual stills for the extraction of the "fifth essence," that is, the essential and ethereal part of medicinal substances, in the workshops of Alexandria.

IN PERSIA, TRIBUTES TO THE CALIPHS WERE PAID WITH ROSE WATER

JABIR IBN HAYYAN, KNOWN AS GEBER

Geber, Rhazes, and Avicenna: Between Magic and Medical Science

I N this period, the distillation of aromatic botanicals was a widespread practice, as evidenced by the Persian custom of paying tribute to the caliphs with bottles of rose water, as roses were widely grown in Persia. Evidence of this can also be found in the detailed writings of the famous Persian Jabir ibn Hayyan, known as Geber, considered by many historians of science to be one of the greatest alchemists of the eighth century and, above all, a link between alchemy as magic and alchemy as chemistry and a pharmaceutical art. His successor, in terms of prestige, was Abu Bakr Muhammad ibn Zakariyya al-Razi, better known as Rhazes, who was the most illustrious practitioner of medieval Arab medicine during the second half of the 9th century to the beginning of the 10th century. Rhazes was a great expert on Hippocrates (a Greek physician and the father of modern chemistry, who lived between the fifth and fourth centuries B.C., and to whom the birth of Western medicine can be traced). It is believed that Rhazes was one of the first to use ethanol, obtained by distillation, as a solvent for the active principles of botany.

In his *Kitab al-Mansouri fi al-tibb*, known in Latin as *Liber medicinalis Almansoris*, Rhazes provided the first official definition of *julab* ("julep," from the Arabic *gul* = "rose" and *ab* = "water"), which consisted of an infusion of violets in water, sugar, and alcohol.

Thanks to his writings and to the new principles of medicine elaborated by the Arab alchemists, this mixture, widespread throughout the Mediterranean, became a vehicle of antifungal, anti-inflammatory, antiseptic, diuretic, and emollient medicines. Another great expert of the fundamentals of Hippocrates's medicine was Abu Ali al-Husayn ibn Abd Allah ibn Sina, the renowned Persian physician known as Avicenna, who lived in the 10th and 11th centuries. Avicenna was very prolific, in fact more than 200 works are attributed to him, including an encyclopedia in 20 volumes, which was unfortunately destroyed. He wrote, among other things, about pharmacology, anatomy, physiology, and pathology. These treatises were collected in the *Kitab al-Qanun fi al-tibb*, translated into Latin as *Liber canonis medicinae*, and known by the title of *The Canon of Medicine*. The volume contained previously unpublished information on more than 700 medicinal drugs, including nutmeg, coconut, camphor, cloves, bitter orange, aloe, ginger, and cinnamon.

The Medical School of Salerno

WHILE the Arab people in the Middle East assimilated and reinvigorated the principles of Hippocratic medicine, in Italy it was the Medical School of Salerno that played a fundamental role in the training of numerous specialists. The details of the genesis of this school are unknown, but it was certainly the oldest European institution for the teaching of medicine and related sciences. Tradition associates its creation to a legend in which Pontus, a Greek pilgrim, found himself seeking shelter for the night in the city of Salerno, under the arches of the ancient Aqueduct dell'Arce. When a thunderstorm broke out, a Latin wayfarer, Salernus, took shelter in the same place. Salernus was wounded, and Pontus, at first suspicious but also intrigued by the dressings that the Latin was placing on his wound, approached him.

Meanwhile, under the ancient aqueduct, two other travelers had stopped: Helinus, a Jew, and Abdela, an Arab. The latter also showed interest in Salernus's wound and so they began to talk about medicine. It is said that after this meeting the four decided to set up a school where all their medical knowledge could be collected, disseminated, and taught.

Some scholars, on the other hand, are inclined to the theory of a monastic origin of the institution, given the presence of numerous Benedictine monasteries with hospitals in the territory of Salerno. The monks had gardens of *semplici*, or medicinal plants (the term *semplici* is derived from the medieval Latin *medicamentum* or *medicina simplex*, which indicated plant varieties with medicinal properties). The cultivation of medicinal botanicals was necessary for the treatment of the sick. Although the founding of the Medical School of Salerno is still the subject of heated debate today, one cannot deny its role as a forerunner of modern science: It was, in fact, the first organization to unite the Western scientific thought of Greek-Latin origin with the Eastern thought of the Arab alchemists. The geographical position of the city of Salerno was, moreover, of enormous advantage for the development of scientific knowledge. Its proximity to Sicily and its lively relations (not only of a commercial nature) with Spain, Africa, and the Holy Land allowed the city to assimilate different currents of thought. Salerno's medical approach, first of Greek-Latin origin, was integrated in the 11th century with Arabic doctrines thanks to the work of Constantine the African, a physician, man of letters, and monk from Cassino who spent most of his life between Egypt, Ethiopia, and India

DETAIL OF THE CATHEDRAL PULPIT IN SALERNO

FREDERICK II WAS PASSIONATELY
INTERESTED IN MEDICINE

translating a large number of Arabic medical texts into Latin. In the same period, medical practice was also increased by pilgrims and the wounded veterans of the Crusades. Having absorbed the best of Greek, Latin, and Arabic knowledge, the medical masters of the Salerno School began to make changes to alchemical techniques, concentrating particularly on improving the instrument for distillation: the alembic still. They understood that the material of which the Arabic distiller was made (terra-cotta) did not allow the right conduction of heat and, after endless research, they perfected the heating phase. Later on, they further improved the alembic still, including the cooling stage. As a result, they were able to make possible a massive production of distillates with a high alcohol content for pharmaceutical use. Between the 12th and 13th centuries, the Salerno School was in its heyday, and they paid particular attention to pharmacology, which at the time made use of the *semplici*.

Treatises were thus written in which herbs were scientifically investigated in every detail. They were measured and mixed according to their different applications and then classified according to their curative properties. In this context, Matthaeus Platearius, maestro of the school and member of an important lineage of physicians from Salerno, wrote the *Liber de simplici medicina*, a treatise on medicinal plants also known under the title *Circa instans*. This text was widely distributed and was so appreciated that in the 14th century, it was referred to simply as *Codex* for herbalists at the Faculty of Medicine in Paris.

The ruler of the time was Frederick II, the King of Sicily, Duke of Swabia, and Emperor of the Holy Roman Empire. Frederick II was passionately interested in medicine and was very health conscious. He was responsible for the extraordinary development of the Medical School of Salerno, an institution that he used extensively to protect public health and to promulgate modern health legislation. Under his reign, the

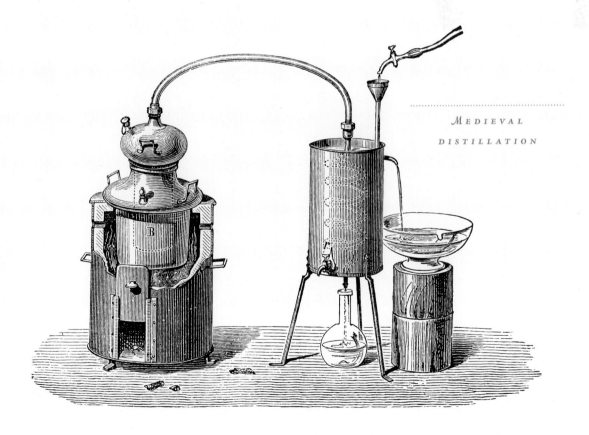

MEDIEVAL
DISTILLATION

so-called *Regimen sanitatis Salernitanum*, or *Flos medicinae scholae Salerni*, was created. This was a collective and anonymous work written in verse. It contained remedies and advice for the protection of health, and it standardized uses and customs to the natural rhythms of the environment and the human organism.

The main precepts of the work were to follow a regimen of long walks, moderate and careful eating, rest, and caution against excesses.

Arnaldo da Villanova and the First Official "Amaro" Created for Boniface VIII

THE Catalan physician and alchemist Arnaldo da Villanova, maestro of the Medical School of Salerno, collected and commented on *Flos medicinae* (the flower of medicine) in the 13th century. In his *Breviarium practicae* (breviary practice), Arnaldo da Villanova described in detail all the diseases known at the time, taking into account the subjective symptoms and their causes, divided into "etiological," "antecedent," and "conjoined." As far as the botanical spectrum was concerned, he focused on the study of *semplici* and the therapeutic use of the extraction of their active ingredients. In his writings, we can also find texts describing the study and use of the "theriac," a very ancient electuary (confection) with supposed miraculous virtues. This cure-all has undergone countless variations over time, conceived first as an antidote against poisons, then as a remedy for numerous diseases. Considered one of the best doctors of his time, "the Catalan" was the personal physician of King James II, brother of Frederick II, at the court of Aragon, where he also played the role of advisor and diplomat. He also served many popes, including Boniface VIII, and successfully treated the pope for kidney stones during the

first Jubilee in the year 1300, thanks to the first official known use of amaro. It was thanks to the resonance created by this event that the infusion of herbs and roots in alcohol for medical purposes spread considerably in monasteries and abbeys.

It was also during this period that the Occitan Franciscan friar, Giovanni di Rucissa, in his *Liber de consideratione quintae essentiae omnium rerum*, described the distillation of wine to obtain the "fifth essence" (which precedes today's brandy and cognac) and its use for the preparation of powerful medicines such as drinkable gold and elixirs for long life.

The Libellus de aqua ardenti *by* Michele Savonarola

ANOTHER important contribution to the spread of distillation was made by the Florentine physician and philosopher Michele Savonarola. Considered one of the most influential figures in Italian Renaissance society, Savonarola was a prolific author. His writings, like his interests, spanned a multiplicity of subjects, including the distillation of alcohol and the effects of aqua vitae on the human body. It was on these last two subjects that he wrote the *Libellus de aqua ardenti* in which he presented the qualities of aqua vitae and advised taking only the recommended dosage. There is also a special chapter in which he described the aqua vitae composite that consisted of alcohol distilled from wine and combined with spices, herbs, roots, and flowers according to the pathologies to be eradicated. During the early 16th century, thanks to the printing of numerous books on the subject, people began to drink and produce these infusions for pleasure and no longer just as medicines.

At the same time, the price of sugar (an ingredient that helped to make the drinks more palatable) began to fall thanks to the greater availability of raw materials from the New World. In addition, the production of amari also began to account for the pleasantness of the final taste.

Catherine de' Medici Introduces Aqua Vitae to the French Court

THE recreational use of spirits seems to date back, more clearly, to the time of Catherine de' Medici, who moved to France in 1533 and brought with her scholars of medicine and pharmacology. The queen consort of Henry II, who went down in history as "the Florentine who led France," revolutionized customs and habits of the French court. She took care to bring the pomp of the Italian courts beyond the Alps, with a view to opening it up to a modern European culture. It is well known that at Catherine's court it was customary and courteous to offer a portion of aqua vitae infused with botanicals to welcome the guests of the royal palace.

Spices Conquer Europe with the Companies of the Indies

THE turning point as far as amari are concerned, on an organoleptic level, came with the easy availability of Indian and South American spices. They began to arrive in Europe, and more precisely in Italian territory, thanks to the flourishing trade of the cities of Venice and Florence and the trading companies of the Indies, founded by the English in 1600, by the Dutch in 1602, and by the French in 1664. These companies were of great mercantile and political importance, and they contributed to the colonial expansion of the major maritime powers of the time, leading the way in the conquest of new territories.

L'Elixir Végétal de la Grande-Chartreuse: A Secret Recipe for More Than 400 Years

MEANWHILE, in France, the Carthusian friars began studies and trials for the first herbal liqueur in history: Elixir Végétal de la Grande-Chartreuse.

The story of this very precious bitter began in 1605, when Marshal François-Annibal d'Estrées, a man trusted by King Henry IV, handed over to the Reverend Father of the Charterhouse of Paris a particular manuscript containing the secret formula of a powerful "elixir of long life." The formula for this elixir called for almost all the medicinal botanicals known until then. The manuscript, which arrived at the monastery of the Grande Chartreuse in Saint-Pierre-de-Chartreuse near Grenoble, underwent diligent study until Father Jerome Maubec, the monastery's wise pharmacist, deciphered the formulas contained in the very precious document. He obtained the recipe for the magnificent bitter in 1737. The original

EAST INDIA COMPANY SHIP

formula of this elixir, still shrouded in a halo of mystery today, contained 69 percent alcohol by volume and the extraction of 130 medicinal botanicals. In 1769, after the great success of the elixir, production began of Chartreuse Verte, which is also known as Liqueur de Santé and is still famous today.

Chartreuse Verte, with 55 percent alcohol, is produced by very slow maceration and distillation of 130 varieties of different botanicals. At the end of maceration and subsequent infusion, sugar is added. The liquid is then left to rest and refine in oak barrels. The typical green color of the Chartreuse Verte is 100 percent natural. Its formulation and its production process are still a well-kept secret today, after 400 years of production history.

The French Revolution Breaks Out: The Art of Creating Religious Liqueur Becomes Popular Practice

THE year 1789 was significant in European history, as this was the year when the French Revolution broke out and France's political order was disrupted. Absolutism, the feudal system, and some centuries-old institutions ceased to exist. This made way for an attempt to achieve ideals typical of the Enlightenment, such as inalienable human rights and popular sovereignty. To remedy public debt, the property, land wealth, and possessions of the Church were made available to the nation with the approval of the Civil Constitution of the Clergy, according to which bishops and parish priests were directly elected by the faithful as religious representatives and, once they swore allegiance to the Constitution, were paid by the State. With the French Revolution, which abolished all the privileges of the clergy, monasteries were closed and conventual orders dissolved. Friars and monks, together with members of the lower clergy, were forced into the diaspora and induced to seek employment within secular society. As a consequence, within a few years, the art of infusion and liqueurs came out from behind the massive walls of religious buildings to become popular knowledge. In this way the foundations were laid for the beginnings of the homemade pharmacopoeia. Hundreds of amari were made by following the instructions provided by the men of the Church. Some amari and elixirs achieved great success after a few years, and this led their creators and some far-sighted entrepreneurs to expand production. Following industrial criteria, dozens of small factories were opened in the first half of the 19th century.

American Prohibition Suppresses Alcoholic Beverages

THROUGHOUT Europe, but especially in Italy and not least in France, liqueurs took a stronger foothold, securing a place of honor among spirit productions of the time, with amari becoming the after-meal digestif beverage *par excellence*. In the United States, however, the state of things was quite different. On February 13, 1826, in Boston, Massachusetts, the American Temperance Society was established. It was one of many temperance societies founded at that time. These societies included political and religious groups. Characterized by preeminent moralism, these societies were engaged in convincing people to restrain themselves from drinking. American women, driven by the belief that alcohol was a destroyer of marriages and families, and often left alone to care for their offspring, played a key role in the temperance societies. The Women's Christian Temperance Union was a particularly powerful force. These societies took up the writings of Benjamin Rush (a signatory of the Declaration of Independence). Rush, who was an influential medical psychiatrist, denied any "alleged" medical benefits of alcohol and stressed the destructive effects of its abuse. The temperance societies pressed the US government to issue an amendment to the US Constitution prohibiting the production, transportation, and sale of alcohol throughout the country. With the ratification of 18th Amendment to the Constitution of the United States, Prohibition became the law of the land in January 1919. The enforcement of Prohibition came through the passage of the Volstead Act, which became law in October 1919 after the ratification of 46 states. The act stated that any liquid containing at least

Beer being poured out during Prohibition

0.5% of alcohol by volume, except for medicinal alcohol, was determined to be an alcoholic beverage. It was precisely this definition that excluded bitters from the vigorous grip of Prohibition: being alcoholic liquids with medical properties, they were sold without too much difficulty in American pharmacies. The effects that Prohibition had, however, despite its good and moral intentions, were catastrophic. Suddenly, alcohol, of very poor quality due to its crude, clandestine production methods, made its appearance on a huge black market. This black market enriched large criminal organizations, which, corrupting the authorities and the police, managed to set up a very efficient distribution network of illicit alcohol throughout the country. These disastrous effects added to the loss of many billions of dollars by the United States government due to the failure to collect taxes on the production of alcoholic beverages. In addition, there was open opposition to Prohibition. Some important women's associations claimed that Prohibition had actually increased the consumption of alcohol. Thus, on December 5, 1933, Prohibition was

ALCOHOL MADE ITS APPEARANCE ON THE BLACK MARKET, ENRICHING LARGE CRIMINAL ORGANIZATIONS

definitively repealed with the ratification of the 21st Amendment to the Constitution.

After this dark period for almost all alcoholic beverages, a time of flourishing began in the United States. Local bitters were once again manufactured, commercialized, and distributed.

Italian Amaro-Mania

In Italy, amaro accompanied the economic boom of the postwar period. New factories were inaugurated and public establishments opened their doors to the entire population. These establishments included sports bars, cafes, betting shops, and coffee roasters with wine service. People could order a *caffè corretto*, or a "correct" espresso (meaning alcohol is added), and *cicchetti* (snacks). Advertising, coming through new types of communication such as television, encouraged the consumption of ancient yet modern drinks. These

drinks increasingly became the protagonists of Italian tables. Around the amari—each one an inimitable expression of its territory of origin—real family rituals were built, generating a deep sense of belonging that would be passed down through entire generations.

Nowadays, it is the United States that has "rediscovered" and relaunched the amaro—neat, with ice, or mixed—putting it at the center of an irresistible new trend in the world of beverages, triggering what can be defined as an authentic amaro-mania!

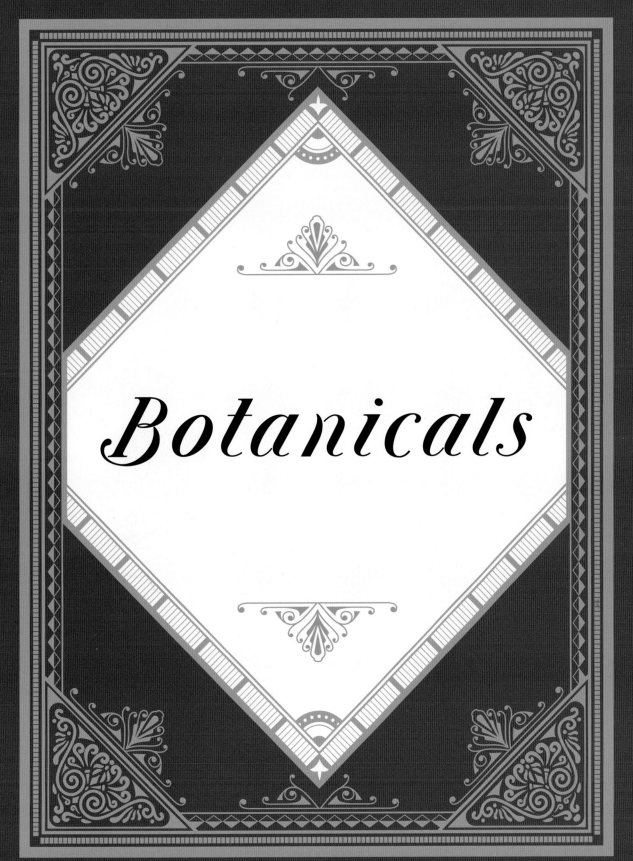

Botanicals

A MARI ARE NOTHING MORE THAN THE PLEASURABLE EVOLUTION of elixirs and herbal preparations with tonic. Acting as a digestive, amaro stimulates the functions of the liver and biliary system. All of this thanks to the use of flowers, leaves, roots, barks, seeds, and fruits with strong bitter characteristics that are associated with greater digestive power.[2] Among the most widely used botanicals in the preparation of an amaro, I identify 50 here. They are divided into two categories: Classic and Aromatic. The latter category includes traditional and innovative aromatic agents and refers to botanicals whose main characteristics are to give the drink a touch of originality, be it in flavor or color.

Classic Botanicals

1. MUSCAT YARROW (*Achillea moschata*)

MUSCAT YARROW is a perennial herbaceous plant of the *Asteraceae* family that grows in the rocky areas of the Alps, from the Aosta Valley to Friuli-Venezia Giulia. In Italy, it is also known as *taneda*, *erba rota*, and *erba iva*. The botanical name of the genus, *Achillea*, is inspired by the Homeric hero Achilles who, according to myth, used the species *Achillea millefolium*—also known as the soldier's herb—to treat the wounds of his comrades during the Trojan War on the advice of his teacher, the centaur Chiron. *Achillea moschata* is appreciated for its delicate scent reminiscent of mint and for its ability to stimulate appetite and boost digestion. These qualities justify its wide use in the production of amari and liqueurs.

---

2. The botanicals listed here are presented as a general guide. The incorrect use and/or overdosage, even minimal, of some of the plant components noted here could cause serious damage to a person's health. For these reasons, for more details on collection, use, and dosage it is always necessary to consult a doctor or a specialist in the field.

MUSCAT YARROW

AN ALOE
SPECIMEN

2. ALOE

ALOE is native to much of central and southern Africa, but the genus *Aloe*—from the *Liliaceae* family, which groups together hundreds of species of succulent plants—can now be found in different areas around the world. Among the best-known species are *Aloe vera* (Barbados aloe) and *Aloe ferox* (Cape aloe). Both have an intense bitter aroma and are rich in benefits that include laxative and antioxidant properties. *Aloe ferox*, in particular, is also known for its digestive and diuretic properties and is an essential ingredient in the production of fernet.

3. ANGELICA (*ANGELICA ARCHANGELICA*)

ANGELICA is an herbaceous species with a two-year or perennial cycle and belongs to the *Apiaceae* family. Very common in central Europe, it prefers marshy soils or, in general, places rich in humidity such as riverbanks and streams. According to legend, it was the archangel Raphael who brought it to Earth so that men could appreciate its infinite merits. Because of its bitter and aromatic qualities, with warm and robust notes, angelica is widely used in the liqueur industry: Its roots, for example, are an essential component to the gin recipe.

4. BITTER ORANGE (*CITRUS AURANTIUM VAR. AMARA*)

BITTER ORANGE is the fruit of the bitter orange tree (*Citrus aurantium var. amara*), also called melangolo, a tree native to the East Indies and South China, and found in many Mediterranean countries. Its cultivation in Italy spread thanks to the Arabs who imported it into Sicily after the year 1000. Bitter orange is often used in cooking, especially in the preparation of delicious jams and marmalades. Given its marked digestive and flavoring properties, it is commonly used in the production of soft drinks and spirits. A good example is curaçao, a liqueur typical of the island of the same name in the Netherlands Antilles, which is made with dried peels of the laraha, a variety of bitter orange imported locally by the Spanish in the 16th century.

5. WORMWOOD (*Artemisia absinthium*)

WORMWOOD is a perennial herbaceous plant of the *Asteraceae* family, referring to the genus *Artemisia* (from Artemis, Greek goddess of hunting and forests), which groups together several species with related aromatic and therapeutic qualities. Wormwood is also called *erba santa* (holy herb) for its high and variegated curative potential, which makes it an excellent tonic and digestive. A highly regarded ingredient in the liqueur industry, wormwood is essential in the formulation of vermouth. Wormwood, also known as absinthe, with its bitter-tannic taste, is also the basis of the famous spirit of the same name that conquered France at the end of the 19th century, with its intoxicating and hallucinogenic effects. In the wormwood plant, there are in fact traces of thujone, a substance that becomes highly toxic if concentrated above a certain threshold: For marketing purposes, the European Union has set a maximum of 10 mg/l for liquors and 35 mg/l for amari.

6. GREATER BURDOCK (*Arctium lappa*)

GREATER BURDOCK is a biennial herbaceous species of the *Asteraceae* family. Native to Europe and the temperate zones of Asia, it is a plant that loves to grow in rugged environments, on the edges of ditches, and along country roads. The scientific name of the genus, *Arctium*, comes from the Greek *árktos* (bear), probably alluding to the shaggy and hairy character of the plant. The name of the species, *lappa*, comes from the Greek *lambánein* (to take, to grasp) due to the presence of hooked spines that snag easily to surrounding objects. Greater burdock, of which the rhizomes and leaves (containing the bitter ingredient of arctiopicrin) are mainly used, has detoxifying and diuretic properties.

7. BOLDO (*Peumus boldus*)

BOLDO is a perennial bushy shrub of the *Monimiaceae* family, native to South America, in particular, Chile. Among the Andean populations, its leaves and bark have been used as a vermifuge and as a remedy for the treatment of gastrointestinal tract disorders. Among the most important functions of boldo is the stimulation of hepatobiliary activity, resulting in effective diuretic and purifying action. The penetrating and woody smell of the leaves means that boldo is often chosen to soften the taste of yerba mate, an energizing and diuretic drink very popular in Latin America.

8. ROMAN CHAMOMILE (ANTHEMIS NOBILIS)

ROMAN CHAMOMILE grows wild in central and western Europe and is certainly known for its calming properties. Belonging to the *Asteraceae* family, its name comes from the Greek words *chamái* (on the ground) and *mêlon* (apple) precisely because of the flowers' scent, which is similar to that of certain apples. Widely used by the Egyptians, Greeks, and Romans, it was in the Middle Ages that it became popular as a healing plant. Its sedative power is actually linked to its antispasmodic qualities that cause muscle relaxation, facilitating sleep and a general state of well-being. Roman chamomile, which is preferred over common chamomile for its intensity and finesse, often plays a significant role in the preparation of nonalcoholic drinks and alcoholic spirits (one of them being vermouth).

9. ARTICHOKE (CYNARA SCOLYMUS)

ARTICHOKE is a perennial herbaceous plant of the *Asteraceae* family. Native to the Mediterranean area, it is famous for its tasty flower heads and for its innumerable benefits. The scientific name of the genus is linked to Greek mythology and more precisely to the nymph Cynara, who was transformed into an artichoke by Zeus because of her capricious temperament. For centuries, used for the treatment of hepatobiliary disorders, the artichoke is rich in bitter substances that are associated with considerable digestive qualities, and it is widely used in the liquor industry. The plant also has diuretic and hypoglycemic effects and is useful in combating problems of hypercholesterolemia.

10. *MILK THISTLE* (*Silybum marianum*)

Milk thistle is a biennial herbaceous species of the *Asteraceae* family that grows wild all across the Mediterranean basin. According to legend, its leaves have characteristic little white spots that originate from the milk of the Virgin Mary, who, during her flight to Egypt, together with Jesus and Joseph, found shelter behind a thistle plant that has been called Marian ever since. The plant contains silymarin, an active ingredient present in the fruit, which plays an important role in protecting the liver from toxins.

11. COMMON CENTAURY (CENTAURIUM ERYTHRAEA)

COMMON CENTAURY, an herbaceous plant with an annual or biennial cycle, belongs to the *Gentianaceae* family. It is widespread throughout Italy, and it prefers growing in wet and grassy areas. The common name *centaury* is inspired by the mythological figure of Chiron, the wisest of the centaurs, who used the plant to try to heal the wound on his foot caused by a poisoned arrow mistakenly shot by Hercules. Interestingly, the species name *erythraea* comes from the Greek *erythrós* (red), in reference to the pink color of its flowers. The common centaury, whose flowering tops are used, is known for its marked and persistent bitter taste and for its great digestive and detoxifying effectiveness. For its febrifuge-like qualities, it is also known as a *cacciafebbre* (fever fighter).

12. CINCHONA

CINCHONA refers to a group of tree species of the genus *Cinchona*, belonging to the family of the *Rubiaceae* and native to the Andes. The name *cinchona* refers to the character of Ana de Osorio, Countess of Chinchón, wife of the Peruvian Viceroy Luis Jerónimo de Cabrera, who, according to legend, after being cured of fever thanks to the bark of this plant, encouraged its introduction into 17th-century Europe by the Jesuit Fathers. A famed antimalarial and febrifuge, cinchona, with its characteristic bitter and astringent notes, is also known for its appetite-increasing and digestive qualities. Red cinchona is the most sought-after in the herbal and phytotherapeutic field. Gray cinchona, on the other hand, is widely used in the production of liqueurs.

13. CHICORY (CICHORIUM INTYBUS)

CHICORY is a perennial herbaceous plant of the *Asteraceae* family. Found throughout Europe and Italy, it grows wild among ruins, in uncultivated fields, and on the edges of roads and paths. Also known by the name wild radicchio (or ugly radicchio, because of its unpleasant appearance), it was famous for its therapeutic efficacy among the ancient Egyptians, Greeks, and Romans. Its culinary use dates back only to the 17th century, however. Chicory has properties that stimulate gastrointestinal, hepatoprotective, and detoxifying activities. The presence of bitter and sugary elements makes it an excellent base for the production of digestive beverages such as the well-known chicory coffee.

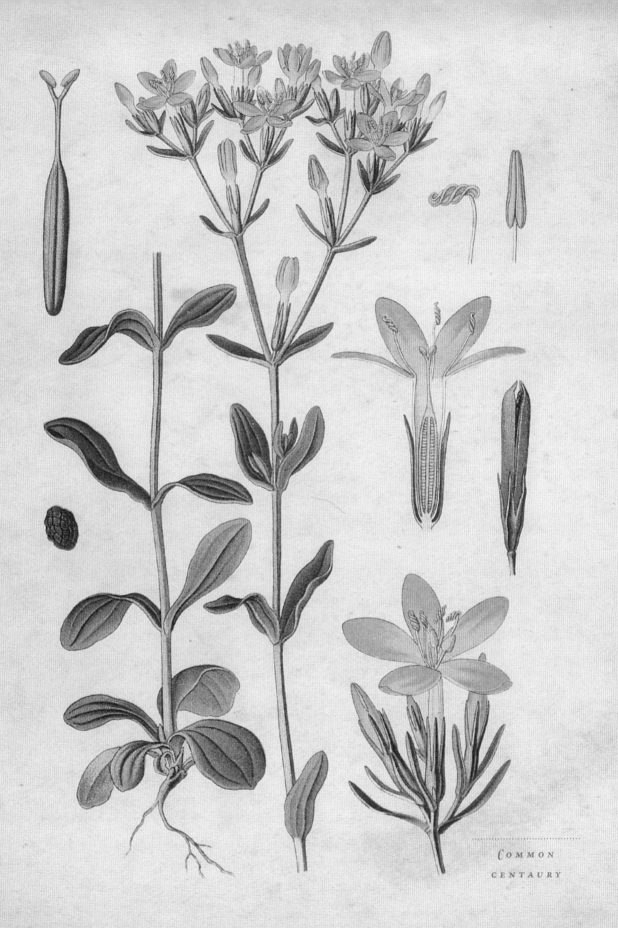

COMMON
CENTAURY

14. CONDURANGO (MARSDENIA CONDURANGO)

CONDURANGO belongs to the *Asclepiadaceae* family and is native to South America. The scientific name of the genus is a tribute to William Marsden, secretary of the English Admiralty of Sumatra who lived between the 18th and 19th centuries, and who studied and wrote the history of the island. The common name *condurango* derives from the union of two indigenous words, *cundur* and *angu* (vine of the condor). The latter, according to the natives, could heal snake bites. The victim simply had to eat the leaves of the condurango plant. Its most important uses, linked primarily to its bitter-tonic and analgesic properties through the use of the bark (with a pungent scent, similar to pepper), are for stimulating digestive processes and treating painful gastric disorders.

15. TURMERIC (CURCUMA LONGA)

TURMERIC, of the family of the *Zingiberaceae*, is a perennial rhizomatous species that is widespread in tropical countries and native to southeast India. Firmly established as a spice, it takes the scientific name *Curcuma* from the Persian-Indian term *kour-koum* (saffron). And in fact, in Europe during the Middle Ages, turmeric was known as the saffron of the Indies due to the similarities in color, which effectively rendered the two spices interchangeable. The higher cost of the floral stigmas of saffron (*Crocus sativus*) likely encouraged its interchangability with turmeric. Turmeric is an essential component of Indian curry, along with coriander, nutmeg, cinnamon, cloves, and ginger. In addition to its uses in cooking and the liquor industry, the turmeric rhizome is widely used in phytotherapy thanks to its digestive, antioxidant, and anti-inflammatory properties.

16. ELECAMPANE (*Inula helenium*)

ELECAMPANE is a perennial herbaceous plant that belongs to the *Asteraceae* family. It is widespread in southeastern Europe, and in Italy it is found in central-northern areas near clearings and wet scrublands. The genus *Inula* derives its name from the Greek *ineo* or *inao* (to purge), thanks to its associated detoxifying potential. The species name *helenium*, is inspired by the character of Helen of Troy, because the plant, in the myth, was supposedly born from her tears. Since ancient times, the elecampane, with its bitter-piquant taste and pleasant floral smell, has been renowned for its bitter-tonic properties. It is widely used in the production of spirit drinks. Enula wine, for example, is used as an aperitif, and it is made by adding dried elecampane roots to the wine.

17. GENTIAN (*Gentiana lutea*)

GENTIAN is a perennial herbaceous plant of the *Gentianaceae* family. It is native to central and southern Europe and Asia Minor, and it grows wild in mountainous areas. Only the root is used, which must be dried because it is poisonous when fresh. The botanical name of the genus, *Gentiana*, comes from Gentius, king of Illyria, who is thought to have been the first to discover its therapeutic qualities in the second century B.C. The species name *lutea* refers to its characteristic yellow flowers. Gentian, with its characteristic bitter flavor, boasts tonic and eupeptic properties with which it stimulates the appetite and digestive functions; in ancient times it was considered an essential vermifuge and anti-poison remedy.

18. GENTIANELLA (*Gentiana acaulis*)

GENTIANELLA is so called because of its small size compared to other species of the genus *Gentiana*: its height is usually around 2 inches (5 cm), and it rarely exceeds 6 inches (15 cm). This plant is typically found in mountainous areas, and in Italy it thrives wild in the Alps and Apennines. Gentianella—also known as Koch's gentian—is distinguished by its large blue-violet, bell-shaped flowers that sit directly on the apex: hence the name *acaulis*, which is from the Greek *ákaulos* (without stem). The flowers and roots of gentianella have a very bitter taste, and the benefits of the plant are of a tonic and digestive nature.

19. JUNIPER (*Juniperus communis*)

JUNIPER is an evergreen shrub of the *Cupressaceae* family. It is widespread in almost the entire northern hemisphere. In Italy it grows from the Alps to Sardinia, although it prefers central-northern regions such as Umbria, Tuscany, and Emilia Romagna. Its name, according to many, derives from the Celtic *juneperus* (acrid). Juniper has long been considered a panacea for all ills, and it is used mainly as a digestive, detoxifier, antiseptic, and expectorant. Its berries are very popular in liqueurs. In fact, they represent the main ingredient of gin, a famous distillate obtained from a base of cereals and juniper berries that is flavored with a special mix of botanicals.

20. HOPS (*Humulus lupulus*)

HOPS are a perennial climbing herbaceous species of the *Cannabaceae* family. It is widespread in the shady areas of central Europe. It is a plant famously used for the production of beer. Hops are what gives beer a more bitter or more aromatic taste, depending on the varieties used in the recipe. Hops also contribute to the preservation of beer thanks to its antiseptic action. The resins present in the hop cones are specifically responsible for its bitter taste, and they can also perform an antifungal action. Hops have digestive, analgesic, and sedative properties.

GENTIANELLA

JUNIPER

HOPS

21. *QUASSIA AMARA OR AMARGO* (*Quassia amara*)

Quassia amara belongs to the *Simaroubaceae* family and is a tree native to tropical areas of Central and South America, including the countries of Guyana, Brazil, and Venezuela. Quassia wood is characterized by a very high bitterness index, which makes it an excellent tonic-digestive remedy. Quassia also possesses antipyretic qualities. It is said that its name derives from a slave from Surinam known as Quassi who recommended it to his master, Colonel Carl Gustav Dahlberg, as a powerful febrifuge. Dahlberg himself then introduced it to Carl Linnaeus, a famous 18th-century Swedish botanist, due to the healing significance of the plant. Quassia, with its intense bitter taste, is called also amargo, which means "bitter" in the Spanish language.

22. CHINESE RHUBARB
(RHEUM PALMATUM)

CHINESE RHUBARB is a rhizomatous perennial herbaceous plant of the *Polygonaceae* family. It grows wild in Mongolia and China where it has been used for medicinal purposes for thousands of years. The genus name *Rheum* is inspired by the ancient name Rha, which refers to the Volga River, which crosses European Russia. There are, in fact, many other species of rhubarb, cultivated for horticultural or ornamental use, that originate from a vast area spanning from Eastern Europe to Central Asia. With a bitter and slightly astringent taste, Chinese rhubarb—whose rhizome is mainly used—is rich in digestive, appetite-inducing, and detoxifying properties.

23. RUE (RUTA GRAVEOLENS)

RUE is a perennial species of the family of the *Rutaceae*. Its herbaceous jets are woody at the base. Native to southern Europe, in Italy it grows in almost all regions—except the major islands—preferring arid and stony environments, at elevations no higher than 3,280 feet (1,000 m) above sea level. In popular tradition, probably because of the repellent smell of its leaves, rue was recognized as having magical and protective powers, able to ward off evil spirits as well as insects and vipers. A medicinal plant with antispasmodic and antioxidant effects, thanks to its aromatic and digestive traits, rue is held in great esteem in the formulation of amari and grappas.

24. DANDELION (*Taraxacum officinale*)

DANDELIONS are a perennial herbaceous plant of the *Asteraceae* family. Widespread in Italy and throughout the northern hemisphere, it prefers growing in meadows, uncultivated land, and wooded clearings. Its scientific name, according to many, refers to the union of the Greek words *tarássein* (to mix) and ákos (remedy) to indicate its numerous medicinal properties. It is known as dandelion, thanks to its toothed leaves (*dent de lion* in French), and puffball for its flowers that turn into a soft white sphere whose achenes (similar to small feathers) are dispersed in the air with a simple puff. Loaded with symbolic meanings linked to lightness and hope, the dandelion, with its bitter-sapid notes, enjoys tonic, detoxifying, and diuretic properties. Not by chance, in peasant culture it is also called *piscialetto* (pee-a-bed).

25. BOGBEAN (*Menyanthes trifoliata*)

BOGBEAN is an aquatic plant of the *Gentianaceae* family that prefers marshy soils and ponds in submontane alpine areas. The Italian name, *trifoglio fibrino*, derives from the Latin *fiber* (beaver), which is also an inhabitant of marshy environments. The botanical name of the genus, *Menyanthes*, recalls the Greek terms *mēn* (month) and *ánthos* (flower), which can be translated into "flower of the month," probably because in the past the plant was considered an essential remedy for hypomenorrhoea. The species name *trifoliata* refers to the trilobed leaves. Bogweed—whose leaves are often used—is rich in bitter substances that stimulate digestive processes and boost gastric and hepatic activity, which prove useful in case of lack of appetite and dyspepsia. Bogbean has long been considered a panacea for all ills, therefore able to cure many diseases, including scurvy, asthma, and gout.

26. VERBENA (*Verbena officinalis*)

VERBENA, belonging to the *Verbenaceae* family, is a perennial herbaceous species native to Asia and Europe. It is widespread throughout Italy. According to some interpretations, its name comes from the Celtic *ferfaen* (stone-breaker), as it was used by druids for the treatment of bladder stones. In ancient times, verbena was considered a sacred plant and therefore played an important role in secular and religious ceremonies. It was also attributed important aphrodisiac properties, so much so that the Romans called it *herba Veneris* and therefore associated it with the goddess Venus. Verbena can have sedative, anti-inflammatory, and febrifuge effects. Its bitter-tonic qualities make it suitable for use in the preparation of digestive liquors.

Aromatic Botanicals

27. CINNAMON (Cinnamomum zeylanicum)

CINNAMON is a spice obtained from the woody parts (left to dry in the sun) of a tree of the *Lauraceae* family. *Cinnamomum zeylanicum* originated in Sri Lanka and it is present throughout tropical Asia. In addition to its proven aromatizing power, with both embracing sweet and spicy notes, for which it has a place in gastronomy and in the food and liquor industry, cinnamon is also an excellent remedy for disorders related to digestion difficulties and the flu. It also helps regulate blood sugar levels and promotes the metabolism of fat.

28. GREEN CARDAMOM (Elettaria cardamomum)

GREEN CARDAMOM is a spice obtained from the tropical plant *Elettaria cardamomum*, which belongs to the *Zingiberaceae* family. Widely cultivated in Central America, it grows wild in southern India, China, and Sri Lanka. The plant bears green capsule-shaped fruits containing black-brown seeds that represent the spice itself. Appreciated by the ancient Egyptians, Greeks, and Romans for its sweet and pungent aromatic qualities, green cardamom is an undisputed favorite in Asian cuisine, and it is not difficult to find it in recipes for alcoholic beverages such as Swedish glogg (mulled wine).

29. CLOVES (*Syzygium aromaticum*)

CLOVES are a spice obtained from the dried buds of the *Syzygium aromaticum* plant (also called *Eugenia caryophyllata*) of the *Myrtaceae* family, native to the Moluccas Islands in east Indonesia. Clove is much loved in the East and has been omnipresent for centuries in the pantries of European kitchens. Clove is also widely used in phytotherapy thanks to its numerous beneficial effects, including anti-inflammatory, antiseptic, and analgesic properties. Clove is part of the botanical blend of the famous Alchermes liqueur, which was served in the late 15th century at the Florentine court of Lorenzo de' Medici.

30. LEMONGRASS (*Cymbopogon nardus*)

LEMONGRASS is a perennial herbaceous plant of the *Poaceae* family. Native to South Asia, lemongrass is thought to have been brought to the West by Alexander the Great's soldiers in the fourth century B.C. The scent of its leaves is strongly citrusy—the Italian name, *citronella*, comes from the French *citron* (lemon)—and for this characteristic it is much sought after as a cooking herb as well as for use in perfumery and cosmetics. Lemongrass helps to combat digestive problems and has an excellent sedative and calming effect on the nervous system. It is also known for repelling mosquitoes.

LEMONGRASS

31. HELICHRYSUM (Helichrysum italicum)

HELICHRYSUM is a shrubby herbaceous species of the *Asteraceae* family that prefers to grow in the arid and stony areas of Mediterranean Europe. It is also widespread in Italy, particularly in the central-southern region. The genus name *Helichrysum* comes from the union of two Greek words, *hélios* (sun) and *chrysós* (gold), thanks to the bright yellow color of its flowers. The color remains even after harvesting and drying. For this reason, in ancient times, the plant was considered to be a symbol of eternity, and it was also associated with the cult of the sun. Helichrysum is distinguished by its strong flavor reminiscent of licorice and curry. It also possesses innumerable virtues; for example, it naturally stimulates liver and gastrointestinal functions and has an anti-inflammatory and antibacterial nature.

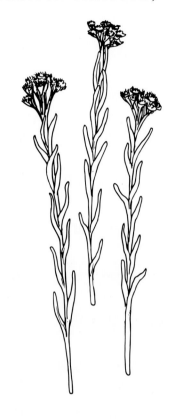

32. WILD FENNEL (Foeniculum vulgare)

WILD FENNEL is a perennial herbaceous plant of the *Apiaceae* family. Typical of the Mediterranean basin, it grows wild in dry and sunny environments, at the edges of fields and country paths. Wild fennel has appetite-inducing, digestive, antispasmodic, and diuretic properties. Its pleasant and unique herbaceous-balsamic scent causes leaves, seeds (which actually correspond to the fruits), and rhizomes to often end up as flavor enhancers for food or as a base for herbal teas and digestive liquors.

33. HIBISCUS FLOWERS (Hibiscus sabdariffa)

HIBISCUS is a perennial plant of the *Malvaceae* family. It is very common in the tropical zones of Africa and Asia, and in Central America. The calyxes of its flowers are naturally rich in vitamin C and antioxidants, and they are able to stimulate digestive processes and to combat hypertension and water-retention disorders. The dried calyxes are also used to produce a famous infusion drink, *karkadè* (red tea), which has a notoriously sour taste. Hibiscus—of which the leaves, seeds, and roots are also used—is also known to have sedative and laxative properties.

34. LICORICE (Glycyrrhiza glabra)

LICORICE is a perennial suffruticose species of the *Fabaceae* family, and it is characteristic of Mediterranean countries. In Italy it grows wild in the southern regions and islands. The genus name *Glycyrrhiza* comes from the meeting of the two Greek words *glykýs* (sweet) and *rhíza* (root) that describe its sweet and pleasant taste and its soothing qualities. The healing properties of licorice were already known to great civilizations such as Egypt, Assyria, and China. However, the plant did not arrive in Europe until the 15th century when it was brought by Dominican friars. Licorice boasts, among many other qualities, digestive, depurative, diuretic, and anti-inflammatory properties; it can be instrumental in the treatment of gastric and duodenal ulcers. For alimentary and therapeutic purposes, the roots are mainly used.

35. MACE (*Myristica fragrans*)

MACE is a spice obtained from an evergreen tree native to the Moluccas Islands of east Indonesia, the *Myristica fragrans*, whose seed is nutmeg. Mace is obtained by drying the aril, which is the fleshy red coating that embraces the seed of the fruit. The taste of mace is similar to that of nutmeg but is more elegant and delicate. Mace, with its spicy and bitter-like taste, also has digestive and anti-inflammatory properties.

36. MINT

MINT refers to a genus of plants belonging to the *Lamiaceae* family, which brings together numerous species and distinguishes itself for its high propensity to hybridization that in turn leads to the birth of new varieties. Its name recalls that of the nymph Mintha, who, according to Greek mythology, was transformed into a plant by Persephone after Mintha tempted her husband, the god Pluto. Widespread in the Mediterranean area, it is one of the best-known aromatic herbs in the world. It possesses important antispasmodic and decongestant properties, as well as digestive and balsamic benefits. Among the most widespread species of mint is peppermint.

37. MYRTLE (*Myrtus communis*)

MYRTLE, an evergreen shrub of the *Myrtaceae* family, is the very definition of Mediterranean vegetation. It is known for its characteristic spherical berries and its unmistakable balsamic scent. In ancient times, as a plant dear to the goddess Venus, it was considered a symbol of love. It was also used for healing purposes for the treatment of certain respiratory and digestive disorders. Myrtle has digestive and anti-inflammatory properties. In Sardinia it is the basis of the liqueur, mirto (the Italian word for myrtle).

38. NUTMEG (*Myristica fragrans*)

NUTMEG is a spice obtained from the peeled seed of the *Myristica fragrans*, an evergreen tree of the *Myristicaceae* family native to the Moluccas Islands in east Indonesia. The nutmeg tree is now widespread in various intertropical regions. Nutmeg is also known as the nut of Muscat, the capital of Oman, where, centuries ago, it began to be marketed by the Arabs. Introduced in Europe only in the 16th century, this spice has had a long reputation as a powerful aphrodisiac and antiseptic. Today it is recognized as also having tonic, appetite-inducing, and carminative properties. Nutmeg, with its hot-pungent taste, should be consumed in small quantities to avoid side effects.

MYRTLE

Rosemary

39. ALLSPICE (*Pimenta dioica*)

ALLSPICE, also known as Jamaican pepper, is a spice produced from the dried berries of the *Pimenta dioica*, an evergreen tree of the *Myrtaceae* family, native to Jamaica. In French it is known as *toute-épice* (or *quatre-épices*) thanks to its peculiar flavor that is reminiscent of cinnamon, cloves, ginger, and nutmeg. Primarily valued on the tables of Central America, allspice is also recognized in phytotherapy for its digestive, carminative, and antiseptic qualities.

40. ROSEMARY (*Rosmarinus officinalis*)

ROSEMARY, an evergreen shrub plant of the *Lamiaceae* family, is characteristic of the Mediterranean basin. Its name comes from the Latin *ros marinus* (sea dew) because of its manner of growing along the coasts and the color of its flowers, which at times recalls that of the sea. Among ancient peoples, rosemary was considered a symbol of immortality of the soul, which is why its small branches were burned during propitiatory and funerary rituals. Moreover, in popular tradition, the plant was attributed aphrodisiac qualities as well as the ability to keep away negative energies. Rosemary, with its intense balsamic flavor, has digestive, tonic, antiseptic, and antibacterial properties, and it is one of the most appreciated aromatic herbs in cooking and in the cosmetics sector.

41. ELDERBERRY (*Sambucus nigra*)

ELDERBERRY is a perennial plant of the *Caprifoliaceae* family. It is found throughout Europe, including Italy. It takes the form of a shrub or small tree, and it grows mostly in damp woods, near ruins or watercourses, from the sea to subalpine areas. Its name derives from the Greek *sambyke,* an ancient stringed musical instrument made from the wood of the plant. Elderberry has purifying, diuretic, anti-inflammatory, and diaphoretic qualities. The dried flowers of the *Sambucus nigra* and *Sambucus racemosa* varieties are used in the liquor industry; its seeds and leaves, as well as unripe fruit and fresh bark, are toxic due to the presence of substances such as *sambucina* and sambunigrin.

42. VANILLA (*Vanilla planifolia*)

VANILLA is a famous spice obtained from the fermentation and drying of the pods of *Vanilla planifolia,* an orchid native to tropical America. It is very common in Mexico and on the islands of the Indian and Pacific oceans. Among the most prized varieties are Bourbon vanilla, typical of the island of Réunion and Madagascar, and Tahiti vanilla produced on the island of the same name in French Polynesia. Always considered an effective aphrodisiac, vanilla is also recognized for its sedative qualities, which are useful to combat stress and insomnia, as well as for its antioxidants that are aimed at fighting cellular aging. Its sweet and embracing aroma makes it a precious spice for preparations in the cosmetic, culinary, and liquoristic fields.

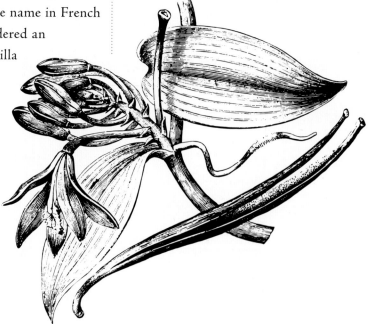

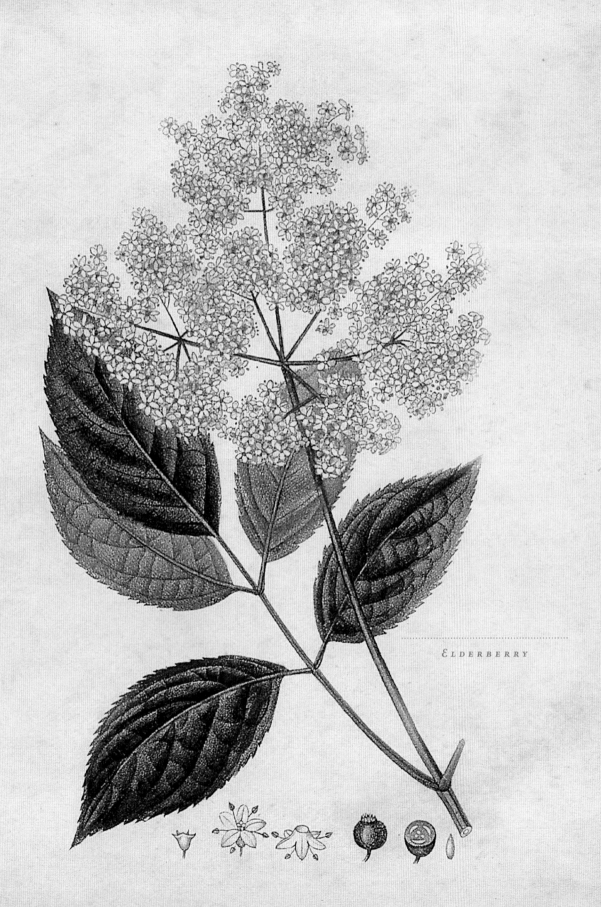

ELDERBERRY

Sea fennel

43. CHINOTTO (CITRUS MYRTIFOLIA)

CHINOTTO, also known as myrtle-leaved orange, is the fruit of the citrus tree *Citrus myrtifolia* of the *Rutaceae* family, which is believed to be native to China. In Italy, chinotto is a typical product of the Western Ligurian Riviera and is also widely cultivated in Calabria and Sicily. The plant itself is most likely the result of a genetic mutation of the bitter orange, and it is distinguished by leaves similar to those of myrtle: This latter characteristic is recalled in the botanical name of the species. Naturally rich in vitamin C, chinotto, given its bitter taste, has digestive properties and is therefore used in many spirits such as Amaro Neri from Chinottissimo.

44. SEA FENNEL (CRITHMUM MARITIMUM)

SEA FENNEL is a perennial herbaceous plant of the *Apiaceae* family. It prefers growing on rocky coasts and in brackish environments, which is why it thrives in Mediterranean areas, on the Atlantic coasts of western Europe, and on the Black Sea coasts. Thanks to its intrinsic link with the sea, it is also called St. Peter's Wort, in reference to the apostle and patron saint of fishermen and sailors. Furthermore, the latter used to eat sea fennel during crossings, as they were aware of its antiscorbutic qualities. In phytotherapy, sea fennel is also known for its purifying, digestive, carminative, and diuretic properties. In gastronomy it is mainly used to flavor salads and fish dishes. Together with golden samphire (*Limbarda crithmoides*), it is part of the formulation of Amaro Crithmum produced in Maratea.

45. OLIVE LEAVES (Olea europaea)

OLIVE LEAVES are from an evergreen tree of the *Oleaceae* family that is probably native to Asia Minor. Very common in the Mediterranean basin and in the temperate zones of America and Australia, the tree is known above all for its tasty fruits, olives, and for the prodigious oil obtained from them, which is the basis of the Mediterranean diet. It also has countless cosmetic and medicinal uses. The leaves of the olive tree also have a curative value of a purifying and antioxidant nature, proving to be a valuable aid in the treatment of hypertension and blood-circulation disorders. As a flavoring agent they are used in the amaro recipes of Amaro Pax from Umbria and Limolivo from Puglia.

46. JUJUBE (Ziziphus zizyphus)

JUJUBE refers to the fleshy fruit of the jujube tree (*Ziziphus zizyphus*), a small tree of the *Rhamnaceae* family, and is also known as the Chinese date. In the culinary field, jujube broth, a hydro-alcoholic infusion of Venetian origin, prepared with autumn fruit, is well known. It was found in Renaissance times at the Gonzaga court. Jujubes are very rich in vitamins and minerals; they help to counteract disorders related to depression, anxiety, and insomnia, and they act as a laxative and as a purifying remedy for the liver. In South Tyrol they give life to Juith, a natural amaro made with jujubes created by master distiller Florian Rabanser.

LAMPASCIONE is a perennial herbaceous plant of the *Liliaceae* family. It is widespread in the Mediterranean area. Its bulbs, similar to small onions, represent a typical product of southern Italy, in particular, Puglia and Basilicata. The typical bitterish taste is made pleasant by a balance of sweetness on the finish, and this means that the bulbs can also be eaten naturally or preserved in vinegar or oil. The choice of the name *lampascione* can be attributed to Oribasius, a Greek physician from Byzantium in the fourth century A.D. In the Late Latin period, it was referred to as *lampadionem* (lamp) in reference to the specific shape of the bulb. Known for centuries for its purifying, purgative, and aphrodisiac effects, lampascione is now part of the recipe of Amaro Imperatore, offspring of the Tavoliere delle Puglie region. This also known as tassel hyacinth.

48. MORINGA

MORINGA refers to a genus of plants belonging to the *Moringaceae* family. It is native to India and widespread in Asia, Africa, and South America. The most well-known and widely used spice for food, medical, and cosmetic purposes is the horseradish tree (*Moringa oleifera*). Moringa trees are also called "miracle trees" because all the elements of the plant—seeds, roots, leaves, flowers, and fruits—have beneficial potential. Ancient peoples like the Egyptians knew of its ability to purify undrinkable water, so it was used to clean up lakes and streams. Its high concentration of nutrients—particularly mineral salts, vitamins, and essential amino acids—means that moringa is considered by many to be a true superfood. The Roman company Earth Mother Project uses its leaves to make Amaro 81.

49. NEPITELLA (CALAMINTHA NEPETA)

NEPITELLA is a perennial herbaceous plant of the *Labiatae* family present in the Mediterranean area and in some areas of central and southern Europe and western Asia. Also known as lesser calamint, nepitella should not be confused with Roman mint (*Mentha pulegium*), which is improperly called *mentuccia* in Rome and the surrounding area. Nepitella has aromatic qualities as well as hepato-stimulant, tonic, and digestive properties. In 2017 it became the main ingredient of Amaro Nepéta produced in the region of Syracuse.

50. RED TREVISO RADICCHIO

RED TREVISO radicchio is a variety of *Cichorium intybus*, the botanical name with which common chicory is identified, of the family *Compositae*. It is a product with Protected Geographical Indication, and it is harvested early or late and finds its terrain of choice in the provinces of Treviso, Padua, and Venice. Rich in vitamins and mineral salts, red Treviso radicchio has the ability to boost digestion and hepatobiliary functions. Its unmistakable bitterish taste enhances countless dishes of local cuisine; in Veneto it enriches the aromatic bouquet of Amaro Negroni.

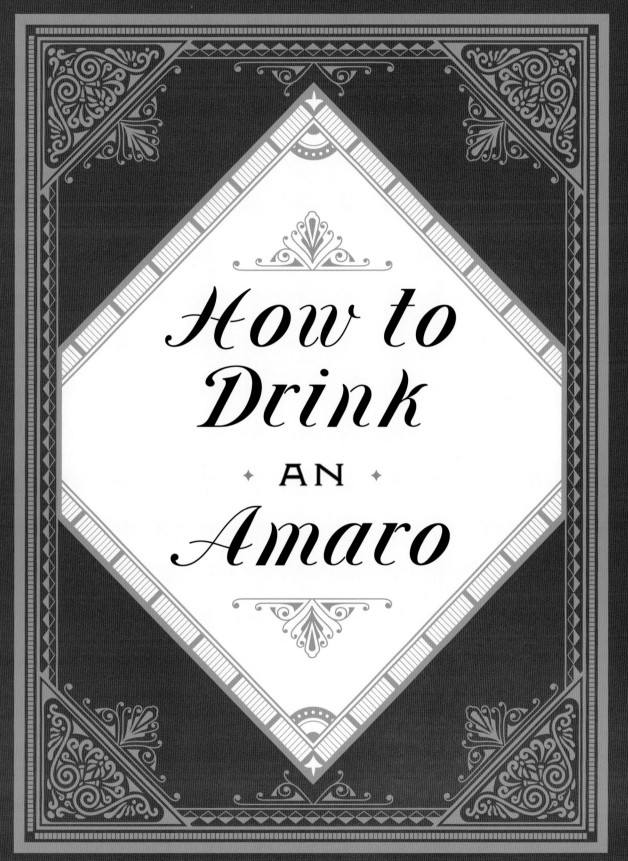

How to Drink
· AN ·
Amaro

When Is the Best Time to Enjoy an Amaro?

I n his 1905 work *Sur la lecture*, Marcel Proust asserted that there is no better friendship than that with a book. I add that there is no better friendship than that with a book and an amaro, to be sipped between pages, flooding the palate with complex and exciting flavors that accompany us in the colorful ocean of moods aroused by reading.

With a glass of amaro and a good book there are no formalities. We often leave them reluctantly. We laugh with them to the extent that they grace our palate and our soul and, once satiated with their company, we put them back in their place, waiting for the next "journey." The ideal conditions to fully enjoy this sincere, selfless, almost touching, relationship are certainly solitude and silence, purer than words.

As D'Annunzio himself admitted, although referring to Amaro Montenegro, amaro is the "liqueur of the Virtues": It regenerates, fills, satisfies, ennobles. But in order for it to carry out its task fully, it is essential to choose the proper temperature of consumption.

In this regard, I am reminded of a long period of my childhood when I attended the neighborhood oratory, that of the church of San Clemente Papa in Rome.

After our soccer matches, the parish priest Don Giuseppe often asked me to stay on to serve Mass as an altar boy.

Don Giuseppe was a great man of the church, affable and original like few others. He was also a great soccer player, he joked like one of us, and every so often asked me to replace the wine in the chalice with the amaro that he kept in the sacristy fridge: According to him it was an amaro of great value, produced by the Benedictine friars and spared by the bombardment that in 1944 hit the abbey of his town, Montecassino, in the province of Latina, during the World War II. It was in that context, between scoring a goal and a stolen sip, that I discovered I loved cold amaro.

Even my grandfather Ferdinando preferred to drink it like this! My mother told me that in 1960, after undergoing an operation to remove throat cancer, grandfather Nandi learned from the doctors that he had at most 15 days left to live. At the news he fell asleep disconsolate and sad, praying and asking for the good Lord's help.

The following morning, he told of having been visited in his sleep by a bearded man, dressed in a long robe and emitting a very strong light, who placed his hand on his sick side and told him to be calm. As a faithful

Venetian, grandfather Nandi recognized that bearded man as Saint Anthony of Padua. Probably many skeptics will not believe it, but the day after the event, thanks to a medical checkup, it was discovered that the tumor had completely reabsorbed. My grandfather lived another 25 years, and they were healthy and happy years. From the day of the miracle, grandfather Ferdinando, before going to sleep, began to drink a drop of St. Anthony's Liquor (always cold), addressing a prayer to the saint to thank him; he often allowed me, as a child, to perform the same ritual, which would have me laid out in bed inebriated.

AMARO IS THE LIQUEUR OF PASSIONS: IT REGENERATES, FILLS, SATISFIES, ENNOBLES.

In truth, however, there is no "right" temperature to best appreciate an amaro. Surely what you should never do is drink it with the addition of ice, unless it is to your express taste or there is a need to lighten the alcoholic effect. Ice, in beverages, is not always an added value; in this case it would cancel the balance and the complexity of the flavors of the amaro, which is created with the idea of not adding other substances because it is perfect at the moment of bottling. Even drinking an amaro straight from just the freezer is not a good habit: Even if it is cold, a temperature below zero would anesthetize the taste, risking making it anonymous to the palate. As it is easy to imagine, when talking with enthusiasts and insiders I have often dwelt on the theme of tasting amaro. Among the theories that I found the most interesting is certainly the one held by Armando Bomba, a great connoisseur of the beverage world but, above all, a refined producer of Amaro Formidabile.

According to Bomba's thesis, there are three ways to best taste an amaro:

- **ON AN EMPTY STOMACH, IN TWO DIFFERENT PHASES:**
  - **AT ROOM TEMPERATURE**
  - **SIPPING IT COLD, BUT NOT ICED**

This double tasting allows you to perceive nuances and aromatic peaks in their entirety thanks to the difference in temperature. In "curative" terms, it also allows you to enjoy the aperitizing power of the amaro and/or as a preparatory to better digestion.

- **WITH A FULL STOMACH AS A PURE DIGESTIVE, IMMEDIATELY AFTER MEALS, WITH A PALATE ALREADY ACCUSTOMED TO THE FLAVORS.**

- **ACCORDING TO OUR EXPERIENCE OR FOLLOWING THE MANUFACTURER'S SUGGESTIONS, PERHAPS RESPECTING THE PRINCIPLES OF A PERFECT SERVE.**

Analytical Tasting

To carry out a sensory analysis of amaro, it is useful to submit it to the practical tasting rules common to wines and spirits. In a technical tasting, for the abovementioned reasons, the amaro must be at room temperature and any vertical tasting must take into account groups of amari of similar bitterness content, starting from the softer and more delicate spirits to the more aromatic and overbearing ones. This begins with a visual examination.

The color will tell us about the type of botanicals used, while clarity will refer to the production technique. An amaro of a darker color, ranging from brown to almost black, is often an indication of a greater presence of roots and barks; by contrast, an amaro that ranges between amber and dark green could reveal a more herbaceous and vegetal essence. If opaque, the amaro will be the result of simpler filtrations, by choice of the producer.

Continue the examination with an olfactory analysis. The glass, at this point, will be slightly heated by the palm of one hand and should be covered with the other to allow the alcohol to evaporate from the liquid and the odorous and volatile molecules to rest on the inner wall of the glass. Carefully approach the glass with both nostrils for a first olfaction. Inhale and exhale deeply to achieve a full overall perception. Then take a sip; on the palate, the amaro should be tasted in small sips such that it pervades the entire oral cavity, then it should be left to rest on the taste buds for a few seconds. The first sensations will be those of bitterness and sweetness; our receptors will then begin to break down the spirit to bring out new elements. At first roots, barks, and citrus fruits emerge, then, little by little, aromatic herbs are defined. When everything seems to vanish, a surprising aftertaste will arrive, perhaps floral, and it could be stunning.

The first sips will always remain impressed in your taste-olfactory memory, and they will correspond to your most authentic perceptions.

The analytical tasting of an amaro is equivalent to the interpretation of a sum of sensations felt simultaneously or subsequently. Its primary purpose is to separate, sort, and identify the different taste impressions that would go unnoticed with a quick, disinterested, and above all, disenchanted approach.

Without love an amaro cannot be understood. However, only by knowing in depth the circumstances from which it was born can one be ready to be truly enraptured by it!

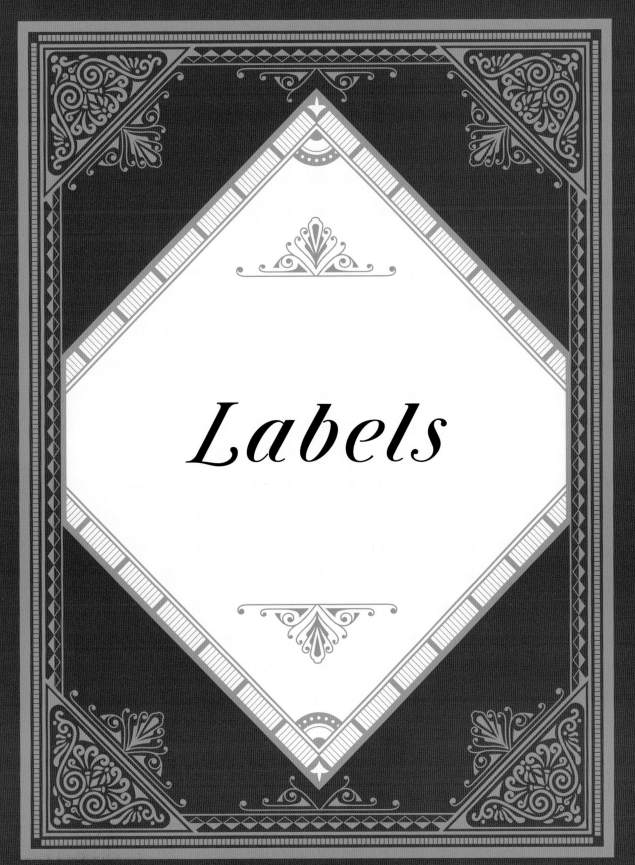

Labels

Aosta Valley

AMARO BENEFORT

Distilleria Alpe
Hone, Aosta

Distilleria Alpe, active for more than 60 years, has always been run with passion and professionalism by the Calvetti family. The production company makes handcrafted spirits and follows the traditions of the centuries-old Aosta Valley distillers. Like every authentic, old-style amaro from a mountain region, Benefort is a completely natural amaro, produced by the mixture of over 20 vegetal sources, including alpine flowers, roots, and herbs, as well as Roman wormwood (called *benefort* in Valdostan patois), rhubarb, cinchona, gentian, yarrow, and cardamom. Standard botanicals are infused in alcohol for about 60 days after which the infusion is steam distilled.

ALCOHOL CONTENT: 38% vol.

COLOR: amber

BOUQUET: distinct alpine notes of bitter herbs

TASTE: bitter and full with clear floral hints

AFTERTASTE: bitter persistence of wormwood

AMARO CIARDON

Vertosan
Châtillon, Aosta

The Vertosan company's new life began in 2007, the year in which the Bernardini family, already operating in the food and beverage sector, took it over. They were well aware of the strength of one of its flagship products created in the 1970s, Amaro Ciardon. *Ciardon* is the name in Valdostan patois of the milk thistle (*cardo mariano* in Italian), whose leaves represent the main ingredient of the eponymous bitter. Yarrow, Roman wormwood, chamomile flowers, gentian, and rhubarb are some of the botanicals that are added to Amaro Ciardon's recipe, which remains mostly secret. We certainly know that the plant mix is infused in neutral alcohol and that the spirit, before bottling, undergoes a period of refinement in steel tanks.

ALCOHOL CONTENT: 36% vol.

COLOR: amber

BOUQUET: intense with citrus and bitterish hints

TASTE: gentle and aromatic, with a distinct and well-integrated bitterness

AFTERTASTE: long vegetal persistence, very clean

AMARO LYS

Distilleria Alpe
Hone, Aosta

The recipe of Amaro Lys was created around the end of the 1970s for those who preferred to drink an amaro with a sweeter taste. With this intent, Armando Calvetti, founder of Distilleria Alpe, decided to add some ingredients with a less bitter taste such as sweet orange, bitter orange, vanilla, and almonds to the tincture prepared to produce Amaro Benefort. These components are cold infused in high-quality grain alcohol produced in Italy. At the end of the process, the spent botanicals are distilled and then added to the infusion. Amaro Lys is the symbol of a perfect balance between sweet and bitter, exalted by a decisive complexity of taste and an appreciable persistence due to the distillation.

ALCOHOL CONTENT: 30% vol.

COLOR: amber

BOUQUET: scent of alpine herbs and flowers

TASTE: balanced between sweet and bitter

AFTERTASTE: excellent, with a soft herbaceous and fresh persistence

EBO LEBO

Ottoz du Val d'Aoste
Quart, Aosta

Tradition, innovation, and a link to its territory distinguish the St. Roch Distilleries, which in 2005 added Ottoz liqueurs to their production. The line of the Ottoz brand originates from an idea by Laurent Ottoz, Valdostan by birth, who emigrated from his homeland with his family to France to make his fortune. Across the Alps, Laurent acquired liquor-making techniques while working for a French producer of Génépy, refining and perfecting them thanks to his immense passion. Ebo Lebo possesses exceptional tonic, invigorating, and digestive properties, hinted at in the historical advertising claim "With Ebo Lebo, I can even digest my mother-in-law." The Ebo Lebo recipe includes 45 botanicals, including yarrow, juniper, and genepy. In the Grand Reserve version, saffron and white genepy are blended to the main ingredients.

ALCOHOL CONTENT: 36% vol.

COLOR: amber

BOUQUET: intense scent of alpine herbs

TASTE: balanced between sweet and bitter

AFTERTASTE: strong bitter connotation with balsamic hints

AMARO DENTE DI LEONE

La Valdôtaine
Saint-Marcel, Aosta

In the Aosta Valley, a region nestled in alpine nature, there is a widespread use of herbs that are then processed and skillfully transformed into authentic liqueur specialties. Among the many small distilleries scattered in the Aosta Valley territory, La Valdôtaine stands out. It was founded as Grapperia in 1947 in Verres in the "lower valley" (the part of the Aosta Valley that goes from Pont-Saint-Martin to Montjovet and Saint-Vincent) and began distilling grappa in small copper stills by traditional discontinuous steam distillation. In 1978, the factory moved its headquarters to Saint-Marcel. The strong presence of alpine botanicals and emerald water coming from the glaciers behind the distillery led the company to bet on the reworking of a recipe for an amaro of mountain herbs, and so Amaro Dente di Leone was born. Among the vegetal components are yarrow, nutmeg, angelica (root and seeds), Roman wormwood, gentian wormwood, Roman wormwood, basil leaves, cnicus, gentian root, hyssop leaves, elderflowers, and savory. The formula is enriched with raw sugar for sweetening, common thyme, and dandelion roots.

ALCOHOL CONTENT: 32.6% vol.

COLOR: very clear with a lovely chestnut color with golden reflections

BOUQUET: delicate with herbaceous hints

TASTE: the tenderness of the dandelion and gentian emerges, attenuated by the flavor of thyme and other herbs

AFTERTASTE: elderflowers prevail; very long finish

Piedmont

ALPESTRE

Distilleria San Giuseppe
Carmagnola, Turin

The history of Alpestre, symbol of the San Giuseppe Distillery, is closely linked to that of the Marist friars, a religious congregation founded in France at the beginning of the 19th century. In 1857 Friar Emanuele, an expert botanist and Marist herbalist, driven by the need to produce a cordial to aid against the most common ailments, developed the formula for a distillate made with 34 different herbs, expertly dosed, and aged for at least four years in Slavonian oak barrels. The very secret recipe did not include, and still does not include, the use of sugar, let alone substances that sweeten the final taste. Thyme, wormwood, lavender, angelica, fennel, tansy, sage, mint, lemon balm, hyssop, cedar, and chamomile are just some of the botanicals necessary for the production of Alpestre. Also available is a version that includes the addition of honey.

ALCOHOL CONTENT: 44% vol.

COLOR: straw yellow

BOUQUET: vegetable and aromatic

TASTE: dry with strong herbaceous connotation

AFTERTASTE: excellent plant persistence

ALPESTRE SPECIAL RESERVE 1983

Distilleria San Giuseppe
Carmagnola, Turin

Alpestre Special Reserve 1983 is an Alpestre selected for its quality and exceptional aging in the Carmagnola cellars of Distilleria San Giuseppe. Like every vintage, it offers distinctive characteristics, both olfactory and taste. During the prolonged aging in Slavonian oak barrels for 10 years, the Alpestre Special Reserve 1983 has developed qualities of a meditation elixir, releasing intoxicating herbaceous and oak wood flavors.

ALCOHOL CONTENT: 49.5% vol.

COLOR: straw yellow with golden reflections

BOUQUET: soft and herbaceous

TASTE: warm and embracing with hints of wood

AFTERTASTE: persistent, clean, and vegetal

AMARO ALBERGIAN

Albergian
Pinerolo, Turin

It was 1908 when the Albergian Hotel was founded in Pragelato (Turin) with a specialty shop inside for local products, Casa Specialità Prodotti Alpestri Albergian. Serafino Ponsat, esteemed hotel concierge, after working in the best hotels in Paris, Lyon, and Nice—dreaming of this day throughout the last 20 years of the 19th century—could finally see his pioneering project realized. The Amaro Albergian is still part of the company's traditional offerings. It is made with a curated infusion of rose hip, elderberry, gentian, and numerous other botanicals, and over the years it has carved out a place for itself in the history of Piedmontese after-dinners, never bending to the rules of mass production.

ALCOHOL CONTENT: 25% vol.

COLOR: caramel with golden reflections

BOUQUET: aromatic scents of alpine herbs and flowers

TASTE: pleasantly bitter and balanced with hints of gentian

AFTERTASTE: floral with almond sensations

AMARO ALPINO

Argalà Liquorificio Artigianale
Boves, Cuneo

To be *argalà*, in the Occitan dialect, means to be satisfied, to be happy. Argalà Liquorificio Artigianale was born in 2011 from the idea of two friends, Piero Nuvoloni-Bonnet and Enrico Giordana, who have been producing liqueurs since January 2016 in an old renovated barn in the heart of the Boves countryside. In the summer of 2018, Piero and Enrico bottled the first batch of their Amaro Alpino, considered the sum of the experience they had gained over the years. The recipe is inspired by an intoxicating walk that lasted two days, from the Maritime Alps to the sea, and it brings together citrus and balsamic notes thanks to the use of components such as orange peel, pine, and lavender. The procedure for making this amaro includes cold maceration of 30 botanicals and dilution with water from the Alps.

ALCOHOL CONTENT: 28% vol.

COLOR: intense amber color with red nuances typical of elderberries

BOUQUET: very fragrant, citrusy, balsamic, accompanied by lavender

TASTE: interesting complexity, intense and warm, full-bodied structure and pleasantly citrusy

AFTERTASTE: persistent bitter and balsamic note of yarrow and pine needles

AMARO BLACK NOTE

Turin Vermouth
Turin

This company, Turin Vermouth, has accomplished great successes in just a few years, achieved thanks to enormous passion, respect for tradition, the continuous search for excellence, and a team of great professionals such as Giuseppe Rabottini and Nicolò Calza. The right combination of flavors and aromas and the selection of the highest quality botanicals characterize the production of Amaro Black Note. It represents the result of modern extraction technology, realized directly by the Turin company in its own factory. The recipe, however, remains secret.

ALCOHOL CONTENT: 21% vol.

COLOR: caramel

BOUQUET: full and spicy

TASTE: sweet and warm with pleasant notes of cloves and cinnamon

AFTERTASTE: persistent and fresh scent of rhubarb

AMARO BOSSO

Bosso
Cunico, Asti

Pierluigi Bosso, born in 1961, grew up in the family distillery and eventually became master distiller, acquiring the secrets of the artisan processes that have distinguished the company since 1888. Pierluigi, a panel leader in sensory analysis, and supported by the passion and strength of tradition, always manages to create spirits full of personality. Alongside the top products by Bosso, which are represented by grappas obtained from the grape marc of the most famous grapes of the Langhe, we find Amaro Bosso. This amaro was brought back on the market in 2017 after five years of ceased production. The recipe for this amaro belongs to the Bosso family heritage, and it includes the use of native Monferrato botanicals with the addition of bitter orange peel and rhubarb.

ALCOHOL CONTENT: 32% vol.
COLOR: mahogany with golden highlights
BOUQUET: herbaceous and citrus perfumes
TASTE: full and well balanced between bitter and fruity
AFTERTASTE: soft and round, rhubarb notes

AMARO CASALE

Distilleria Magnoberta
Casale Monferrato, Alessandria

From an ancient recipe of the Luparia family of San Martino di Rosignano (Alessandria) comes Amaro Casale. A symbol of liquor production of the Magnoberta Distillery (taken over by Rinaldo and Giuseppe Luparia in 1937), Amaro Casale is a dedication to Casale Monferrato, which is the city that since 1918 has hosted the distillery. Amaro Casale possesses remarkable tonic, digestive, and regenerating properties, thanks to the skillful alcoholic maceration of 12 botanicals, including saffron, ambrette, cinchona, and zedoary. In 2015 this amaro was updated and restyled, while remaining tied to the tradition that has made it unequivocally the pride of the company.

ALCOHOL CONTENT: 25% vol.
COLOR: amber
BOUQUET: vegetal and citrusy
TASTE: balanced between bitter and sweet
AFTERTASTE: medium persistence, slightly herbaceous

AMARO D.CO ULRICH

Distilleria Santa Teresa Fratelli Marolo
Alba, Cuneo

With a successful combination of tradition and innovation, Distilleria Santa Teresa, founded in 1977 by Paolo Marolo together with his brother, works with passion and respect for artisan traditions and local culture without giving up experimentation. In 2015, Paolo, after an enlightening conversation with an advertising representative, decided to bring Amaro D.co Ulrich back to life, reinterpreting the 1854 recipe developed by Dr. Domenico Ulrich. Amaro D.co Ulrich contains the active ingredients of 19 botanical herbs, flowers, fruits, and roots that make it an effective and invigorating digestive stimulant. In the aromatic bouquet, notes of genepy, gentian, anise, yarrow, and wormwood stand out.

ALCOHOL CONTENT: 32% vol.
COLOR: brown
BOUQUET: intense herbaceous notes
TASTE: full and bitter with a strong alpine connotation
AFTERTASTE: excellent persistence with vegetal character

AMARO D'ERBE BÒN DA BÈIVE

Grapperia Artigianale Alì
Canelli, Asti

Recognized as an Artisan Excellence by the Piedmont region since the 1950s, Grapperia Artigianale Alì has maintained its strong artisan and traditional practices. In the product line, different qualities of grappa and typical and innovative liqueurs stand out. These include Amaro Vecchia Canelli and Amaro d'Erbe Bòn da Bèive. The latter, with its fresh and warm character, was introduced at the beginning of the 2000s in response to the evolution of consumers' tastes. Amaro d'Erbe Bòn da Bèive was created from a historic recipe with cinchona, juniper, and gentianella to which artichoke and mint were added. The name on the label was the suggestion of the loyal customers of the grapperia: *bòn da bèive*, which in Piedmontese dialect means "good to drink."

ALCOHOL CONTENT: 17% vol.

COLOR: dark brown

BOUQUET: herbaceous with distinct shades of mint

TASTE: sweetish and slightly bitter with an evident note of freshness

AFTERTASTE: balsamic and sweet persistence

AMARO DEL CENTENARIO

Punto Bere
Canelli, Asti

In 1957, Aldo and Maria Cerutti began to produce liquors thanks to their shared passion for the cultivation of medicinal herbs. They came up with an amaro that used extracts from the distillation of various plant components with beneficial properties. The latter was produced for the first time in 1961 and called Amaro del Centenario (Amaro of the Centennial) on the anniversary of the Unification of Italy. The Amaro del Centenario remained on the market until the 1980s, when production was suspended due to the cessation of the company's activities. But, in 2014, thanks to the will and enthusiasm of Aldo and Maria's children and grandchildren, the product was revived in its original form, in strict compliance with the traditional recipe that includes a mixture of selected botanicals that include orange, vanilla, rhubarb, gentian, and angelica.

ALCOHOL CONTENT: 25% vol.

COLOR: intense and bright copper

BOUQUET: scents of herbs and citrus fruits

TASTE: bitter and velvety with distinct notes of orange, vanilla, and rhubarb

AFTERTASTE: round and bitter flavor of gentian

AMARO DELLA SACRA

Antica Torino
Turin

The formulation of the Amaro della Sacra is the result of historical-scientific research into the monastic traditions of the Middle Ages. The ingredients are all natural: leaves, flowers, seeds, roots, resins, spices, and barks. Some are typical of the Piedmont region, such as gentianella and hops; others are "exotic," in that they were discovered during the exploration of new lands, such as vanilla from Madagascar, green cardamom from the Indies, myrrh from the Middle East, and cinchona from South America. Amaro della Sacra is obtained by separately macerating the various botanicals in grain alcohol; the macerates are then blended and aged for five months before bottling.

ALCOHOL CONTENT: 35% vol.

COLOR: amber

BOUQUET: notes of bitter botanicals and spices

TASTE: bitterness mitigated by notes of cinnamon and vanilla

AFTERTASTE: persistence of gentian with hints of resin

AMARO DEL MULINO

Distilleria Vieux Moulin
Costigliole d'Asti, Asti

In 1933, in an old, 16th-century mill, Ugolino, son of Lorenzo Grosso and Countess Luigia Asinari di San Marzano, began distilling the grape marc from the hills of Langhe, Monferrato, and Roero. Today, under the guidance of Elena Borra, the Distilleria Vieux Moulin has reached the third generation of distillers who continue to produce and seek the best in the tradition of craftsmanship that has always characterized it. Amaro del Mulino is made using a secret recipe of many botanicals in a cold infusion in alcohol. Sugar is then added to the mixture, which is then filtered and left to age before bottling.

ALCOHOL CONTENT: 30% vol.
COLOR: mahogany
BOUQUET: scented and spicy with hints of alpine botanicals
TASTE: full and embracing medicinal herbs
AFTERTASTE: distinct and persistent notes of licorice

AMARO DI LANGA

Valverde di Birello Carlo & C.
Cortemilia, Cuneo

Valverde is a family business run by founder Carlo Birello, together with his wife Maria Rosa, their daughter, Francesca, a pharmacist who is passionate about herbs, and two invaluable and irreplaceable collaborators, Franco and Franca. The beating heart of the company is the workshop where the expert hand of grandfather Carlo, who gives life to the whole production, works. Amaro di Langa, revisited and improved several times over the years, is considered a historic label of Valverde. Among the botanicals used, mostly from the hills of Langa, are gentian, helichrysum, and lemon balm as well as bitter orange, damask rose, cinnamon, star anise, ginger, and saffron. Before being bottled, Amaro di Langa is put to settle in wooden barrels for at least four months.

ALCOHOL CONTENT: 26% vol.
COLOR: intense brown
BOUQUET: typically herbaceous
TASTE: strongly aromatic and balanced
AFTERTASTE: embracing and persistent

AMARO DILEI

Bordiga 1888
Cuneo

The history of the Bordiga distillery is above all a family history. Since its inception, the company has never betrayed its most cherished values. Among these is the attention paid to the choice of the best raw materials (from the wine to the herbs, from the sugar to the mountain water), the importance attributed to the territory, and the craftsmanship of the processing. Amaro Dilei, a poetic name, describes a product that, despite its robust alcohol content, is designed to be appreciated by more delicate palates. It is a spirit with a captivating taste and complex bouquet that evokes the scents of flowers and herbs of the splendid Piedmontese valleys.

ALCOHOL CONTENT: 30% vol.
COLOR: dark brown with emerald shades
BOUQUET: strong smell of roots and bitter herbs with a slightly fresh scent of peppermint
TASTE: sweet but balanced by the aroma of alpine herbs
AFTERTASTE: mentholated, almost balsamic, long and persistent

AMARO ESSENZIALE

Forum Vini di Franco Cavallero
Asti

Previously at the helm of the Sant'Agata Winery, Franco Cavallero inaugurated Il Cicchetto, a wine and cocktail bar in Asti in 2010. The bar was inspired by his great passion for gin; he now produces his own line with the project, Gin Agricolo. On 10 acres of his property, Franco uses a biodynamic style to cultivate all the necessary botanicals for the production of his distillates. The natural evolution of the project was the realization of the Amaro Essenziale, which is obtained from melilot, gentian, cinchona, angelica, sage, hyssop, mint, and orange. This spirit stands as the perfect link between the background of Franco's oenological production and his new love of essential herbs.

ALCOHOL CONTENT: 30% vol.

COLOR: amber with orange reflections

BOUQUET: prevalent herbaceous aroma with balsamic notes

TASTE: bitter, with fresh and citrus nuances

AFTERTASTE: fresh and spicy finish

AMARO FORTE

Mazzetti d'Altavilla
Altavilla Monferrato, Alessandria

Mazzetti d'Altavilla have been distillers since 1846 and theirs is a well-known historical name to lovers of grappa and distillates. Following the latest beverage trends, Mazzetti d'Altavilla has also dedicated itself to the production of amari. From a secret recipe created in the Benedictine monastery that stood at the top of Altavilla Monferrato, Amaro Forte, an authentic concentrate of the *Hortus Simplicium*, a botanical garden where medicinal plants were cultivated and selected by the monks to prepare compounds and medicines, has been handed down. Licorice, rhubarb, dandelion, cinchona, and peppermint are among the notes that most stand out.

ALCOHOL CONTENT: 30% vol.

COLOR: amber yellow

BOUQUET: decisive herbs and roots

TASTE: embracing, with strong notes of cinchona and licorice

AFTERTASTE: persistent and fresh

AMARO GAMONDI

Gamondi Spirits di Toso
Cossano Belbo, Cuneo

Gamondi Spirits, owned by the Toso company, has always distinguished itself with its production of traditional herbal liqueurs from the highest quality raw materials. Founded around 1890 in Acqui Terme (Cuneo), at the behest of Carlo Gamondi, an expert herbalist, the distillery was first engaged in the production of tonic and bitter drinks, and later in the production of vermouth, grappa, and amari. Among these is Amaro Gamondi, conceived in the wise mind of Carlo, whose recipe is very secret and characterized by the cold maceration of different types of botanicals in alcohol and excellent craftsmanship.

ALCOHOL CONTENT: 27% vol.

COLOR: mahogany with reddish highlights

BOUQUET: herbaceous with fresh and citrusy notes

TASTE: perfectly balanced between sweet and bitter

AFTERTASTE: sweet persistence, with hints of bitter herbs

AMARO GENTILE

Mazzetti d'Altavilla
Altavilla Monferrato,
Alessandria

Amaro Gentile, produced by Mazzetti d'Altavilla, is inspired by an ancient Piedmontese elixir based on 13 botanicals collected from the hills of Basso Monferrato. Every single variety of herbs, berries, and roots used in this amaro brings digestive properties and peculiar scents to the drink. For the production of Amaro Gentile, some of the plant components are macerated for 12 months in aged muscat grappa; the rest undergo a period of infusion in alcohol together with orange and lemon peels. The aromatic notes include sage, marjoram, gentian roots, and thyme.

ALCOHOL CONTENT: 30% vol.

COLOR: straw yellow

BOUQUET: fresh and citrusy

TASTE: clean and delicate with hints of gentian

AFTERTASTE: soft-medium persistence of citrus fruits and medicinal herbs

AMARO GRINTA

Glep Beverages
Borgomanero, Novara

The adventure of the young Glep Beverages began between trials, tastings, and a lot of experimentation. Ezio and Luca, the first a sommelier and lover of vermouth, the second a creative and visual innovator, began to produce liqueurs to enhance the taste of their favorite cocktail: the Milano Torino. In the company's line, Vermouth Vandalo and Bitter Spinto are joined by Amaro Grinta, which is obtained through a single infusion of roots, plants, herbs, and mountain flowers, including genepy, juniper, gentianella, yarrow, gentian, peppermint, quassia, eucalyptus, and thistle. The creation of the unique label has been curated by Luca, who chose to take inspiration from the Tasmanian devil, an animal now extinct, which symbolizes strength and tenacity.

ALCOHOL CONTENT: 28% vol.

COLOR: bright green

BOUQUET: decisive balsamic tones

TASTE: notes of gentian and juniper stand out from the bitter and vegetal character

AFTERTASTE: long, fresh herbaceous persistence with hints of eucalyptus

AMARO LUIGI FRANCOLI

Casa Francoli
Ghemme, Novara

The Francoli family has been working with distillation since 1875, when Luigi Guglielmo Francoli began his experiments with a rudimentary still, giving birth to his first grappa. The alchemical art that Luigi passed down to his descendants lives again today in Amaro Luigi Francoli, which is dedicated to the founding father of the company. The recipe for this spirit, developed in 2015, includes the hydro-alcoholic infusion of gentian, gentianella, rhubarb, wormwood, sweet and bitter orange, artichoke, yarrow, genepy, cardamom, cinnamon, nutmeg, and mint.

ALCOHOL CONTENT: 31.5% vol.

COLOR: intense dark amber

BOUQUET: penetrating and harmonious in which you can perceive all the herbs used

TASTE: soft and sweet taste with hints of citrus fruits, rhubarb, and nutmeg

AFTERTASTE: good fresh and bitter persistence of gentian and wormwood

AMARO MANDRAGOLA

Compagnia dei Caraibi
Vidracco, Turin

Among the many families who have made vermouth history in Turin, a leading role is held by the Baracco family. They are at the helm today of the company Compagnia dei Caraibi. The indissoluble bond with the territory and a strong attention to raw materials have led the Baracco family to rediscover ancient traditional recipes such as Amaro Mandragola. The formula of this digestive, which dates back to 1873, was passed on to the Baracco family by an established pharmacist who was an heir to a setmin (Piedmontese healer). This amaro includes 15 botanicals, of which only 8 are publicly known: laurel, bitter orange, mint, lemon balm, sage, rosemary, cinnamon, and cloves.

ALCOHOL CONTENT: 45% vol.

COLOR: brown with golden reflections

BOUQUET: intoxicating scent of bitter herbs

TASTE: overwhelmingly bitter and balsamic

AFTERTASTE: excellent bitter persistence with notes of cloves and cinnamon

AMARO MARTINA

Ditta Claudia Lagossi
Turin

Amaro Martina was created in 1908 by Salvatore Martina, an apothecary from the province of Lecce, with the intention of producing a spirit that would combine digestive qualities with the strength of a corroborant. In spite of the numerous awards at major national and international exhibitions, the production of Amaro Martina ceased in the late 1930s with the death of Salvatore. His great-grandson Valentino Martina relaunched it. After finishing his career as a doctor, in 2015, together with his wife Claudia Lagossi, he decided to reestablish the production and sale of the historic amaro. The recipe involves, now as then, the infusion in alcohol of seven botanicals, including cardamom and gentian.

ALCOHOL CONTENT: 38% vol.

COLOR: amber with red highlights

BOUQUET: hints of herbs

TASTE: clean and appealing with distinct notes of gentian

AFTERTASTE: persistent, with the bitter note tempering itself

AMARO MENTHA

Luigi Fassio
Chieri, Turin

Amaro Mentha's story originates from two mysterious notebooks found at home by Monica Buzio, Luigi Fassio's great-granddaughter, in which the latter had written down about a hundred recipes for liquors, bitters, vermouths, and elixirs that he produced and served in the elegant cafés he ran in the center of Turin, from the beginning of the 20th century until 1958. In 2018 Monica decided to bring back to life some of those wonderful recipes, giving birth to the Luigi Fassio brand. Amaro Mentha stands out, able to perfectly combine the taste of the golden age of Turin's liquor industry with a touch of freshness typical of the Piedmontese territory. The main botanicals are aloe, quassia, coriander, mace, gentian, cinchona, and, of course, Piedmontese mint.

ALCOHOL CONTENT: 30% vol.

COLOR: brown

BOUQUET: strong herbaceous notes

TASTE: bitter and mentholated with hints of mace and cinchona

AFTERTASTE: excellent persistence of gentian and freshness of mint

AMARO MOTTARONE

La Bottega del Morni 1948
Gravellona Toce, Verbania

La Bottega del Morni 1948 was established with the aim of providing continuity to the historic artisan workshop founded in 1948 by Fermo Morniroli, a passionate and capable herbalist. In 2005, close to retiring and without the possibility to continue his work, Fermo decided to sell the business to the Guglielminetti family, who acquired the original processing techniques. Developed after years of study and research by Fermo, Amaro Mottarone takes its name from the mountain on whose slopes the production site is located and is considered the company's main product. The original recipe includes the slow, cold maceration of a selection of about 20 botanicals, including orange, gentian, cinchona, licorice, and juniper.

ALCOHOL CONTENT: 28% vol.

COLOR: bright mahogany

BOUQUET: delicate hints of flowers and roots

TASTE: bitter note of cinchona mitigated by citrus nuances

AFTERTASTE: sweet and spicy

AMARO PALÈNT

Palènt
San Damiano Macra, Cuneo

Palènt is a small hamlet of the municipality of Macra (Cuneo) perched on rocks at about 5,000 feet (1,500 m) that has two residents: Matteo and Virginia. In Palènt, a fascinating and bucolic hermitage, Matteo Laugero follows the principles of biodynamics as he grows many medicinal herbs with which, together with roots and small fruits harvested in the surrounding woods, he produces Amaro Palènt. At the base of the recipe there is the cold infusion in organic grain alcohol of 18 botanicals, including the native genepy of the Cuneo valleys and rhubarb, yarrow, blueberry, raspberry, and cherry.

ALCOHOL CONTENT: 26% vol.

COLOR: garnet

BOUQUET: distinct scent of herbs and fruits

TASTE: bitter with pleasant hints of berries

AFTERTASTE: bitter persistence with toasted notes of rhubarb

AMARO PERUZZO

Erbaflor Peruzzo
Basaluzzo, Alessandria

Amaro Peruzzo, created by the fervid mind of Iginio Peruzzo, is inspired by an ancient recipe typical of the Ligurian Apennines. Iginio dedicated his life to the study of plants, becoming an expert botanist and acquiring fame as a healer known in the Ovadese region under the name of Wizard of the Orba Valley. In 1950, the great herbalist set up a workshop next to his house where he first taught his children about the secrets of herbal medicine. It was Sebastiano, his most faithful pupil, who later founded the Erbaflor company, which is still family-run today and in the hands of Irene Peruzzo, Iginio's granddaughter. The botanicals that make up Amaro Peruzzo's mix are yarrow, angelica, anise, gentian, licorice, sage, rhubarb, artichoke, wormwood, and juniper.

ALCOHOL CONTENT: 23% vol.

COLOR: brown with reflections

BOUQUET: fresh hints of gentian and wormwood

TASTE: bitter and balanced medicinal herbs

AFTERTASTE: persistent, bitter, and balsamic

AMARO SAN

La Canellese
Calamandrana, Asti

La Canellese, a company producing vermouth and liquors, nestled between the Langhe and Monferrato districts, is a company founded in the first half of the 20th century thanks to the passion of Francesco Sconfienza, an artisan cooper, and his wife Rosa Bertello, a botanical expert. The Sconfienza family, now represented by Alfredo, Bruna, and Lucia, has distinguished itself over the years thanks to its products with a traditional soul, among which Amaro San stands out. This amaro comes to life from a blend of selected white wines to which the extract of 18 different botanicals is added, including wormwood, bitter orange, rhubarb, coriander, and juniper.

ALCOHOL CONTENT: 17% vol.
COLOR: dark amber
BOUQUET: intense with delicate scents of cinnamon and rhubarb
TASTE: bitter and spicy with hints of juniper
AFTERTASTE: persistent with notes of cinchona and wormwood

AMARO SAN CARLO

Distilleria Beccaris
Boglietto di Costigliole d'Asti, Asti

It was 1951 when Cavalier Elio Beccaris, undecided whether to start a distillery, a wine cellar, or a vinegar cellar, left the decision to Carlo, then only a few months old. Cavalier put three pieces of paper, each containing one of the three options, in a hat and gave the little one the choice to extract one, thus resolving the dilemma. Distilleria Beccaris was therefore founded almost thanks to a "game"! One of its flagship products has always been Amaro San Carlo. It is obtained by macerating a mix of botanicals that include rhubarb, tansy, cinchona, wormwood, thyme, gentian, aloe, and gentianella. The name of this amaro, San Carlo, calls to mind one of the most fascinating panoramic areas of Costigliole d'Asti.

ALCOHOL CONTENT: 30% vol.
COLOR: brown with orange highlights
BOUQUET: fragrant scents of herbs and roots
TASTE: soft bitterness of cinchona and aloe
AFTERTASTE: well-rounded and persistent rhubarb and orange

AMARO SAN FELICE

Distilleria Dellavalle
Vigliano d'Asti, Asti

The oenologist Roberto Dellavalle, after years of experience in the world of wine and grappa, in 1983 decided to found his own company, Distilleria Dellavalle, in Vigliano d'Asti, in the heart of the great wine-producing Piedmont. Amaro San Felice was inspired by a recipe developed by Roberto's grandfather, Felice Dellavalle, in 1891. In the production process, the extraction of the botanicals, including wormwood, gentian, elderberry, nutmeg, and angelica, takes place by cold maceration in a hydro-alcoholic solution for about 60 days. This is followed by a light pressing and then aging in small barrels for six months.

ALCOHOL CONTENT: 25% vol.
COLOR: brown with orange highlights
BOUQUET: strong hints of herbs, including wormwood and rhubarb
TASTE: harmonious and gentle with bitter notes of cinchona and gentian
AFTERTASTE: soft, spicy persistence of cinnamon and nutmeg

AMARO SIBONA

Distilleria Sibona
Piobesi d'Alba, Cuneo

Located near an old kiln, Distilleria Sibona is a historical company located in Roero, one of the most prestigious areas of the Piedmont wine country. Always considered an excellent example of regional distillation, the company retains an artisan character, creating grappas and refined distillates. Amaro Sibona, inspired by an ancient Piedmontese recipe, involves the use of 34 botanicals, including gentian, cinchona, and rhubarb, macerated with a slow and patient bath in alcohol of the highest quality.

ALCOHOL CONTENT: 28% vol.
COLOR: dark amber
BOUQUET: intense notes of roots and spices
TASTE: soft and embracing with bitter hints of cinchona
AFTERTASTE: pleasantly bitter with rhubarb dominance

AMARO SOLDATINI

Distilleria Gualco
Silvano d'Orba, Alessandria

In 1870, Paolo Gualco founded the first of three Gualco distilleries, subsequently joined by Susanna Gualco, who has valued traditions and experience.

Susanna's husband, Marcello Soldatini, a liquorist from Genoa, was dedicated to the preparation of traditional spirits and liquors, including Amaro Soldatini, whose original recipe included 12 botanicals, including medicinal plants, spices, and citrus fruits. Today the distillery is in the hands of Marcello's grandchildren, Giorgio and Marcella Soldatini, and the current formulation of this amaro, reinterpreted by Giorgio, includes the addition of other plant elements such as chinotto di Savona and Ligurian basil.

ALCOHOL CONTENT: 30% vol.
COLOR: amber
BOUQUET: scent of citrus and cinchona
TASTE: delicately bitter with fresh and citrus notes
AFTERTASTE: clean persistence with hints of star anise

AMARO VECCHIA CANELLI

Grapperia Artigianale Alì
Canelli, Asti

The foundation of Grapperia Artigianale Alì dates back to the early 1950s and is owed to the passionate oenologist Giuseppe Aliberti. Specializing in the production of liqueurs and syrups, the company has always operated in an artisan and family dimension, and today it is run by the Poglio family. Amaro Vecchia Canelli, one of the first products of the grapperia, is obtained, according to an ancient recipe, from the maceration of many and mostly secret botanicals, including gentian, juniper, cinchona, genepy, and gentianella.

ALCOHOL CONTENT: 30% vol.
COLOR: medium amber
BOUQUET: intense and herbaceous
TASTE: bitter with an appropriate sugar balance
AFTERTASTE: aromatic persistence of herbs with gentian and juniper overtones

AMARÒT

Amaròt
Turin

The recipe for Amaròt—a young, artisan product from Turin—is inspired by the bootleg liquors produced by the farmers who moved to the Piedmontese capital in search of employment at the beginning of the 20th century in the neighboring valleys and consumed at the end of an exhausting day's work. Amaròt, made with a chinotto base, puts together fragrant citrus fruits from the Ligurian Riviera and bitter and aromatic Piedmontese herbs. In its secret formulation you can recognize other plant sources such as worm-wood, cardamom, aniseed, gentian, and bergamot.

ALCOHOL CONTENT: 28% vol.
COLOR: intense brown with orange highlights
BOUQUET: citrus notes with hints of vanilla and cardamom
TASTE: bitter notes of gentian and wormwood balanced by softer sensations
AFTERTASTE: round, embracing, and fresh with licorice and aniseed

BARATHIER

Bernard & C.
Pomaretto, Turin

The Bernard family has been producing liquors since 1902, the year in which Giacomo Bernard began to macerate mountain herbs and flowers in top-quality alcohol. Today the company is in the hands of Enrico, Giacomo's great-grandson, who with the same passion dedicates himself to the artisan production of the Bernard house. The herb elixir Barathier, invented in 1902, is a historical specialty included in the list of Prodotti Agroalimentari Tradizionali Piemontesi (Traditional Piedmontese Agri-food Products). The recipe, jealously guarded by the Bernard family for four generations,

includes seven secret botanicals, including spices, wild herbs, and mountain flowers picked by hand in the Cottian Alps.

ALCOHOL CONTENT: 26% vol.
COLOR: limpid brown
BOUQUET: scent of alpine herbs
TASTE: soft and slightly bitter with spicy notes of angelica
AFTERTASTE: sweet and floral persistence

CARDAMARO

Casa Tosti
Canelli, Asti

The formula for Cardamaro by Casa Tosti, dating back to the early postwar years, was developed by Rachele Bosca, an illustrious scholar and connoisseur of the beneficial qualities of numerous wild herbs. Blessed thistle, milk thistle, and artichoke leaves are the main ingredients of Cardamaro, which, skillfully dosed, enhance all the aromatic properties of the thistle. The very secret recipe also includes the single extraction in wine of columbo, juniper, yellow gentian, cloves, licorice root, cardamom, lemon, and marjoram.

ALCOHOL CONTENT: 17% vol.
COLOR: tawny, almost amber, with bright reflections
BOUQUET: spicy notes of thistle and licorice stand out
TASTE: full and harmonious, balanced between sweet and bitter
AFTERTASTE: long spicy persistence with hints of tobacco

CHINA MARTINI

Bacardi
Pessione, Turin

Ernesto Calindri and Franco Volpi, in a sketch entitled "Dura Minga" on the famous Italian TV show *Carosello*, while enjoying their cinchona aperitif, China Martini, either neat or hot in a punch, sang a nice jingle: "Since the times of Garibaldini... China Martini China Martini!" China Martini was in fact created in 1847 with the foundation in Turin of the National Distillery of Spirits and Wines, forerunner of Martini & Rossi. This elixir, having become an icon in the history of Italian culture, is created through the marriage of alcoholic extracts of herbs and cinchona bark, long known for its important bitter-tonic and anti-malarial qualities. The manufacturing process, followed by master herbalist Ivano Tonutti, involves the maceration of the botanicals in a neutral spirit

base. The extraction of the flavors and active ingredients takes place through a process called *la girata lenta* and takes place "slowly" in rotating drums, three times a minute, for several weeks. Afterward, the botanical extracts rest for two months to ensure a balanced and rounded taste. Among the components of the recipe are rhubarb, turmeric, sweet orange, gentian, and licorice.

ALCOHOL CONTENT: 25% vol.

COLOR: brownish bronze, slightly viscous

BOUQUET: hints of Middle Eastern spices emerge

TASTE: predominant note of cinchona accompanied by flavors of licorice and rhubarb; light but pleasantly warm persistence

AFTERTASTE: citrusy

CHIOT MONTAMARO

Bordiga 1888
Cuneo

Pietro Bordiga, an expert herbalist and founder of Bordiga 1888, was born in Val di Grana and then moved with his family to Turin, which was then the capital of the newborn Kingdom of Italy. Here, with his strong training, he created a variant of vermouth that immediately became a success. Returning to Cuneo in 1888, he started a business that occupied him for the rest of his life: a distillery for wine, vermouth, liqueurs, and syrups made with

the best mountain herbs, in full respect of the purest artisanal traditions. Chiot Montamaro is one of these, obtained from a skillful combination of a multitude of herbs from the territory, which are macerated and then distilled.

ALCOHOL VOLUME: 18% vol.

COLOR: light brown

BOUQUET: strong notes of roots and bitter herbs with a slight hint of peppermint

TASTE: overbearing, despite the low alcohol content, mint opens to the flavors

AFTERTASTE: persistence of gentian with an herbaceous finish

ELISIR DEL PRETE

Albergian
Pinerolo, Turin

Elisir del Prete is the sum of ancient liquoristic and herbalist knowledge, prepared from a careful selection of herbs and roots left to macerate for long months in alcohol. An exclusive amaro for which the Albergian company has received the prestigious "Dino Villani" award by the Accademia Italiana della Cucina "to the producer who has distinguished himself in the artisan processing of a food product of notable organoleptic quality, made with prime quality ingredients, with a well-identified local, not industrial, typicality." Cinchona and gentian are some of the botanicals used in this very secret recipe.

ALCOHOL CONTENT: 45% vol.
COLOR: dark caramel
BOUQUET: overpowering hints of bitter herbs and roots
TASTE: extremely bitter and aromatic
AFTERTASTE: excellent herbaceous persistence embracing the palate

FERNET ALBERGIAN

Albergian
Pinerolo, Turin

Nowadays, it is Giacomo, a member of the fourth generation of the Tillino family, who leads the more than 100-year-old Albergian, a company specializing in the handmade production of typical Piedmontese delicacies. The company caters as much to lovers of authentic flavors as to those on the lookout for novelties who find themselves discovering tastes so ancient that they are surprisingly modern. From an ancient recipe of the Albergian tradition comes Fernet Albergian, based on cinchona, gentian, and rhubarb, which are combined with many other botanicals and cold macerated

for many months in alcohol of exceptional quality.

ALCOHOL CONTENT: 45% vol.
COLOR: dark amber with orange highlights
BOUQUET: strong scents of herbs and roots
TASTE: markedly bitter; rhubarb and cinchona stand out
AFTERTASTE: persistent and aromatic with a long note of gentian

FERNET GANCIA

F.lli Gancia & C.
Canelli, Asti

In 1850, after a long experience in the wine sector, Carlo Gancia founded Fratelli (F.lli) Gancia with his brother Edoardo. They began to experiment with the production of the first "Champagne Italiano," using techniques he learned during his stay in Reims, France. F.lli Gancia, however, also boasts a great liquoristic knowledge and relevant professionalism in the processing of botanicals. This is demonstrated by Fernet Gancia, an alcoholic infusion of herbs and spices that include cinchona, gentian, saffron, mint, and licorice.

ALCOHOL CONTENT: 40% vol.
COLOR: intense amber with golden highlights
BOUQUET: intense and aromatic medicinal herbs
TASTE: marked bitterness and fresh shades of mint and gentian
AFTERTASTE: persistent, warm, and spicy with notes of licorice

FERNET MAGNOBERTA

Magnoberta Distillery
Casale Monferrato, Alessandria

Fernet Magnoberta is obtained following an old recipe of the Luparia family, which became part of the great Magnoberta project in 1937. This amaro, composed of more than 16 precious herbs and spices carefully mixed, draws inspiration from the formula of the ancient and renowned Swedish sacred tincture. All the (secret) botanicals used to create Fernet Magnoberta act effectively on the functionality of the digestive system, and for this reason this spirit is recommended as an effective digestive aid.

ALCOHOL CONTENT: 40% vol.
COLOR: intense brown
BOUQUET: pleasant notes of herbs and roots
TASTE: distinctly bitter with fresh mentholated hints
AFTERTASTE: good bitter and balsamic persistence with hint of wormwood

FERNET TUVÈ

Turin Vermouth
Turin

The Tuvè line from the young Turin company Turin Vermouth expresses a deep passion for the liqueur tradition of the *bel paese* (beautiful country) and a strong link with the Piedmontese territory. All the plant components at the base of the Tuvè product recipes are carefully selected, analyzed, and then processed "according to modern tradition." Such exclusive attention in the production process distinguishes Fernet Tuvè, a prestigious and refined digestif from a very secret recipe.

ALCOHOL CONTENT: 39% vol.

COLOR: dark amber

BOUQUET: medicinal aroma with notes of gentian

TASTE: bitter with strong and fresh hints of roots and barks

AFTERTASTE: lingering coffee and cloves

FERNET VIEUX MOULIN

Distilleria Vieux Moulin
Costigliole d'Asti, Asti

Yesterday, as today, in the historic and almost century-old Distilleria Vieux Moulin, among the stills and barrels of fine oak, the ancient gestures of the art of liquor and distillery passed down in the Borra family for three generations are repeated, unchanged. In 1948, Alberto Borra, grandfather of Elena who is currently at the helm of the company, created the Fernet Vieux Moulin, which still sees great care and passion in its production. The recipe includes the maceration of many aromatic botanicals, including anise and fennel together with—we can imagine—licorice, cinchona, gentian, and aloe.

ALCOHOL CONTENT: 43% vol.

COLOR: deep black

BOUQUET: overbearing and pleasant herbal notes

TASTE: distinctly bitter with spicy and tamarind scents

AFTERTASTE: fresh and persistent with hints of aniseed

IL 28 DI VIA SAN NICOLAO

Distillerie Berta
Mombaruzzo, Asti

A third-generation exponent of expertise in the spirits industry, Paolo Berta, continuing and developing the work of his father Giovanni and his grandfather Francesco, founded the first family distillery in 1947 at number 28 Via San Nicolao in Nizza Monferrato. Right at the beginning of this wonderful adventure, the amaro Il 28 di Via San Nicolao came to life. This amaro uses Distillerie Berta's own 1986 Acquavite di Vino Casalotto, and it follows a secret recipe of infusions and distillates of herbs and aromatic roots, including rhubarb, cinchona, and gentian.

ALCOHOL CONTENT: 30% vol.

COLOR: mahogany with red highlights

BOUQUET: embracing roots and barks

TASTE: rich and warm with hints of rhubarb, gentian, and berries

AFTERTASTE: persistence of cinchona with notes of tobacco and vanilla

L'AMARO

Opificio Il Reale
Chieri, Turin

Opificio Il Reale was created following an encounter between Paola Pressi and "Maestro Alfre," an aromatic expert. The name Il Reale is a tribute to Prince Serge of Yugoslavia, nephew of the last king of Italy, Umberto II of Savoy, as evidenced by the family's coat of arms clearly visible on the label of their products. L'Amaro, launched on the market in 2018, is obtained by macerating various plant components in herbs, spices, and roots. These include gentian, orris, Roman wormwood, and blue violet. It's a combination that

makes this product so unique and agreeable.

ALCOHOL CONTENT: 30% vol.
COLOR: brown with red highlights
BOUQUET: scents of spices and roots
TASTE: agreeable and balanced with notes of wormwood and gentian
AFTERTASTE: persistent herbaceous hints

LIQUORE FERNET

Contratto
Canelli, Asti

Contratto's production of fernet began in the early 1920s, then stopped in the early 1960s and finally resumed in December 2012, thanks to Giorgio Rivetti who relaunched it using the original graphics designed by Leonetto Cappiello in 1925. Today, Liquore Fernet is made strictly following the traditional method that includes the cold maceration for 30 days of 33 botanicals, including aloe, saffron, aniseed, licorice, ginger, mint, myrrh, juniper, nutmeg, fennel, rhubarb, quassia, milk thistle seeds, cloves, and cinnamon.

ALCOHOL CONTENT: 30% vol.
COLOR: brown
BOUQUET: overbearing herbaceous aromas
TASTE: bitter and spicy with a predominance of licorice and cloves
AFTERTASTE: fresh and balsamic with hints of juniper and mint

ST. HUBERTUS

Bordiga 1888
Cuneo

Inside each Bordiga 1888 product you can find the soul of its place of origin, enhanced by the unique and aromatic character of mountain herbs. With every sip, tradition and innovation meet in a blaze of flavors that testify to the excellence of spirits created with artisan methods, made in Italy for over 130 years. Bordiga 1888's St. Hubertus amaro takes its name from the patron saint of hunters, and its recipe—from secret botanicals—includes the use of various infusions and distillates. It is striking for its complex and harmonious taste, sustained by a high alcohol content, and for its incomparable digestive properties.

ALCOHOL CONTENT: 38% vol.
COLOR: rust with glints of orange
BOUQUET: intense nose characterized by roots, barks, and alpine flowers
TASTE: powerful, bitter, aromatic, initially soft on the palate
AFTERTASTE: balsamic, with long licorice finish

TOCCASANA

Toso Spa
Cossano Belbo, Cuneo

In the best years of his profession, Teodoro Negro, an herbalist and "healer" born in Cessole (Asti) in 1910, began to think about the possibility of creating a "universal remedy," a broad-spectrum elixir for long life. Thus was born a special mixture of herbs infused in hot water, white wine, or cognac, depending on the specific case. Toccasana can also be drunk after meals to aid digestion. In 1970, Teodoro began to produce the bitter Toccasana, which is made from 37 botanicals, subjected to cold maceration, that include rosemary, lemon balm, green anise, basil, Chinese rhubarb, Roman wormwood, and yarrow.

ALCOHOL CONTENT:
21% vol.

COLOR: mahogany
with orange
highlights

BOUQUET: pleasant
floral aroma

TASTE: moderately
bitter with distinct
hints of gentian and
chamomile

AFTERTASTE:
excellent persistence
with notes of
rhubarb and yarrow

WUNDERBAR

Distilleria Magnoberta
Casale Monferrato,
Alessandria

The Distilleria Magnoberta of
Casale Monferrato owes its creation to two partners: Domenico Magno and Paolo Berta. In
1937, Giuseppe and Rinaldo
Luparia, father and son, joined
the company as true experts in
viticulture. In 1970, a cousin
of the Luparia family brought
a recipe for a German amaro
to the attention of the distillers that was discovered on a
business trip to Germany. This
amaro had hit him so hard that
he exclaimed, *"Wunderbar!"*
("wonderful") at the first sip.
Magnoberta's Wunderbar is
obtained following the ancient
and secret recipe taken from
Germany, which includes the
infusion of seven botanicals
aged in oak barrels.

ALCOHOL CONTENT: 35% vol.
COLOR: brown
BOUQUET: delicate scent of herbs
TASTE: sweet and herbaceous
herbs with notes of vanilla
AFTERTASTE: cloves and
caramel

Lombardy

AMARO BRAULIO

Campari Group
Bormio, Sondrio

Amaro Braulio is without doubt the most important example of Italian alpine amaro. It is in fact a jewel in its category, still produced by hand using herbs and botanicals typical of the surrounding area dominated by Mount Braulio, nestled in the heart of the Alps and the Valtellina. It all began in the second half of the 19th century, when Dr. Giuseppe Peloni, a renowned pharmacist and member of one of the most noble and historical families of Bormio, began using local botanicals to create experimental galenic mixtures. Giuseppe passed on his passion for herbal medicine to his son, Attilio. The latter, who became a pharmacist, helped to make the product known at trade fairs, obtaining prestigious awards. The family tradition was then carried on by Egidio Tarantola Peloni, Attilio's grandson, and his son Edoardo, who helped to expand the production of Braulio, which continues to be produced according to the same process of 140 years ago, with aging in barrels of Slavonian oak 4,000 feet above sea level (1,200 m). Only the four main ingredients of the secret formula are known: gentian, juniper, wormwood, and yarrow.

ALCOHOL CONTENT: 21% vol.
COLOR: amber with ruby shades
BOUQUET: wood and root scents emerge, of which the gentian root stands out, rounded by refreshing scents of juniper and aromatic herbs with wormwood on the finish
TASTE: robust and intense flavor of herbs and essential oils, followed by notes of wood and roots, with a pleasant bitterness on the finish
AFTERTASTE: full-bodied and persistent with delicate bitter notes of gentian root and wormwood

AMARO 18 ISOLABELLA

Illva Saronno
Saronno, Varese

Amaro 18 Isolabella, produced today by Illva Saronno, was conceived by Egidio Isolabella in 1871 and was soon recognized by many as a "tonic aperitif" thanks to its eupeptic and appetizing properties made possible by the botanicals used in its manufacture. Amaro

18 Isolabella became famous all over the Italian Peninsula thanks to the numerous and creative campaigns advertisements including on the famous Italian TV program *Carosello* with Corrado Mantoni. This amaro, with a very secret recipe, is produced by cold infusion of 18 plant components including herbs, rhizomes, roots, barks, and citrus.

ALCOHOL CONTENT: 30% vol.

COLOR: intense brown

BOUQUET: wide and rich herbaceous hints, slightly citrus

TASTE: round and bitter

AFTERTASTE: soft persistence with notes of cinchona

AMARO D'ANGERA

Rossi d'Angera
Angera, Varese

The recipe for Amaro d'Angera is the Rossi d'Angera distillery's oldest and involves alcoholic maceration for a period of 30 days of 30 alpine herbs, including yarrow, star anise, sage, gentian, lemon balm, lesser calamint, and Breckland thyme. The compound obtained is then slowly distilled for three hours and then left to rest in barrels of Allier oak for at least three months, a practice that gives

the product a full-bodied and decisive flavor.

ALCOHOL CONTENT: 30% vol.

COLOR: deep mahogany

BOUQUET: complex bouquet reminiscent of the essences of medicinal herbs and roots

TASTE: broad and round, with herbaceous hints and notes of oriental spices, from patchouli to nutmeg, and date to bitter almond

AFTERTASTE: lingering bitterness

AMARO DEL FARMACISTA

Farmacia Minelli
Toscolano Maderno, Brescia

Amaro del Farmacista is made according to the traditional recipe formulated by the Farmacia Minelli, active in Toscolano Maderno since 1948. This drink, with a proven digestive action, is distinguished by notes of bitter orange, gentian, wormwood, and cinchona root, which combine with the balsamic tones of mint. The five botanicals that give life to Amaro del Farmacista all have stomachic properties, that is, they are able to stimulate the appetite and digestive functions. They also promote bile production and combat post-prandial bloating.

ALCOHOL CONTENT: 27% vol.

COLOR: light brown

BOUQUET: the citrus notes given by the bitter orange stand out

TASTE: well balanced between sweet and bitter with clear hints of gentian

AFTERTASTE: bitter persistence, with notes of wormwood

AMARO GUELFO

Torricella63
Brescia

In 2016, during the traditional Christmas dinner, Andrea Ronconi thought of involving his cousins Diego, Paola, and Stefano in the production of an amaro inspired by their grandfather Guelfo. Following that Christmas, the four cousins met every Monday, for a whole year, to taste a spirit that was improving over time. The composition of Amaro Guelfo has about 20 botanicals, including rhubarb, gentian, licorice, Roman wormwood, coriander, rosemary, red thyme, mint, lemon, juniper, and tonka bean. A characteristic of this amaro is the presence of brandy aged 36 months, the real backbone of the product.

ALCOHOL CONTENT: 30% vol.

COLOR: dark amber with golden highlights

BOUQUET: spicy, herbaceous, and aromatic

TASTE: aromatic, bittersweet, and spicy with hints of rhubarb

AFTERTASTE: good persistence with notes of licorice and wormwood

AMARO LAGO MAGGIORE

Rossi d'Angera
Angera, Varese

Lake Maggiore is among the most beautiful lakes in Italy, with a territory rich in history. It is where the Rossi d'Angera distillery has been producing schnapps and other spirits capable of best expressing the local traditions and flavors since 1847. And it was out of a feeling of belonging that at the end of the 19th century, Amaro Lago Maggiore was created. It is an agreeable amaro with a marked alpine character, thanks to the infusion of herbs, roots, and mandarin peels in a hydro-alcoholic solution.

ALCOHOL CONTENT: 30% vol.

COLR: dark brown

BOUQUET: bitterness very present with citrus notes

TASTE: well balanced with hints of tangerine citrus

AFTERTASTE: bitter persistence

AMARO RAMAZZOTTI

Pernod Ricard
Milan

Amaro Ramazzotti was produced for the first time in Milan in 1815. It was born as Amaro Felsina Ramazzotti from a secret recipe by Ausano Ramazzotti, a pharmacist from Bologna who moved to Milan in the early 19th century. It was the first aperitif not to have wine as a base. Driven by the desire to produce an aromatized drink, perfect for every moment of the day, Ausano created a harmonious blend of 33 spices, herbs, flowers, and fruits. The recipe is still secret today and has been handed down over time. Among the botanicals used are the Sicilian orange peel, star anise, cardamom, and cloves, which are, together with the other elements, reduced to a powder and mixed with caramelized sugar and alcohol.

ALCOHOL CONTENT: 30% vol.

COLOR: dark brown

BOUQUET: spicy and herbaceous

TASTE: balanced between sweet and bitter

AFTERTASTE: bitter persistence

AMARO TANEDA

Carlo Ericini
Bormio, Sondrio

Amaro Taneda is a one-of-a-kind digestif, made with yarrow (*Achillea millefolium*), of which it preserves both scent and taste. *Taneda* is, in fact, the term used in the Bormino dialect to indicate the beautiful "white gold" plant named after the hero of Greek mythology Achilles. Also known as *erba iva*, yarrow grows above 6,500 feet (2,000 m) up to the edges of the glaciers. Each family in Valtellina has their own recipe for *taneda*, which varies in flower weight, alcohol content, and degree of sweetness.

ALCOHOL CONTENT: 21% vol.

COLOR: dark brown

BOUQUET: distinctly floral

TASTE: agreeable, with strong floral and balsamic hints

AFTERTASTE: bitter persistence with floral notes

AMARO TASSONI

Cedral Tassoni
Salò, Brescia

Cedral Tassoni was built by Paolo Amadei in 1884 along Lake Garda. He acquired an old pharmacy in Salò, and he decided to spin off the distillery, giving it an industrial setup. The company's production is based on the citron fruit, which has been used for centuries along the Lake Garda Riviera to make distillates obtained from hydro-alcoholic infusions obtained from the peel. The complete recipe of Amaro Tassoni has always remained secret; some of the botanicals used are wormwood, galangal, and bitter orange peel.

ALCOHOL CONTENT: 30%. vol.
COLOR: light amber
BOUQUET: citrus notes of bitter orange
TASTE: well balanced between bitter and sweet with hints of wormwood
AFTERTASTE: good bitter persistence

AMARO VENTI

Magi Spirits
Como

Magi Spirits is a young family business founded by Marco Rivolta and his mother, Gianna Percassi. Their adventure began with the production of Rivo Gin (together with the first Italian sloe gin, characterized by blackthorn berries) and continued with Amaro Venti, a modern interpretation of the classic amari, created following traditional liquoristic methods. The name Amaro Venti (Amaro Twenty) refers to the number of botanicals included in the recipe, each representing one of the 20 regions of Italy. The main

botanicals are myrtle, basil, lemon, orange, juniper, olive, tansy, yarrow, and gentian.

ALCOHOL CONTENT: 26% vol.
COLOR: bronze with green-gold reflections
BOUQUET: perfumed with vegetal tendency
TASTE: the citrus fruits wrap the palate at the first sip and then give way to the delicate flavor of basil
AFTERTASTE: long and persistent where the bitter yarrow and gentian dominate

AMARO ZEROTRENTA

Amarcor
Brescia

Amaro Zerotrenta originates from the strong and sincere friendship between Andrea Corezzola and Alessandro Ortogni, fans of soccer and endless card games. In fact the "witty" project came about almost as a joke between one hand and another at the card table. The recipe is based on a hydro-alcoholic infusion of star anise, gentian, licorice, rosemary, lemon balm, chamomile, and juniper. The name Zerotrenta translates as zero-thirty, and it suggests the alcohol content of the amaro. It is also a tribute to Brescia, the hometown of Andrea and Alessandro, as zero-thirty is the telephone area code.

ALCOHOL CONTENT: 30% vol.
COLOR: deep brown with amber and honey highlights
BOUQUET: warm and intense with notes of hay and balsamic herbs
TASTE: strong and very warm with hints of cinchona, chamomile, and licorice
AFTERTASTE: persistent and soft with cool and mentholated sensations

AMARO ZEROTRENTA IN BARRIQUE

Amarcor
Brescia

Amaro Zerotrenta in Barrique features herbaceous and woody essences that are combined with hints of amber and vanilla from the oak wood in which the amaro itself is left to rest for a whole year. At the end of the aging period, a small amount of the amaro is replaced by Reserve of Grappa di Amarone. The main botanicals included in the recipe are star anise, rosemary, licorice, and gentian.

ALCOHOL CONTENT: 30% vol.
COLOR: dark brown
BOUQUET: warm and round with hints of vanilla
TASTE: full and harmonious with woody and aromatic sensations
AFTERTASTE: persistent, soft, and fresh

FERNET-BRANCA

Fratelli Branca Distilleries
Milan

Fernet-Branca was invented in 1845 by Bernardino Branca in his shop in Milan. He then founded a factory for industrial production, starting the family business with his brother Stefano in 1862. The recipe is still secret, and it is handed down from father to son. This amaro contains a total of 27 botanicals, and its basic known botanicals are cinnamon, aloe, rhubarb, chamomile, cinchona, zedoary, galangal, linden, bitter orange, iris, saffron, and myrrh. All the components of the plants involved become part of the Fernet-Branca formula. Flowers, leaves, roots, and stems are used to make alcoholic infusions, extracts, and decoctions that, when mixed together, create the famous product.

ALCOHOL CONTENT: 39% vol.
COLOR: dark brown
BOUQUET: distinct herbaceous hints
TASTE: very bitter, characterized by herbaceous notes
AFTERTASTE: lingering bitter persistence

FERNET-BRANCAMENTA

Fratelli Branca Distilleries
Milan

Fernet-Brancamenta is inspired by the 1960s, a period characterized by great changes: an economic boom, a new way of life, more individualism and less conformism, and, consequently, a greater desire for novelty, including tastes and flavors. So, riding on the wave of these changes, Fratelli Branca Distilleries decided to start the production of a drink perfect for every season by creating Fernet-Brancamenta, a reinterpretation of the eponymous house product, characterized by the addition of essential oils of peppermint from Piedmont.

ALCOHOL CONTENT: 28% vol.
COLOR: dark brown
BOUQUET: herbaceous and mentholated hints
TASTE: very bitter, with herbaceous and mentholated notes
AFTERTASTE: bitter persistence

RAMAZZOTTI IL PREMIO

Pernod Ricard
Milan

In 1850, after leaving the reins of the business to his sons Eugenio and Giuseppe, Ausano Ramazzotti paid homage to them by creating a product that combined Amaro Ramazzotti with Grappa di Nebbiolo Riserva. The recipe for Ramazzotti il Premio, preserved until today in the company's historical archives, combines the herbaceous and fruity candied-orange notes of amaro with the soft and enveloping nuances of vanilla and caramel typical of Grappa di Nebbiolo Riserva; aged 36 months.

ALCOHOL CONTENT: 35% vol.
COLOR: amber
BOUQUET: pungent notes with hints of vanilla
TASTE: well balanced with presence of licorice
AFTERTASTE: bitter with notes of licorice on the finish

Trentino-South Tyrol

ALPLER

Roner Distilleries
Termeno sulla Strada del Vino, Bolzano

Roner Distilleries, created in 1946 from an idea by Gottfried Roner, includes a product range of grappa, fruit distillates, and liquors. They all line up with Alpler, an amaro made from alpine herbs. Alpler is a truly bitter amaro. Its recipe was developed in the Middle Ages in a convent near Bolzano where it was considered an elixir of long life thanks to its many healing properties. The current formulation, which differs from the original only in the lower alcohol content, includes chamomile, gentian, and licorice.

ALCOHOL CONTENT: 40% vol.

COLOR: amber brown

BOUQUET: intense notes of herbs and roots

TASTE: bitter, full, and clean

AFTERTASTE: lingering bitter persistence

ALTA VERDE

Antica Erboristeria Dr. Cappelletti
Aldeno, Trento

The main ingredient of Alta Verde amaro is wormwood, whose renowned bitterness is balanced with a complementary blend of brilliant alpine herbs, spices, and citrus fruits, including eucalyptus, mint, cumin seeds, and verbena. The different botanicals, macerated individually in alcohol for at least 90 days, evoke the image of a forest in all its verdant splendor. The recipe for Alta Verde was created in 2017, but it was only in 2019 that Antica Erboristeria Dr. Cappelletti decided to distribute the product on the Italian market.

ALCOHOL CONTENT: 24% vol.

COLOR: yellow-green

BOUQUET: strong hints of bitter herbs and roots

TASTE: bitter, fresh, and clean

AFTERTASTE: distinctly bitter with a persistent hint of gentian

AMARO ALPINO

Distilleria Alpina
Trento

Distilleria Alpina of Trento links its fame to Amaro Alpino, created in 1930 by Dr. Agostino Pontillo. It is a spirit based on alpine herbs and roots. The company wanted to keep the list of ingredients mostly secret, but it includes gentian roots, juniper berries, cinchona, rhubarb, and calamus. Like the recipe itself, the production process is unchanged, and it remains inspired by the most authentic artisan tradition that has always characterized the parent company.

ALCOHOL CONTENT: 18.5% vol.

COLOR: dark brown

BOUQUET: sharp hints of juniper and gentian

TASTE: balanced, with bitter notes of cinchona and rhubarb

AFTERTASTE: bitter persistence

AMARO DAKAPO

**Azienda Vitivinicola
Castello Rametz**
Merano, Bolzano

The formula of Amaro Dakapo was created in 1992 on the basis of a historical recipe reinterpreted by Karl Schmid. Schmid, a skillful liquorist and botanist, decided in 1972 to purchase the Castello Rametz Winery and to expand its portfolio, which at the time included oenological products plus high-quality liqueur specialties. Amaro Dakapo (*daccapo* means "from scratch") does not aim to be an end point. Rather, as the name suggests, it aims to be a new adventure. By mixing aromatic botanicals that include gentian, cinchona, orange, and licorice, Karl gave life to this young amaro, while drawing on ancient tradition.

ALCOHOL CONTENT: 30% vol.
COLOR: brown with orange highlights
BOUQUET: intoxicating scents of herbs and citrus fruits
TASTE: soft, slightly sweet with hints of herbs
AFTERTASTE: sweet persistence with notes of orange and licorice

AMARO DELLO SPEZIALE

A. Foletto
Ledro, Trento

The history of the A. Foletto pharmaceutical laboratory began in 1850 with the founder Giovanni, a pharmacist from Ledro, in the province of Trento. In 2010 a few yards from the company's office the Foletto family opened a botanical garden of apothecary (*speziale*), where the botanicals used for the production of amari are grown. This includes Amaro dello Speziale, whose formulation is inspired by an *elixir di China* from 1938, which was then enriched with aromatic herbs for a total of 22 botanicals used, including gentian, licorice, coriander, rhubarb, mint, and wormwood. The production of this amaro, while complying with modern production standards, maintains the artisan character of the original recipe.

ALCOHOL CONTENT: 30% vol.
COLOR: intense caramel with golden highlights
BOUQUET: citrusy and complex
TASTE:
aromatic,
balsamic, and
astringent
AFTERTASTE:
lingering
gentian and
rhubarb notes

AMARO GIORI

Giori Distillati Trentini
Volano, Trento

Giori Distillati Trentini was founded by Ferruccio Giori in 1946. Over the years their activity has grown progressively, and they have achieved an international dimension thanks to the passion and professionalism of the Giori family, which today is enriched by the presence of Marella and Alessandro, Ferruccio's grandchildren. Among the products of the distillery, Amaro Giori, with its secret recipe, stands out. Among the various botanicals, rhubarb is mainly used.

ALCOHOL CONTENT: 35% vol.
COLOR: light brown
BOUQUET: soft with rhubarb finish
TASTE: well balanced between sweet and bitter
AFTERTASTE: bitter finish with presence of rhubarb

AMARO MARZADRO

Distilleria Marzadro
Nogaredo, Trento

The history of Distilleria Marzadro began in a scenario where there was no escaping poverty: postwar Italy. Sabina Marzadro, possessing a firm will to change her life, cultivated the dream of dedicating herself to the art of distillation. So, in 1949, she began her adventure together with her brother Attilio. Passionate about botany, Sabina did not miss the opportunity to go up to the mountains to collect and study the wild alpine herbs, roots, and local berries and to combine them with her beloved grappa. It was from this strong passion for herbs, handed down from generation to generation, that Amaro Marzadro was born. Alpine rhubarb, gentian, white briony, chamomile, fennel, holy thistle, galega, and various varieties of yarrow, after being carefully handpicked, are left to macerate in alcohol for 20 to 30 days.

ALCOHOL CONTENT: 30% vol.
COLOR: red with mahogany shades
BOUQUET: aromatic and herbaceous
TASTE: bitter and fresh with a prevalence of gentian
AFTERTASTE: persistence of rhubarb and chamomile

AMARO MUGO GIN

Villa Laviosa
Sette Querce-Terlano, Bolzano

Villa Laviosa produces liqueurs, grappas, and other distillates capable of expressing the irresistible scents of South Tyrol. Their range of products includes Amaro Mugo Gin, which recalls the characteristics of a fortified grappa. This amaro

is the result of careful processing in which juniper, mountain pine, licorice, and other roots are subjected to cold infusion, blending their characteristics in a harmonious way.

ALCOHOL CONTENT: 38% vol.
COLOR: dark amber
BOUQUET: prevalent notes of grappa
TASTE: bitter, well balanced to sweet
AFTERTASTE: lingering juniper

AMARO PASUBIO

Antica Erboristeria Dr. Cappelletti
Aldeno, Trento

In 2017, Antica Erboristeria Dr. Cappelletti, inspired by an ancient local recipe, launched Amaro Pasubio onto the market. This amaro is based on wine reminiscent of the flavors of the forest. Prepared with aromatic plants and roots harvested on the slopes of Mount Pasubio and Col Santo, this spirit represents the perfect combination of the typical bitter scents of alpine herbs, and among them you can recognize mountain pine, wormwood, gentian, centaury, yarrow, mint, and the sweet notes of blueberry.

ALCOHOL CONTENT: 17% vol.
COLOR: brown with emerald highlights

BOUQUET: typical forest scents, among which the mountain pine stands out
TASTE: marked bitterness mitigated by the sweet notes of blueberry
AFTERTASTE: excellent persistence of bitter herbs

AMARO PROIBITO

A. Foletto
Ledro, Trento

In 1943, the pharmacist and botanist Achille Foletto, a lieutenant at the military hospital of Riva sul Garda, used the language of botanists to interpret the feelings of hope and renewal in his patients. Amaro Proibito, which was drunk secretly by guests and soldiers in the basement of the hospital, is composed of over 24 botanicals including angelica, lavender, chamomile, peppermint, gentian, primrose, and gentianella. The aromatic freshness of the lemons of Lake Garda, combined with the floral elegance of the mountains of Trentino and the herbaceous character of the Dolomite roots, gives life to this refined bitter elixir.

ALCOHOL CONTENT: 30% vol.
COLOR: deep amber
BOUQUET: fresh, woody, and resinous
TASTE: bold and velvety
AFTERTASTE: lingering bitter persistence

AMARO ROSSI D'ANAUNIA

Distilleria Rossi d'Anaunia
Revò, Trento

Distilleria Rossi d'Anaunia has always stood out for its attention to detail and for the artisanal methods used in the production of its products in a virtuous balance between tradition and innovation. Located in the heart of the Val di Non, the company has been producing aquavits, grappas, and liqueurs for more than a century. Their logo contains the number 137, which refers to the old house number of the building that houses their alembic still and where great-grandfather Armando began distilling. One of the company's leading products is the Amaro Rossi D'Anaunia, made from a mix of medicinal herbs with marked digestive and aromatic properties.

ALCOHOL CONTENT: 30% vol.
COLOR: deep mahogany
BOUQUET: hints of medicinal herbs and roots prevail
TASTE: broad and round, with herbaceous notes and aromas of patchouli, nutmeg, date, and bitter almond
AFTERTASTE: lingering bitter notes

AMARO SFUMATO

Antica Erboristeria Dr. Cappelletti
Aldeno, Trento

The Italian term *sfumato* (gradient) indicates a painting technique typical of the Renaissance: delicate plays of chiaroscuro, darkness, and light harmoniously mixed. This is how Amaro Sfumato presents itself, describing a more-than-perfect balance among the bitterness of alpine herbs with the unique taste of rhubarb and the sweet notes of berries. This young Cappelletti product came to life in 2016 to make up for the lack of a rhubarb-based bitter that did not have an excessive amount of sugar. This is how Amaro Sfumato was born, and the percentage of rhubarb in it is very high, at least 25 kg per 1,000 L.

ALCOHOL CONTENT: 20% vol.
COLOR: opaque brown
BOUQUET: distinct hints of rhubarb
TASTE: pleasant and agreeable
AFTERTASTE: lingering bitter-sweet persistence

AMARO SVEDESE

Distilleria Alfons Walcher
Frangarto, Bolzano

In 1966, Alfons Walcher, using just a small artisanal still, began distilling at the Turmbachhof farm in Appiano on the famed Wine Road near Bolzano. The farm had been owned by the Walcher family for nine generations. Since then, the distillery has come a long way, inspired by the concepts of tradition and innovation, with the utmost respect for the environment. Among Walcher's products, a standout is Amaro Svedese, a famous elixir made according to an ancient recipe using carlina root, angelica root, aloe, myrrh, Chinese rhubarb root, Venetian theriac, and saffron. It also features senna leaves, camphor, turmeric, and flowering ash.

ALCOHOL CONTENT: 32% vol.
COLOR: dark brown
BOUQUET: distinct notes of rhubarb and angelica
TASTE: balanced between sweet and bitter
AFTERTASTE: bitter rhubarb finish

ELISIR DELLO SPEZIALE

Antica Erboristeria Dr. Cappelletti
Aldeno, Trento

This amaro went into production at the end of the 1950s in honor and memory of Giuseppe Cappelletti, who founded the distillery Antica Erboristeria Dr. Cappelletti. It was the personal elixir of the herbalist from Trentino, made to be enjoyed with friends. To date, the recipe has remained unchanged, as has the care in the preparation. It is made with individual botanicals that include wormwood, centaury, gentian, angelica, anise, coriander, cloves, cinnamon, and quassia that are macerated in alcohol for at least 90 days.

ALCOHOL CONTENT: 32% vol.

COLOR: mahogany

BOUQUET: intense herb and spice

TASTE: rich, full, and spicy

AFTERTASTE: persistent and very agreeable

ELISIR NOVASALUS

Antica Erboristeria Dr. Cappelletti
Aldeno, Trento

Giuseppe Cappelletti was born in 1880 in Ciago di Vezzano (Trento), on the slopes of the Brenta Dolomites. As a true lover of medicinal herbs, he earned his diploma as an herbalist and apothecary and then, together with his brothers, he started a company for the sale of wholesale and retail colonial goods, which over the years has developed into what is today an established company producing syrups, liqueurs, amari, and grappas. Elisir Novasalus, a historical product of Antica Erboristeria Dr. Cappelletti, is an "elixir of health" obtained from a harmonious combination of infusions, decoctions, and macerated herbs, flowers, and roots in wine that is still aromatized and crafted by hand. The recipe, conceived at the end of World War I, involves the use of more than 30 botanicals including aloe, angelica, anise, orange, wormwood, burdock, cinnamon, cardamom, centaury, cloves, ivy, eucalyptus, fennel, buckthorn, ash, gentian, juniper, orris, lavender, lemon balm, mint, licorice, rhapontic rhubarb, rhubarb, dandelion, valerian, saffron, zedoary, and ginger. For collectors, it is impossible to find bottles of Elisir Novasalus that were put on the market before the 1980s, demonstrating how it has always been difficult to keep it for a long time in the cupboard or in the cellar.

ALCOHOL CONTENT: 36% vol.

COLOR: amber

BOUQUET: intense scent of alpine herbs

TASTE: strong bitter connotation with balsamic hints

AFTERTASTE: persistent alpine taste

GHIMPEN MAT L'AMARO DI PINÈ

Distilleria Paolazzi Vittorio
Faver Altavalle, Trento

Distilleria Paolazzi Vittorio was founded in 1962 in Faver, in Valle di Cembra. The family distilling tradition is carried on today by Martino, Vittorio's son. In accordance with the Trentino and Cembran customs, the company uses the discontinuous steam distillation method, with a production philosophy aimed at supporting classic products of the highest quality. Ghimpen Mat L'Amaro di Pinè, an amaro made from mountain and scrub herbs of the Pinè Plateau, follows an ancient recipe created by the great-great-grandfather Tommaso Tomasi, who was called Ghimpen Mat, a wizard and botanist who lived between 1828 and 1898.

ALCHOL CONTENT: 35% vol.

COLOR: garnet

BOUQUET: bitter herbal notes

TASTE: balanced between sweet and bitter

AFTERTASTE: decisive bitter persistence

JUITH

Attimi Perfetti
Castelrotto, Bolzano

Juith is produced from an agricultural alcohol base in which the botanicals are infused following a well-defined rhythm. Thanks to this process, the spirit acquires its characteristic roundness. Juith is a natural bitter wherein Italian jujubes are married to sweet chamomile flowers, using a recipe developed by combining scientific knowledge and passion by the great master distiller, Florian Rabanser, founder of Distilleria Zu Plun in Castelrotto.

ALCOHOL CONTENT: 33% vol.

COLOR: dark amber

BOUQUET: fresh and flowery notes of jujube

TASTE: soft with a pungent finish; the alcoholic note gives harmony to the body

AFTERTASTE: soft finish with mentholated peaks

K32 AMARO

Roner Distilleries
Termeno on the Wine Road, Bolzano

For this amaro, *K* stands for the German word *Kräuter*, (herbs) and the number 32 denotes the alcohol content. The experience gained in the use of herbs through decades of production has been, for the master distiller of Roner Distilleries, the inspiration for the development of an amaro with a modern spirit. Typical alpine botanicals are combined with other distinctively Mediterranean ones, producing an amiability and richness of scents. K32 Amaro is the latest addition to the Roner family, with chamomile, lemon balm, mint, juniper, gentian, licorice, cornflower, heather, and citrus fruits, united with a distillate of pine cones from Swiss pine. This amaro is full-flavored, but not intrusive, with a pleasant sweetness and roundness.

ALCOHOL CONTENT: 32% vol.

COLOR: amber

BOUQUET: fresh with bitter and citrus notes

TASTE: full, bitter, and fruity

AFTERTASTE: harmonic persistence

KAISERFORST

Valentini
Tassullo, Trento

In 1872, in the splendid Val di Non, Von Damian Valentini began to dedicate himself to the production of aged distillates for his family and community. In the wake of this tradition, in 1921 Rodolfo Valentini, Von Damian's eldest son, returned from Colorado and founded the first of the Valentini distilleries in Tassullo. The Kaiserforst amaro was created from 47 carefully selected botanicals, skillfully infused and distilled. The subsequent aging process in French oak barrels gives the product a soft and round character.

ALCOHOL CONTENT: 32% vol.

COLOR: dark brown

BOUQUET: distinct herbaceous notes

TASTE: well balanced between sweet and bitter

AFTERTASTE: bitter persistence

L'AMARO SCHMID

Azienda Vitivinicola Castello Rametz
Merano, Bolzano

The first documents referring to Azienda Vitivinicola Castello Rametz date back to 1227, in which the estate is defined as situated on a moraine hill as a "significant possession in the field of viticulture." It was here, in fact, that the pinot noir vine was cultivated for the first time in South Tyrol, in 1860. Thanks to the guidance of Karl Schmid, a great expert in spirits, the company began to produce Italian liqueur specialties in 1972. The latest addition to the production range is L'Amaro Schmid, handcrafted with skillful alcohol infusions of numerous botanicals including licorice, gentian, and cinchona.

ALCOHOL CONTENT: 43% vol.
COLOR: deep brown
BOUQUET: sharp herbaceous notes
TASTE: balanced between sweet and bitter, distinctly herbaceous and spicy with notes of licorice
AFTERTASTE: warm and embracing with light citrus scents

RUTABEN

Antica Erboristeria Dr. Cappelletti
Aldeno, Trento

The formulation of Rutaben belongs to an ancient herbarium of 1617. As reported on the label, it is "for a few learned and judicious people," and, among the many virtues, it possesses those of "chasing away the wind" and "taking a good breath." Rutaben does not contain rue: Its name, of Trentino dialectal derivation, is in fact a wish for good digestion, an invitation to burp! It is a product for those who love an intense bitter taste. It does not contain sugar, and the predominant botanical is gentian along with cinchona, wormwood, centaury, cloves, and saffron.

ALCOHOL CONTENT: 45% vol.
COLOR: brown with golden highlights
BOUQUET: intense mountain herbs
TASTE: very bitter and decisive
AFTERTASTE: fresh and clean

SALTNER

Distilleria Alfons Walcher
Frangarto, Bolzano

Distilleria Alfons Walcher is situated in a large orchard, and the many sunny days and cool nights in spring and summer allow the fruit there to develop intense and unmistakable scents. Walcher's Saltner amaro is distinguished by its seductive aroma, in which the scent of bitter orange emerges clearly, as it intertwines with those of the finest herbs and spices. The result is a drink with an intense, pleasant, and distinctly bitter taste.

ALCOHOL CONTENT: 28% vol.
COLOR: dark brown
BOUQUET: distinct hints of bitter orange
TASTE: bitter part very apparent
AFTERTASTE: bitter persistence

TINTURA STOMATICA

A. Foletto
Ledro, Trento

Tintura Stomatica is a historical tincture of botanicals of alpine medicinal herbs created by the pharmacist and botanist Angelo Foletto in 1898. Until 1990, it was a product registered as a pharmaceutical specialty. Today it is made with the same artisanal method of maceration of medicinal substances in "small batches" of 475 quarts (450 l). Tintura Stomatica is composed of only seven botanicals in an oversaturated concentration to create the maximum organoleptic expression of each one. The original recipe includes lady's mantle, orange, clove, trumpet gentian, willow gentian, yellow gentian, and rhubarb. The percolation and maceration processes last 24 months.

ALCOHOL CONTENT: 32% vol.
COLOR: deep brown
BOUQUET: citrusy, tannic, and astringent
TASTE: strong, with predominance of gentian and rhubarb
AFTERTASTE: astonishing persistence

Veneto

AMARO '900

Liquoreria Carlotto
Valdagno, Vicenza

The history of Liquoreria Carlotto is linked to that of the Potepan family, of Hungarian origin, who came to the Hapsburg court around 1820. Anton Potepan, as an exponent of central European pastry and liquor art, together with his son Giovanni Onesto, began to produce the famous Bulgarian Rose Rosolio. This drink immediately found the extraordinary approval of Francis Joseph I of Austria who decided to donate a bottle to the king of Italy, Vittorio Emanuele II. Teresa, daughter of Giovanni Onesto, married Girolamo Carlotto, owner of a liquor factory. As a dowry, Teresa gave her new husband the family recipes that still inspire the Carlotto production today. The formula of Amaro '900 dates back to the early 20th century and includes the skillful infusion of 39 botanical-aromatic herbs, among which sage prevails.

ALCOHOL CONTENT: 34% vol.

COLOR: bright mahogany with orange highlights

BOUQUET: aromatic notes of flowers and medicinal herbs

TASTE: aromatic and floral with predominance of sage

AFTERTASTE: vegetal persistence with aromatic notes

AMARO 33

Distilleria Andrea Da Ponte
Conegliano, Treviso

Like every product of Distilleria Andrea Da Ponte, Amaro 33 is the result of a perfect combination of study and experimentation. Created by Francis, descendant of the Da Ponte–Fabris family, and launched onto the market after more than two years of research in collaboration with the oenologist Graziano Freschet, Amaro 33 can count on an alcoholic base of fine, aged Prosecco grappa that is exalted by the delicate yet striking notes of ginger, the main ingredient of this original amaro with an exotic character.

ALCOHOL CONTENT: 33% vol.

COLOR: pale straw yellow

BOUQUET: strong notes of ginger

TASTE: warm and pleasant alcoholic tip of grappa combined with spicy hints of ginger

AFTERTASTE: velvety, embracing, and exotic with good persistence

AMARO 107

Antiche Distillerie Mantovani
Pincara, Rovigo

Quality, creativity, and attention to image are the strong points of the Antiche Distillerie Mantovani. Today, the activity is carried on with enthusiasm and dynamism by siblings Anna and Paolo, based on a wise union between tradition and innovation. In the museum area, inaugurated in 2004 within the company, some ancient manuscripts containing precious recipes for the preparation of intriguing liqueurs and distillates are preserved with painstaking care. Among the many, there is also that of Amaro 107, number 107 in the ancient recipe book, whose production began in the 1920s by Renato Mantovani.

ALCOHOL CONTENT: 30% vol.

COLOR: dark caramel

BOUQUET: herbaceous hints with a prevalence of gentian

TASTE: bittersweet, with notes of rhubarb and gentian

AFTERTASTE: soft, fresh, and herbaceous with lingering hints of mint

AMARO ABANO

Girolamo Luxardo
Torreglia, Padova

Girolamo Luxardo founded the company of the same name in 1821 in Zadar, on the coast of Dalmatia. After years of flourishing production, World War II imposed heavy restrictions and led to the almost total destruction of the factory, which was severely hit by American bombardments. In 1947, Giorgio and Nicolò III resumed the family business, inaugurating the new company headquarters in Torreglia, in the province of Padua. Created in 1952, the recipe for Amaro Abano includes an alcoholic infusion of condurango, cardamom, cinnamon, bitter orange peel, cinchona, and other botanicals. Amaro Abano is also produced in a dry version that features a higher alcohol content (35% vol.) and a markedly more bitter taste.

ALCOHOL CONTENT: 30% vol.

COLOR: dark amber

BOUQUET: intense notes of medicinal herbs

TASTE: warm, harmonious

AFTERTASTE: distinctly bitter with citrus persistence

AMARO ASIAGO

Antiche Distillerie Riunite
Ponte di Barbarano, Vicenza

Antiche Distillerie Riunite can boast over 150 years of history, and today its distilleries are under the wise guidance of Francesco Dal Toso and his children Nicola and Patrizia. It all began thanks to Giovan Battista Rossi, a young and talented botanist and pharmacist of Asiago who in the second half of the 19th century developed the recipe of the company's first iconic amaro, China Rossi, an excellent restorative, invigorating, and digestive aid based on cinchona and royal jelly. Another symbolic product of the company, strongly expressive of the territory, is Amaro Asiago, which is based on an alcohol infusion of botanicals and alpine herbs that include gentian, chamomile, fern, coriander, wormwood, and rhubarb.

ALCOHOL CONTENT: 30% vol.

COLOR: deep amber

BOUQUET: distinct hints of herbs and roots

TASTE: amiable and slightly bitter with a predominance of gentian

AFTERTASTE: soft balsamic and vegetal persistence

AMARO CENT'ANNI

Gagliano Marcati
Sommacampagna, Verona

The Gagliano Marcati company was started in 1919, when brothers Pietro and Luigi Marcati began as liquorists in the family pharmacy, in whose small artisan workshop the skillfully crafted spirits were being created. Pietro, at the same time, began to compile a refined recipe book that today, in the hands of siblings Pietro, Andrea, and Maria Paola—currently at the helm of the company—is an inexhaustible source of inspiration. Among the products in the ancient collection, Amaro Cent'anni stands out as the result of cold alcoholic infusions of secret digestive and aromatic botanicals that include medicinal herbs, barks, and roots.

ALCOHOL CONTENT: 35% vol.
COLOR: dark brown with golden highlights
BOUQUET: pleasant and delicate scents of alpine herbs
TASTE: aromatic and balanced
AFTERTASTE: slightly bitter with sensations of wormwood

AMARO CHINOL PADOVA

Sipla Royal Drink
Campodarsego, Padua

The result of an ancient recipe developed by Caterino Dondi Pinton, based on cinchona, chamomile, artichoke, rhubarb, yarrow, thyme, gentian, bitter orange, wormwood, juniper, and 15 other herbs and roots, Amaro Chinol Padova, the Venetian amaro of the postwar period, brings with it a long history of wisdom and tradition. Caterino, an expert liquorist, after having traveled all over the world as the right-hand man of the Dalle Molle brothers to build factories dedicated to the production of Amaro Cynar, began a personal adventure with Sipla Royal Drink that today boasts a large production plant also engaged in subcontracting production.

ALCOHOL CONTENT: 16% vol.
COLOR: dark ruby
BOUQUET: herbaceous and aromatic perfume
TASTE: hints of chamomile and artichoke with well-integrated sugary notes
AFTERTASTE: soft vegetal persistence with notes of rhubarb

AMARO CORTINA

1895 Liquori Frescura
Sedico, Belluno

The Liquori Frescura company was founded by Primo Frescura in 1895. His son Ezio, his successor at the helm of the company, between the two World Wars, transferred part of the production to Cortina d'Ampezzo. Amaro Cortina was born there when its recipe was filed in 1952. This spirit with a lively body is made by cold infusion in alcohol of numerous botanicals that include gentian, wormwood, cinchona bark, cardamom, dandelion, mint, bitter orange peel, and valerian.

ALCOHOL CONTENT: 38% vol.
COLOR: mahogany with orange highlights
BOUQUET: prevalent hints of herbs and roots
TASTE: agreeable with herbaceous notes and hints of cinchona and citrus fruits
AFTERTASTE: fresh persistence and vegetal

AMARO DEL LUPO

Antiche Distillerie Mantovani
Pincara, Rovigo

The birth of the Antiche Distillerie Mantovani dates back to 1824 when Cesare Mantovani decided to make his passion for the art of liquor a profession. The company, started in Mirabello di Ferrara, was transferred in 1970 to Pincara, keeping intact the love for tradition, with an eye toward innovation. Amaro del Lupo has always stood out among the Antiche Distillerie Mantovani–branded products, created from the alcoholic infusion of gentian, quassia, aloe, coriander, angelica, and other numerous botanicals.

ALCOHOL CONTENT: 38% vol.

COLOR: amber with golden highlights

BOUQUET: strong and intoxicating scent of herbs and roots

TASTE: dry and bitter with strong hints of gentian

AFTERTASTE: dry and clean with long and fresh persistence

AMARO DEL PALAZZONE

Distilleria Fratelli Brunello
Montegalda, Vicenza

Distilleria Fratelli Brunello owes its flourishing, which took place in the early 20th century, to Maria Marzari, one of the first women entrepreneurs in the world of grappa. Today the company is under the guidance of Giovanni, Paolo, and Stefano Brunello. The recipe of Amaro del Palazzone was created in the 1970s to meet the demands of customers tired of watching the production of bitters destined exclusively for pharmacies. Amaro del Palazzone takes its name from the 16th-century building that is now the headquarters of the distillery, and the amaro itself is composed of two varieties of cinchona, boldo, cascara, bitter orange, and rhubarb, which, together with other botanicals, have been subjected to maceration in alcohol without undergoing mechanical treatment and filtration.

ALCOHOL CONTENT: 30% vol.

COLOR: brown with mahogany highlights

BOUQUET: delicate and herbaceous

TASTE: soft and harmonious

AFTERTASTE: agreeable with hints of citrus and rhubarb

AMARO D'ERBE

Distilleria Zamperoni
Galliera Veneta, Padua

Distilleria Zamperoni was founded in the 1950s in San Martino di Lupari (Padua) by Domenico Zamperoni, who was already active in the distillation sector. Today, in Zamperoni's range of products—in addition to grappas and distillates—there is Amaro d'Erbe. This amaro, which is based on a historical recipe handed down from father to son, is made from the infusion in alcohol of herbs, roots, and citrus fruits. The specific ingredients include gentian, rhubarb, Roman wormwood, mint, lemon balm, cinchona, juniper, rosemary, bitter orange, and sweet orange.

ALCOHOL CONTENT: 30% vol.

COLOR: brown with mahogany highlights

BOUQUET: herbaceous and spicy

TASTE: full, with a pleasant bitter note

AFTERTASTE: fresh and aromatic persistence that envelops the palate

AMARO EUGANEO

Sipla Royal Drink
Campodarsego, Padua

Amaro Euganeo was born in the early 2000s, thanks to Alberto, the master herbalist of Sipla Royal Drink and grandson of distillery founder Caterino Dondi Pinton. The formulation, inspired by an ancient Euganean recipe, includes botanicals such as artichoke, nettle, chamomile, licorice, aloe, thyme, mint, mallow, and lemon balm, which are infused in alcohol.

ALCOHOL CONTENT: 32% vol.

COLOR: brown with orange highlights

BOUQUET: hints of roots and barks

TASTE: moderately bitter with fresh and floral hints

AFTERTASTE: persistent and spicy with notes of licorice and cinnamon

AMARO FELSINA SCHIAVO

Distilleria Schiavo
Costabissara, Vicenza

Distilleria Schiavo is a "small" family business founded in 1887. The company had the idea of bringing Amaro Felsina Schiavo, once used as an aperitif by adding it to white wine, back onto the market in 2010. They took the old recipe and modified it with the introduction of fruit alcohol for infusion and three types of sugar as sweeteners: white, powdered, and demerara. Among the botanicals in the secret recipe are sweet orange, bitter orange, gentian, licorice, and rhubarb.

ALCOHOL CONTENT: 28% vol.

COLOR: dark amber with orange highlights

BOUQUET: notes of orange, gentian, licorice, and rhubarb

TASTE: embracing, bitter, with hints of herbs

AFTERTASTE: good persistence with sweet finish

AMARO FRESCURA

1895 Liquori Frescura
Sedico, Belluno

The Liquori Frescura company was founded in 1895 by Primo Frescura, who had learned the secrets of the art of liqueur-making in Bologna while working at the historic Distilleria Buton. From the very beginning, Primo focused on quality in the processing and selection of raw materials, a choice that won him numerous awards throughout Europe in the early 20th century. Amaro Frescura, the first Amaro Elisir, is inspired by an ancient recipe made by the infusion in alcohol of herbs and roots such as gentian, wormwood, chamomile, cinnamon, mint, lemon balm, and licorice.

ALCOHOL CONTENT: 20% vol.

COLOR: dark

BOUQUET: fresh and aromatic nose

TASTE: bitter hints of gentian and notes of cinnamon stand out

AFTERTASTE: agreeable with hints of licorice and wormwood

AMARO LEON

Castagner
Vazzola, Treviso

Amaro Leon was created after two years of studies and research carried out by in-house oenologists, with the hope of surprising great lovers of amari. More than 45 medicinal botanicals are processed with slow cold infusions according to precise and specific times, in order to extract the most noble aromas from each raw material. Amaro Leon's production method has been baptized the Reff Method, as it aims to get the best out of *radici, erbe, foglie,* and *fiori* (roots, herbs, leaves, and flowers) to make the most out of what nature offers. Among the botanicals used are hops, peppermint, dandelion, milk thistle, rhubarb, angelica, myrrh, and green citrus.

ALCOHOL CONTENT: 33% vol.

COLOR: opaque brown

BOUQUET: intense and varied with hints of fruit and roots

TASTE: intense, rich, and complex

AFTERTASTE: full-bodied and spicy with gentian and rhubarb

AMARO NARDINI

Bortolo Nardini s.p.a.
Bassano del Grappa,
Vicenza

It was April 16, 1779, when Bortolo Nardini, originally from Trentino, opened his distillery in Bassano del Grappa (Bassano Veneto at the time). Ten years before the French Revolution and three years after the American Revolution, a revolutionary event in the history of Italian distillation took place: Up to that moment, in fact, grappa was produced in an itinerant way, on wooden gigs equipped with a mobile distiller that moved from farm to farm. Nardini's distillery was the first fixed Italian distillery with an adjoining grapperia. This changed the way things were done, pushing farmers to go to Ponte Vecchio in Bassano to acquire grappa made from their pomace. More than 240 years after its founding, the Nardini distillery remains a reference point for grappa lovers and others. The impressive Amaro Nardini features in their product line; it was created in the second half of the 19th century for digestive purposes, although it was endowed with a very pleasant taste. Among the botanicals included in the recipe are gentian root, orange, and peppermint, which, together with the others, are naturally infused in grain alcohol.

ALCOHOLIC CONTENT: 31% vol.

COLOR: coffee, clear, and nonviscous

BOUQUET: hints of licorice and caramel

TASTE: mint, cream, and licorice aromas predominate

AFTERTASTE: persistence of orange

AMARO NEGRONI

Distilleria Negroni
Mareno di Piave, Treviso

Distilleria Negroni was founded in 1919 in Emilia Romagna by Guglielmo Negroni. In the 1960s, Guglielmo's sons continued the enterprise undertaken by their father, moving it to Veneto but with unchanged passion and attention to the products of the territory. In the mid-1980s the company was sold to the Palla family, the current owners, already operating in the beverage sector. Amaro Negroni was created by Giancarlo Palla to satisfy the palates of the most demanding amaro lovers. The recipe combines the organoleptic characteristics of red radicchio from Treviso with those of ginseng, rhubarb, gentian, Roman wormwood, dandelion, sweet orange, and bitter orange.

ALCOHOL CONTENT: 27% vol.

COLOR: brown with coppered highlights

BOUQUET: fine, medium intense aroma with hints of ginseng and rhubarb

TASTE: soft, balanced, and pleasantly bitter

AFTERTASTE: good persistence with citrus and bitter notes

AMARO PRATUM

Distilleria Bonaventura Maschio
Gaiarine, Treviso

Distilleria Bonaventura Maschio boasts over a century of history with five successive generations in charge. Work, constant research, and quality are the core values that the Gaiarine business has always been committed to in order to manufacture very high-quality products like Amaro Pratum. Also known as the amaro of stable meadows, Amaro Pratum is created by the careful selection of seven botanicals taken from the stable meadows of Friuli-Venezia Giulia, which are authentic sources of biodiversity.

ALCOHOL CONTENT: 29% vol.

COLOR: intense amber with golden pink highlights

BOUQUET: full and harmonious herb bouquet with notes of thyme and mint

TASTE: harmonic, balanced, and fresh with hints of sage and chamomile

AFTERTASTE: lovely and persistent with notes of yarrow

AMARO TENACE

About Ten
Padua

Dave Garzon, a former globe-trotting bartender, and Francesco Mortai, who has always been in the food and beverage sector, founded About Ten, an artisanal company producing liquors and spirits, in 2011. Dave and Francesco only use natural extractions from the selected botanicals for their blends, and they define themselves as "their own artisans." About Ten works beyond territorial boundaries, proposing new recipes inspired by typical aromas that come from all over the world. The latest creation is Amaro Tenace, made with 16 different botanicals that include rhubarb, cinchona, Roman wormwood, artichoke, gentian, tonka bean, pink ginger, and bergamot.

ALCOHOL CONTENT: 25% vol.

COLOR: amber with golden highlights

BOUQUET: intense and fresh scent of herbs

TASTE: decidedly bitter with a strong herbaceous and spicy connotation

AFTERTASTE: slightly floral and citrusy persistence

AMARO TREVISANO

Distilleria Negroni
Mareno di Piave, Treviso

The recipe for Amaro Trevisano was born in the 1960s after Distilleria Negroni in Veneto moved to Mareno di Piave in the province of Treviso. The founder's sons, Giovanni and Carlo Negroni, continue the operation undertaken by their father Guglielmo with passion and attention, maintaining a deep bond with the territory: The base of Amaro Trevisano is in fact the red radicchio of Treviso. The historical recipe of this amaro, taken from the tradition of Treviso, is still valid today. It provides the hydro-alcoholic infusion of "late" quality red radicchio from Treviso for about 90 days, with the addition of rhubarb, gentian, dandelion, ginseng, and Roman wormwood.

ALCOHOL CONTENT: 27% vol.

COLOR: intense dark red with garnet reflections

BOUQUET: strong scent with a dominant fragrance of red Treviso radicchio

TASTE: soft, balanced, and pleasantly bitter

AFTERTASTE: good persistence with citrus and bitter notes

AMARO VACA MORA

Poli Distillerie
Schiavon, Vicenza

In 1885, Gio Batta Poli decided to move to Schiavon, buying a house and land and opening the Al Cappello tavern. A few years later, the Vaca Mora, the long-awaited steam train, arrived nearby. The passengers of the Vaca Mora would wait for their ride in the tavern while sipping a glass of wine or a drop of what later became Amaro Vaca Mora. The recipe, today reinterpreted in a modern key, provides for the use of 16 botanicals with marked digestive properties: lemon balm, hops, cinchona, wormwood, calamus, bitter orange, cardamom, blood orange, cinnamon, coriander, mint, hyssop, chamomile, iris, angelica, and mace.

ALCOHOL CONTENT: 32% vol.

COLOR: mahogany with red highlights

BOUQUET: spicy with a hint of mint

TASTE: bitter-medicinal

AFTERTASTE: very good bitter persistence

CYNAR

Campari Group
Padua

Produced from the leaves of the artichoke (*Cynara scolymus*) and with versatile character, thanks to its low alcohol content, Cynar can be considered an Italian icon that is known around the world. Its unmistakable taste derives more precisely from the infusion of 13 botanicals according to a recipe that's been a secret since 1948. Created by Angelo Dalle Molle, this spirit was born as a bitter aperitif at the Pezziol company. Cynar reached popularity thanks to the numerous advertising initiatives following one after another over the years. On *Carosello*, an Italian television show that ran for decades, advertisements for Cynar starred the actor Ernesto Calindri and the unforgettable slogan "Against the wear and tear of modern life."

ALCOHOL CONTENT: 16.5% vol.

COLOR: ebony with copper reflections

BOUQUET: artichoke with floral hints

TASTE: bitter and firm, pleasant and balanced

AFTERTASTE: full, with a vegetal note that becomes bitter and persists in the finish

FERNET CARLOTTO

Carlotto
Valdagno, Vicenza

The Carlotto brand boasts a history of quality craftsmanship for over 100 years. Among its most prestigious collaborations is with the great chef Gualtiero Marchesi, who, in 1980, falling in love with liqueurs, commissioned the creation of a series of spirits, helping to relaunch the company after a difficult phase due to the dynamics of large-scale distribution. Among the many specialties of the house is Fernet Carlotto, an amaro with a strong taste and secret recipe that reveals hints of gentian, chamomile, rhubarb, cardamom, and saffron.

ALCOHOL CONTENT: 42% vol.

COLOR: bright amber

BOUQUET: intense scents of roots and bitter herbs

TASTE: strongly bitter and balanced with hints of chamomile and gentian

AFTERTASTE: vigorous bitter persistence and balsamic with notes of rhubarb

FERNET LUXARDO

Girolamo Luxardo
Torreglia, Padua

Fernet Luxardo was born in 1889 in the company's original factory in Zara, Dalmatia. This amaro is still produced today, following family tradition, by the Privilegiata Fabbrica Maraschino "Excelsior" Girolamo Luxardo, in Torreglia. It is an amaro with a strong character and marked bitter qualities. The original recipe, jealously guarded, calls for a prolonged infusion of various botanicals including licorice, which is particularly present in the taste, cardamom, gentian, and saffron.

ALCOHOL CONTENT: 40% vol.
COLOR: glossy dark brown
BOUQUET: astringent with shades of saffron and mint
TASTE: full-bodied with distinct notes of cinchona and aloe
AFTERTASTE: herbaceous, persistent, dry, and elegant

FERNET NARDINI

Ditta Bortolo Nardini
Bassano del Grappa, Vicenza

Fernet has always been considered to be the King of Amari. Corroborant and digestive, already in the early 19th century fernet had a reputation as being an elixir with many healing properties. The Nardini company produces its fernet the old-fashioned way, with great skill and herbal wisdom. Fernet Nardini is a spirit with a balanced and intense taste. The citrus notes of orange stand out in this amaro, combined with notes of licorice, gentian root, and peppermint.

ALCOHOL CONTENT: 40% vol.
COLOR: dark brown with ruby highlights
BOUQUET: strongly vegetal profile with notes of licorice and gentian
TASTE: bitter and dry with citrus hints of orange and balsamic notes of peppermint
AFTERTASTE: licorice finish

GAGLIARDO FERNET RADICALE

Distilleria Schiavo
Costabissara, Vicenza

Founded in 1887, Distilleria Schiavo has maintained family management and high-quality standards over the years. In 2012, the company inaugurated a project called *Gagliardo* (robust, gallant), which was a new line of artisan products based on the infusion of herbs, roots, and spices. Gagliardo Fernet Radicale entered the market in 2013, winning over the palates of many enthusiasts and insiders. With a low sugar content of 8 percent, this fernet includes, among its base botanicals, saffron, green chiretta, licorice, gentian, cinchona, and glacial mint.

ALCOHOL CONTENT: 40% vol.
COLOR: dark with amber and hints of orange reflections
BOUQUET: herbaceous and spicy with a hint of glacial mint
TASTE: strongly herbaceous with notes of licorice, gentian, and saffron
AFTERTASTE: excellent persistence with hints of glacial mint

LIQUORE DEL POLESINE

Antiche Distillerie Mantovani
Pincara, Rovigo

The art of liquor making at the Mantovani distilleries began in the first half of the 19th century with Cesare, who decided to make his passion for the preparation of liqueurs a profession. Ugo, great-grandson of Cesare, together with his wife Gabriella, put down roots in Polesine and so, in 1970, the Mantovani distilleries were moved to Pincara. Dandelion, aloe, coriander, saffron, cinchona, myrrh, chamomile, mugwort, and rhubarb are the main ingredients of the Liquore di Polesine, the company's flagship product. Its artisan character reflects all the peculiarities of the magnificent territory that hosts the Mantovani family.

ALCOHOL CONTENT: 25% vol.
COLOR: brown with orange highlights
BOUQUET: intense, fresh, and herbaceous with citrus hints
TASTE: round and herbaceous with important notes of cinchona and dandelion
AFTERTASTE: excellent vegetal persistence of rhubarb and citrus fruits

THE BITTER NOTE

The Bitter Note
Campodarsego, Padua

The Bitter Note was born in 2018, following the new worldwide trends of low- or no-alcohol drinks. The Bitter Note is the result of three different botanical processing methods: maceration, distillation, and extraction. The mixture obtained is then dealcoholized through an innovative process that at the same time enhances its organoleptic qualities. On a sensory level, the herbaceous base given by aloe and artichoke is enriched by the balsamic notes of tallow and the spicy notes of juniper berries. The citrus tones of bitter orange blend with the softness of chamomile and the fresh notes of mint and star anise. A sip finishes with the aromatic intensity of wormwood and gentian, which gives a persistent and pleasant bitter taste.

ALCOHOL CONTENT: 0% vol.
COLOR: brown with mahogany highlights

BOUQUET: herbaceous and spicy
TASTE: full, with a pleasant bitter note
AFTERTASTE: persistent and delicate

Friuli-Venezia Giulia

AMARO DI ERBE TRIESTE

La Piccola Bottega Spiritosa di Piolo & Max
Trieste

Friendships can lead to great projects, as has happened with Paolo and Massimiliano who, in 2002, gave life to the artisanal liqueurs of Piolo & Max. The company enhances the great Triestine tradition of alcohol processing, without giving up the most innovative techniques. One of the main products of Piolo & Max is the Amaro di Erbe Trieste, created with the infusion of top-quality botanicals such as hops, gentian, eucalyptus, orange peel, and Roman wormwood.

ALCOHOL CONTENT: 40% vol.

COLOR: amber with emerald highlights

BOUQUET: vegetal and floral perfumes

TASTE: herbaceous and bitter, with notes of chamomile and hops

AFTERTASTE: persistent and floral

AMARO DI SPILIMBERGO

Liquoreria Friulana Opificium
Spilimbergo, Pordenone

Liquoreria Friulana Opificium, founded in 2004, resulted from a passion for the production of liqueurs by three food technologists who came into contact with the ancient traditions concerning the collection and transformation of botanicals during their time at university. Amaro di Spilimbergo takes its name from the town where the company is located, and this amaro combines the intense scent of the hay of the Friulian "stable meadows" and the most classic spices and herbs. There are around 20 botanicals used in the recipe, with a clear predominance of mint, minor centaury, Breckland thyme, and yarrow mixed with rhubarb, gentian, bitter orange, cardamom, and chiretta.

ALCOHOL CONTENT: 30% vol.

COLOR: deep amber

BOUQUET: herbaceous and spicy

TASTE: firm and slightly savory

AFTERTASTE: astringent persistence

AMARO D'UDINE

Ditta Colutta Antonio
Udine

Amaro d'Udine is an amaro made from herbs, roots, and fruit. The origin of this drink dates back to the 15th century and was inspired by an ancient recipe of the Friars of Udine. In 1846, Amaro d'Udine was produced by Domenico De Candido, an expert pharmacist, who developed the formula (still secret today), which was handed down decades later to the Colutta family. The herbs, spices, and all the other botanicals in the mixture, after being carefully selected, are subjected to cold alcoholic infusion for several weeks in order to allow the total and slow extraction of the active principles contained in them.

ALCOHOL CONTENT: 15% vol.

COLOR: dark amber with orange highlights

BOUQUET: herbaceous and spicy scents

TASTE: very bitter with overbearing herbaceous notes

AFTERTASTE: bitter and persistent

AMARO FOENUM BIO

Liquoreria Friulana Opificium
Spilimbergo, Pordenone

Foenum in Latin means "hay," and in fact this amaro is a tribute to the "stable meadows" of Friuli, meadows that have existed for centuries and have never been fertilized, let alone treated. These meadows are dedicated exclusively to fodder production, which makes them exceptional for grazing, and they are protected by a strict regional law. The hay that comes from the meadows is particularly precious and its scent is what Liquoreria Friulana Opificium wanted to capture inside the organic Amaro Foenum Bio. There are only five botanicals in the mix of this amaro: yarrow, mint, Breckland thyme, thistle, and minor centaury.

ALCOHOL CONTENT: 30% vol.
COLOR: caramel with mahogany highlights
BOUQUET: pleasant hay aroma
TASTE: balanced and balsamic
AFTERTASTE: persistent with fresh mint notes

AMARO GIOVANNINA

Premiata Distilleria Pagura
Castions, Pordenone

Premiata Distilleria Pagura (the only one left today in the province of Pordenone) was founded in 1879 by Domenico Campagna who chose the young Lindo Pagura as a shop boy and "honorary son." In 1919, the distilleria passed into the hands of Lindo, who changed the name of the company to what it is today. Among the firm's products, Amaro Giovannina stands out. It is a spirit made with grappa to which seeds and fruits are added, according to the ancient family tradition. The original recipe is still kept secret today.

ALCOHOL CONTENT: 40% vol.
COLOR: dark amber
BOUQUET: distinct fruity and citrusy notes
TASTE: well balanced between sweet and bitter
AFTERTASTE: soft finish with fruity hints

AMARO LUSÔR

Buiese Distillerie
Martignacco, Udine

Amaro Lusôr was created in 2009 by the efforts of Cristiano Buiese, thanks to the experimentation conducted by the research group of the Department of Food Science of the University of Udine coordinated by Carla Da Porto, professor of Alcoholic Beverage Technology. This Friulian amaro, the result of the reworking of an ancient recipe exclusively owned by Buiese Distillerie, is made by cold maceration of 17 botanicals including peppermint, lemon balm, rosemary, cloves, and cinnamon. But the main ingredient of this young bitter is the great yellow gentian, which, in this case, comes directly from the experimental cultivations of the University of Udine.

ALCOHOL CONTENT: 26% vol.
COLOR: dark brown with copper highlights
BOUQUET: intoxicating and fresh with herbs and roots
TASTE: distinctly bitter with a predominance of gentian and cloves
AFTERTASTE: fresh and clean finish with persistent hints of cloves

AMARO NONINO QUINTESSENTIA

Nonino Distillatori
Pavia di Udine, Udine

In 1897, Orazio Nonino, itinerant distiller, decided to inaugurate his first distillery in Ronchi di Percoto, in the province of Udine. It was the beginning of a long series of successes that led the Nonino company and its grappas to become a symbol of excellence in Italy and around the world. Over the years, the company has made great progress in the art of distillation, first producing the innovative Monovitigno Nonino, a single-varietal grappa obtained from the separate distillation of marc from Picolit grapes, then the revolutionary ÙE Acquavite d'Uva or brandy obtained by distilling the whole grape. In 1992, Amaro Nonino Quintessentia was produced for the first time, enabled by the use of ÙE Acquavite aged in barriques and small barrels. The original recipe remains secret, but we can imagine, knowing the territory of origin, that the herbs in its preparation might include lavender, mountain pine, mint, sage, dandelion, thyme, and other botanicals of alpine origin. Moreover, when sipping it, it is easy to capture on the palate that exotic touch from allspice, black pepper, citrus, and probably bitter orange.

ALCOHOL CONTENT: 35% vol.

COLOR: amber tending to orange

BOUQUET: delicate but with hints of orange, lemon, vanilla, and chamomile

TASTE: very soft with notes of citrus fruits and chamomile

AFTERTASTE: exotic cardamom aromas

AMARO TOSOLINI

Distillerie Bepi Tosolini
Marsure di Povoletto, Udine

In the wide product portfolio of Distillerie Bepi Tosolini, founded in 1943, you can find Amaro Tosolini, a refined herb amaro with an original blend of Mediterranean botanicals, prepared according to the recipe by the company's founder, Bepi. Angelica, bitter orange, gentian, star anise, cloves, sea wormwood, lemon balm, mint, ginger, glasswort, sea lavender, sea fennel, rosemary, rhubarb, and calamus are macerated in grape spirit in ash wood vats and then distilled.

ALCOHOL CONTENT: 30% vol.

COLOR: intense brown with orange highlights

BOUQUET: pleasant herbaceous aroma

TASTE: rich and aromatic

AFTERTASTE: hints of bitter orange and spicy notes

FERNET CIEMME

Ciemme Liquori
Gorizia

Thanks to the company's firm policy of active attention to quality, Ciemme Liquori has established itself in the spirits market with great success, reaching even beyond the boundaries of the Italian Peninsula. The territory where the company is based, Friuli-Venezia Giulia, inspires almost all Ciemme-branded products, including Fernet Ciemme. The latter is the ruler of the house amari, and its composition, which follows the guidelines of the more traditional fernet, is full of secret aromatic botanicals. After careful alcoholic maceration of its ingredients, Fernet Ciemme is made to rest and age so as to better stabilize its characteristics that are released at the first sip.

ALCOHOL CONTENT: 40% vol.
COLOR: black licorice
BOUQUET: broad aromatic mountain bouquet
TASTE: distinctly bitter with floral notes
AFTERTASTE: pleasant freshness supporting the persistent bitterness

IL SEMINATORE

Buiese Distillerie
Martignacco, Udine

Il Seminatore is one of the most representative products of the Buiese family's liqueur tradition, which has been producing spirits since 1918, the year in which the distillery of the same name was founded by Giuseppe Buiese, after a period of apprenticeship at Fratelli Branca in Milan. Today, three generations later, the company remains synonymous with excellence and, despite modern production practices, does not forget its artisanal origins. The recipe for the herbal amaro, Il Seminatore, is jealously guarded. Among the botanicals present are a variegated mixture of alpine herbs and sweet and bitter orange leaves.

ALCOHOL CONTENT: 30% vol.
COLOR: dark amber with red reflections
BOUQUET: scents of bitter orange, mint, and alpine herbs
TASTE: round and bitterish aroma
AFTERTASTE: fresh bitterness and long herbaceous persistence

L'AMARO ADELIA

Adelia Di Fant
San Daniele del Friuli, Udine

Signora Adelia Di Fant made her debut in the world of spirits in the 1980s with the aim of offering her customers products of high quality while firmly maintaining their roots in Friulian tradition. The careful and accurate selection of the best raw materials, combined with continuous research of new flavors, has made Adelia Di Fant a symbol of Friuli craftsmanship excellence. One of her products is L'Amaro Adelia, the result of a careful hydro-alcoholic infusion of alpine herbs and other digestive botanicals including rhubarb, Breckland thyme, sage, gentian, gentianella, and lemon balm.

ALCOHOL CONTENT: 25% vol.
COLOR: amber with coppered highlights
BOUQUET: scents of spices and alpine herbs
TASTE: prevalently bitter, well balanced in sweetness; prevalent notes of gentian and rhubarb
AFTERTASTE: warm, embracing, and spicy with distinct hints of sage

PIOLINKOMAX

La Piccola Bottega
Spiritosa di Piolo & Max
Trieste

Piolo (whose real name is Paolo) and Max are modern alchemists who call themselves "drinking stylists". They have experimented a great deal, playing with flowers, spices, and botanicals to arrive at unusual and surprising combinations that have led them to stand out in the regional liquor scene. The products of Piolo & Max are synonymous with high craftsmanship: The Chamber of Commerce of Trieste has in fact included the company in the Register of Artisan Companies, recognizing it as operating in the field of artistic and traditional processing. PiolinkoMax is made from an alcoholic infusion of different varieties of wormwood, lemon balm, and bitter orange peel, with the addition of caramel and homemade sugar syrup. In short, it is a Pelinkovac (traditional Croatian wormwood liqueur) in the manner of Piolo & Max.

ALCOHOL CONTENT: 40% vol.
COLOR: amber with orange highlights
BOUQUET: soft and herbaceous
TASTE: bitter with notes of wormwood
AFTERTASTE: long, citrusy persistence

STORICA AMARO

Domenis 1898
Cividale del Friuli, Udine

Domenis 1898's more than 100 years of passion and mastery began in 1898, when Pietro Domenis received a still as a gift from his father and began to practice the art of distillation. Storica Amaro, the result of more than 120 years of experience and craftsmanship of the Domenis family, brings to the market a product that is as classic as it is captivating. The recipe is the result of long and intense work, and making this amaro involves the maceration and distillation of botanicals that include licorice, vanilla, coffee, anise, cinnamon, cloves, and ginger.

ALCOHOL CONTENT: 35% vol.
COLOR: ebony with red highlights
BOUQUET: delicate and round
TASTE: full, with hints of spices and licorice
AFTERTASTE: good herbaceous persistence

Liguria

AMARO ALPICELLA

Sangallo Distilleria delle Cinque Terre
Monterosso al Mare, La Spezia

Amaro Alpicella is one of the many products of Sangallo Distilleria delle Cinque Terre. All of its products are created with carefully prepared recipes and impeccable choices of raw materials. This herbal amaro is inspired by an alchemist monk's creation in 1630, and it is obtained from the maceration and distillation of 32 particularly selected mountain herbs. The monk used to offer this healthy drink to pilgrims visiting the ancient monastery on Colle di Velva.

ALCOHOL CONTENT: 35% vol.
COLOR: dark amber
BOUQUET: sharp herbaceous and balsamic notes
TASTE: well balanced between sweet and bitter
AFTERTASTE: persistent bitterness

AMARO CAMATTI

Sangallo Distilleria delle Cinque Terre
Monterosso al Mare, La Spezia

Sangallo Distilleria delle Cinque Terre is a family-run business that since 1964 has produced amari, liqueurs, and spirits according to ancient Ligurian recipes. Among these is Amaro Camatti, a well-known Genoese specialty obtained from the infusion of botanicals with aromatic and tonic properties. It is made according to the secret recipe prepared in the first half of the 20th century by the pharmacist Umberto Briganti whose name still appears on the label.

ALCOHOL CONTENT: 20% vol.
COLOR: light brown
BOUQUET: pungent herbaceous note
TASTE: well balanced between bitter and sweet; cinchona and gentian stand out
AFTERTASTE: persistent bitterness with hints of cinchona

AMARO DEI SARACENI

Distillerie Pasquale Balzola
Alassio, Savona

It was in 1902 when Pasquale Balzola took over a tavern with stables in the Piazza del Commercio of Alassio. Shortly afterward, Aperitivo di Alassio and Amaro dei Saraceni were born, which soon conquered the palates of their first patrons. Later, Pasquale, Rinaldo's son, specialized in the refined art of pastry making. In 1919 he patented the famous Baci di Alassio, and in 1929 he became head pastry chef of the Royal House of Savoy. In the meantime, the tavern opened up to fashionable concert cafés. It regularly hosted famous industrialists, artists, poets, and intellectuals visiting the city of Alassio, and it became a sought-after showcase for the most prominent personalities of the moment. Today, 110 years after its birth, the café pastry shop Balzola is designated a historic café of Italy, and it remains a landmark for the entire peninsula and beyond. Amaro dei Saraceni was invented by Pasquale Balzola himself, a liquorist at Martini & Rossi in Pessione (Torino), who, after a long and difficult experience in the Americas, returned to Italy. He used the aromatic herbs of the Riviera to create his herbal liqueur, and his recipe includes lemon balm, mint, sage, yarrow, thyme, lavender, chamomile flowers, and gentianella. Since 2018, Amaro dei Saraceni, whose name is inspired by the historical presence of Ottoman pirates in Liguria, has become a Municipal Denomination of Origin (De.CO.).

ALCOHOL CONTENT: 40% vol.

COLOR: amber, slightly viscous

BOUQUET: floral scents with predominance of lavender

TASTE: balanced between herbaceous and floral; persistent

AFTERTASTE: bitter

AMARO DI S. MARIA AL MONTE

Caffo
Genoa

It was 1858 when the Fathers of the Convento di S. Maria al Monte donated to Vincenzo Castrovillari, the official cook of the Duke of Aosta, the recipe for a *lissire miraculoso*, a miraculous elixir capable of warding off all illnesses. Vincenzo dedicated himself to the creation of the Amaro di S. Maria al Monte, completing it with aromatic products typical of the Alps. In the early 20th century the recipe was taken over by the liquorist Nicola Vignale. The Vignale family took care of its production for three generations in the Distillerie dei Dogi. Even today, the cold infusion of felty germander, juniper, gentian, saffron, wormwood, rhubarb, and many other botanicals takes about two months. After eight months of aging, alcohol and sugar are added to the preparation and another six months of refinement is needed to create Amaro di S. Maria al Monte.

ALCOHOL CONTENT: 40% vol.

COLOR: mahogany with red highlights

BOUQUET: prevalent note of bitter herbs

TASTE: bitter and well balanced in aromaticity with distinct hints of cinchona and aloe

AFTERTASTE: vegetal with persistent bitterness

Emilia Romagna

AMARERBE

Gorfer Liquori 1955
Mirandola, Modena

Amarerbe is a typical *Centerbe-* style bitter, for which the Gorfer company wanted to limit the alcohol content to 40% vol. Created in 2019, Amarerbe is made from the infusion of over 25 botanicals including Roman wormwood, carnation, chamomile, and mint. The raw materials, carefully selected and processed, are the main elements of this young amaro, which bring out all its character thanks to a coarse filtration process that affects the active ingredients contained in the plant components as little as possible.

ALCOHOL CONTENT: 40% vol.

COLOR: soft opalescent yellow

BOUQUET: very intense scent of alpine herbs

TASTE: dry, balsamic, and mentholated

AFTERTASTE: persistent pungent note

AMARO CASONI HERITAGE

Casoni Fabbricazione Liquori
Finale Emilia, Modena

With Amaro Casoni Heritage, which was formulated in 1814 and offered to Casoni family friends as an after-meal digestif, the historic company in Finale Emilia rediscovers and proposes a product that features a round and intense flavor. The cold extraction of 17 botanicals that make up the Amaro Casoni Heritage mix takes place separately for each one. These botanicals include sweet orange, bitter orange, cardamom, wormwood, and St. John's wort.

ALCOHOL CONTENT: 36% vol.

COLOR: dark blond

BOUQUET: citrusy scents with hints of herbs and roots

TASTE: floral and embracing with decisive citrus notes

AFTERTASTE: soft and herbal with notes of wormwood

AMARO CLANDESTINO

Azienda Agricola Mistico Speziale
Reggio Emilia

Azienda Agricola Mistico Speziale is a farm founded in 2010 by Saverio Denti in Reggio Emilia with the aim of cultivating medicinal plants for the production of high-quality liqueurs and spirits. Amaro Clandestino is produced by hand in small batches through the natural maceration of more than 25 botanicals in smooth grain alcohol and spring water. The main components present in the plant mix are wormwood, rhubarb, juniper, helichrysum, sage, lemon balm, cedar, hyssop, mint, bergamot, mandarin, cardamom, cinnamon, coffee, and nutmeg.

ALCOHOL CONTENT: 23.5% vol.

COLOR: deep amber

BOUQUET: robust herbal scent

TASTE: full and balanced with balsamic and citrus hints

AFTERTASTE: long and spicy finish

AMARO DEL CICLISTA

Casoni Fabbricazione Liquori
Finale Emilia, Modena

Tradition and know-how are the cornerstones of Casoni Fabbricazione Liquori's tradition of more than 200 years. One of the flagship products of the historic Modena liquor factory is Amaro del Ciclista, created in 2017 and inspired by an old tradition of the Casoni family that consisted of offering guests a small glass of amaro as a refreshing drink after a long bike ride. Amaro del Ciclista is produced from a mix of 15 botanicals, ground and infused in hydro-alcohol, that include rhubarb, cinchona, licorice, gentian, juniper, yarrow, nutmeg, and Benedictine thistle.

ALCOHOL CONTENT: 26% vol.
COLOR: brown with mahogany highlights
BOUQUET: warm herbal scent
TASTE: full and round with strong herbaceous hints
AFTERTASTE: long, warm, and embracing finish

AMARO FELSINA GORFER

Gorfer Liquori 1955
Mirandola, Modena

The Gorfer company was founded in 1950 in Mirandola di Modena as a vinegar factory. Subsequently converted into a distillery, under the management of Giuseppe Miotto and Giuseppe Digito, it became a liqueur factory. Amaro Felsina Gorfer was created in the early 1960s. Among the main ingredients are orange peel, galanga, cloves, myrrh, cardamom, star anise, rhubarb, cinchona, and gentian.

ALCOHOL CONTENT: 30% vol.
COLOR: dark amber
BOUQUET: intense, harmonious with notes of aromatic herbs, citrus fruits, and spices
TASTE: full-bodied with hints of Mediterranean spices
AFTERTASTE: pleasantly bitter with a soft persistence

AMARO MONTENEGRO

Montenegro s.r.l.
Zola Predrosa, Bologna

Stanislao Cobianchi was born in the second half of the 19th century in Bologna, where he received a strict clerical education imposed by his family that he soon rebelled against. An iconoclastic genius, passionate about alchemy and new discoveries, Stanislao soon abandoned the ecclesiastical habit in favor of that of a traveler, even embarking as an adolescent on a merchant ship in search of the True Flavor. Continent after continent, Stanislao collected a treasure made of 40 different botanical specialties. Back in Bologna, after years of experiments, he founded the Cobianchi Stanislao Distilleria a Vapore, which saw the creation of the famous Amaro Montenegro (the name was chosen as a tribute to Elena di Montenegro, wife of King Vittorio Emanuele III of Savoy). For the production of this historic amaro, 40 different botanicals from the four corners of the world are used. These include Mediterranean coriander, oregano, bitter orange and sweet orange, exotic nutmeg, cloves, and cinnamon. To complete the formula, the makers add a secret ingredient called Premio that is obtained from the microdistillation of five aromatic herbs carried out in a reserved area of the distillery.

ALCOHOL CONTENT: 23% vol.
COLOR: light brown with golden highlights
BOUQUET: delicate and aromatic
TASTE: soft and pleasant; skillfully citrusy
AFTERTASTE: slightly bitter

AMARO OLANDESE GORFER

Gorfer Liquori 1955
Mirandola, Modena

The Gorfer company, respecting the Italian liqueur tradition, has recently decided to revisit some old recipes, creating new amari in the belief that the amaro macrocosm can, today more than ever, satisfy consumers. Therefore, in 2019, Amaro Olandese Gorfer was created. It is made with the skillful infusion of over 25 aromatic and digestive botanicals, among which are rhubarb, Roman wormwood, sweet orange, and bitter orange.

ALCOHOL CONTENT: 40% vol.

COLOR: deep brown

BOUQUET: floral and herbaceous aromas, with hints of cherry and cocoa bean

TASTE: decisively bitter, but balanced with notes of gentian, rhubarb, and ginger

AFTERTASTE: long and soft persistence

AMARO TARASSACO

Liquorificio Osvaldo Colombo
Salsomaggiore Terme, Parma

For over a hundred years in Salsomaggiore Terme, the Osvaldo Colombo company has been producing handcrafted distillates and amari using selected herbs, flowers, and fruits according to homemade recipes. Among the leading products is Amaro Tarassaco, made from flowers, roots, and medicinal plants. The mix includes dandelion, rhubarb, cinchona, calendula, wormwood, ginger, and quassia.

ALCOHOL CONTENT: 20% vol.

COLOR: light brown

BOUQUET: pungent herbaceous note with hints of rhubarb

TASTE: well balanced between sweet and bitter, with hints of cinchona and ginger

AFTERTASTE: bitter finish

AMARO ZARRI

Villa Zarri
Castel Maggiore, Bologna

Amaro Zarri was created from a traditional recipe of the Zarri family. Its preparation involves the infusion in cold alcohol of 28 precious herbs and roots with a bitter and elegant taste, among which we can mention quassia, rhubarb, wormwood, columbo, licorice, mint, cinchona, gentian, and bitter and sweet orange peel. The extract is left to rest for several months in steel containers before being brought to an alcohol content of 35% vol. At this point the amaro is ready to be filtered and bottled.

ALCOHOL CONTENT: 35% vol.

COLOR: dark brown with green-gold shades

BOUQUET: scents of medicinal herbs, orange peel, licorice, and coffee

TASTE: soft and balanced with notes of coffee and licorice

AFTERTASTE: balsamic and persistent

FERNET GORFER

Gorfer Liquori 1955
Mirandola, Modena

Despite the availability of technological innovation, much of Gorfer Liquori's work is still carried out manually—as was the case in the past—allowing for the natural transformation of the botanicals. The recipe for Fernet Gorfer dates back to the mid-1950s and is still followed closely today. Its main ingredients include rhubarb, cinnamon, chamomile, vanilla, gentian, cinchona, licorice, and saffron.

ALCOHOL CONTENT: 50% vol.

COLOR: bright mahogany

BOUQUET: intense, complex, and spicy balsamic

TASTE: sharp bitter notes and balsamic

AFTERTASTE: long and fresh persistence

Tuscany

AMARO ARANCIA

Liquorificio Morelli
Palaia, Pisa

For a few years now there has been a novelty in the wide range of products offered by Liquorificio Morelli: Amaro Arancia, with a pleasant and unusual history. Marco Morelli tells us that, some time ago, an employee of the liquor factory during a transfer mistakenly combined the preparation of the orange liqueur with that of Amaro Etrusco. The mixture remained unused until Marco decided to give it a chance and was won over. So the Morelli family began to scrupulously analyze this mistakenly created drink in order to produce Amaro Arancia, which is based on orange, licorice, gentian, and cinchona.

ALCOHOL CONTENT: 30% vol.

COLOR: bright orange with amber reflections

BOUQUET: intoxicating citrus scent

TASTE: distinct notes of orange and hints of bitter herbs

AFTERTASTE: fresh and aromatic with hints of rhubarb

AMARO CHIANCIANO

Gabriello Santoni
Chianciano Terme, Siena

Gabriello Santoni, founder of the company of the same name, has always had a passion for the distilling art and has always been guided by the search for quality. In 1961, in fact, Gabriello realized his greatest dream: to create in Chianciano Terme amaro from a careful mixture of herbs and roots that were precious expressions of this territory of origin. Amaro Chianciano is made from 34 secret botanicals that have undergone a long maceration before being pressed.

ALCOHOL CONTENT: 16% vol.

COLOR: deep brown

BOUQUET: refined, rich, and broad with roots and medicinal plants

TASTE: balanced between sweet and bitter

AFTERTASTE: persistent notes of rhubarb and licorice

AMARO DELL'ELBA

Smania Liquori
Campo nell'Elba, Livorno

The Smania brand was founded in the 1980s on the island of Elba, thanks to the decision of a group of entrepreneurs to take over a small liqueur factory that used traditional methods of processing and raw materials from the territory. Amaro dell'Elba is a bitter liqueur, produced by infusion, which comprises the scents of the island. Among the plant essences used are licorice, myrtle, mastic, bitter orange, sweet orange, Roman wormwood, cinnamon, cardamom, coriander, gentian, quassia, and elderflower.

ALCOHOL CONTENT: 28% vol.

COLOR: intense brown

BOUQUET: strong citrus hints with herbaceous notes

TASTE: harmonious and balanced with hints of licorice and citrus fruits

AFTERTASTE: medium sweet persistence

AMARO DI TOSCANA

Gabriello Santoni
Chianciano Terme, Siena

Artisanal care and a fervent spirit of innovation have distinguished the Gabriello Santoni company since its beginnings in the 1960s. Among its leading products is Amaro di Toscana, which is highly expressive of its wonderful territory of origin. The original recipe has been jealously guarded for generations and includes the infusion in cold alcohol of 27 secret medicinal herbs carefully selected by the company.

ALCOHOL CONTENT: 30% vol.

COLOR: intense brown

BOUQUET: characteristic of roots and herbs

TASTE: harmonic, full, and warm

AFTERTASTE: bitter, well balanced by sweet notes

AMARO ETRUSCO

Liquorificio Morelli
Palaia, Pisa

Liquorificio Morelli was founded in 1911 by Leonello Morelli, an expert liquorist, in the center of Forcoli (Pisa). In 2009, the company left its historic headquarters to expand a few miles away in the town of Palaia. Modernity and functionality inspire the new spaces, yet their production philosophy continues to keep alive their attention to tradition. Amaro Etrusco has been produced since 1911. Today the Morelli family still follows the original recipe that uses botanicals, including rhubarb, licorice, cinnamon, cinchona, and gentian.

ALCOHOL CONTENT: 30% vol.

COLOR: bright brown

BOUQUET: intense scent of rhubarb and herbs

TASTE: bitter with intense notes of licorice

AFTERTASTE: persistent taste of rhubarb and licorice

AMARO HERBARUM

Nunquam
Tavola, Prato

At Nunquam, Cristina and Fabio are dedicated to the production of Amaro Herbarum. Its recipe has been studied and perfected by Fabio, an expert "alchemist" who grew up under the strict guidance of his grandfather Gustavo. In order to produce Amaro Herbarum it is necessary to undertake cold infusion of nine different botanicals in high-quality neutral alcohol inside a steel macerator. These botanicals are wormwood, aromatic calamus, common centaury, angelica, elecampane, cinnamon, juniper berries, iris, and gentian.

ALCOHOL CONTENT: 41% vol.

COLOR: light green

BOUQUET: dry and herbaceous

TASTE: soft and warm with strong vegetal notes

AFTERTASTE: good bitter persistence

AMARO NUNQUAM

Nunquam
Tavola, Prato

Among the varied offerings of Nunquam, Amaro Nunquam stands out. It is the result of 24 different types of botanicals that all come from biodynamic and organic farming. Cristina and Fabio, owners of the factory, personally take care of all the processes that give life to their products. Among these is the White Vermouth of Prato, saved from oblivion and prepared according to the original recipe from 1750.

ALCOHOL CONTENT: 41% vol.

COLOR: amber

BOUQUET: floral and fruity scents

TASTE: warm and full-bodied with bitter notes

AFTERTASTE: herbaceous with hints of citrus

AMARO STILLA

Lombardi & Visconti
Abbadia San Salvatore, Siena

Lombardi & Visconti was started in 1992 with the intent of giving continuity to the production tradition of Amaro Stilla of Mount Amiata that was made from a recipe of the Cistercian monks of the Amiatina Abbey of Abbadia San Salvatore. Today the family-run business, led by Attilio Visconti, produces many types of liqueurs and distillates, all naturally processed on the basis of impressive herbalist knowledge that often refers to ancient recipe books or homemade practices. Among Lombardi & Visconti's "herbal liqueurs," which come from a cold maceration of herbal mixtures without adding artificial flavors and substances, Amaro Stilla

stands out. It is produced with the use of only five botanicals that include mint, lemon balm, hibiscus flowers, and rhubarb rhizome.

ALCOHOL CONTENT: 30% vol.
COLOR: amber with ruby highlights; clear
BOUQUET: fresh and mentholated hints
TASTE: full, slightly sweet, but balanced; starts with hibiscus flowers but the palate is soon enveloped by pleasant balsamic scents
AFTERTASTE: floral

ANTICO ELIXIR DI CHINA CLEMENTI

Antica Farmacia Clementi
Fivizzano, Massa

The recipe of the Antico Elixir di China Clementi was conceived in 1884 and handed down from generation to generation. It is still made today according to the dictates of the great-grandfather, Dr. Giuseppe Clementi, and the recipe calls for the use of the bark of *Cinchona calisaya* and *Cinchona succirubra*, bitter orange peel, and other secret medicinal herbs. The herbs are crushed in an old hammer mill, and their flavors are extracted by maceration for about 50 days. The mixture obtained is then set aside for about 6 months, then added to the sugar part and aged for about 10 months in steel casks.

ALCOHOL CONTENT: 33% vol.
COLOR: orange and bright

BOUQUET: aromatic and intense with hints of medicinal herbs and citrus fruits
TASTE: warm and soft with light ferrous notes
AFTERTASTE: persistent and balanced between sweet and bitter

CENOBIUM

Aurelio Visconti
Abbadia San Salvatore, Siena

For more than 20 years, Aurelio Visconti has been producing macerated herbs from Mount Amiata. Most of the botanicals used by the company are in fact of local origin. The Cenobium amaro is characterized by 0 percent added sugar and is obtained by the infusion in alcohol of 10 different plant components (many of them with a distinctly bitter character). Among these you can taste cloves and sage, juniper and wormwood.

ALCOHOL CONTENT: 30% vol.
COLOR: brown
BOUQUET: vegetal and very intense freshness
TASTE: bitter and structured with notes of sage, wormwood, and cloves
AFTERTASTE: excellent vegetal persistence with hints of lavender and juniper

ESILIO BRANDY AMARO

Smania Liquori
Campo nell'Elba, Livorno

Esilio Brandy Amaro is the pride and joy of Smania Liquori. This amaro is the result of the artisan workmanship of a fine brandy aged 10 years in oak barrels together with botanicals that come from the lush vegetation on the island of Elba, which is typical of the entire Tuscan Archipelago. This exclusive amaro, produced in limited quantity and dedicated to the historical figure of Napoleon Bonaparte, who spent the last part of his life on Elba, is the fruit of Elban tradition. The main botanicals used are licorice, myrtle, bitter orange, and mastic.

ALCOHOL CONTENT: 28% vol.

COLOR: deep brown with mahogany highlights

BOUQUET: intense herbaceous and citrus scent

TASTE: warm and embracing, balanced in sweet notes

AFTERTASTE: good fruity and slightly astringent persistence

IMPERIAL TONIC

Aurelio Visconti
Abbadia San Salvatore, Sienna

Imperial Tonic by Aurelio Visconti was created in honor of Charlemagne, the first emperor of the Holy Roman Empire, who, in his time, stayed near Mount Amiata, where the company is located. This amaro is the result of the alcoholic maceration of 15 types of botanicals, including cardamom, bitter orange, and sweet orange that nicely balance the sweet sensations of cinnamon and vanilla. Imperial Tonic has a 5 percent sugar content.

ALCOHOL CONTENT: 30% vol.

COLOR: light brown

BOUQUET: prevailing spicy notes

TASTE: balanced in sweet and bitter notes

AFTERTASTE: good spicy persistence reminiscent of tobacco

Umbria

AMARO AL TARTUFO NERO DI NORCIA

Italiana Liquori e Natura
Ponte Nuovo di Torgiano, Perugia

In 1976, Ugo Nicolini opened his factory and created a product unusual for those times—an amaro made with the black truffle of Norcia. Ugo began to produce and distribute this amaro on his own. In a few years, Amaro al Tartufo Nero di Norcia became the company's leading product, and it is strongly representative of the Umbrian territory in general and Norcia in particular. It is made according to an ancient recipe that combines the unmistakable aromatic qualities of truffles and those of various medicinal herbs.

ALCOHOL CONTENT: 30% vol.

COLOR: hazelnut with hints of copper

BOUQUET: fresh and citrusy hints and vegetal notes

TASTE: herbaceous and aniseed notes prevail

AFTERTASTE: vegetal and persistent

AMARO CERBERUS

Barberani
Orvieto, Terni

Amaro Cerberus by Barberani combines tradition and novelty in a beautifully packaged bottle. Bernardo and Niccolò Barberani are the heirs of one of the most important families of fine winegrowers in Umbria, which, since 1961, has wisely renewed the ancient harvesting ritual in total respect of the territory and tradition. Bernardo, an intelligent and modern manager, and Niccolò, with a degree in agriculture, have been able to combine family experience with personal skills and to put them at the service of the company's progress through quality actions that embrace new market trends. A tangible outcome includes the creation of Amaro Cerberus, which was made in collaboration with a team of beverage experts. Amaro Cerberus is made with 50 percent Nocino Riserva liqueur aged 10 years and 50 percent of a mix of botanicals that include artichoke, arugula, walnut husk, cinnamon, clove, nutmeg, cinchona bark, angelica, aromatic calamus, blessed thistle, centaury, tonka bean, gentian, mace, mint, rhubarb, muscatel herb, tansy, and saffron. The two bases are mixed and left to rest for about 20 days; then the amaro is ready to be bottled. The recipe also contains, in infinitesimal doses, wolfsbane, an overwhelmingly poisonous plant that should only be processed by qualified professionals. According to Greek mythology, Cerberus (hence the name of the amaro), the dog that guarded the underworld, carried the seeds of wolfsbane in his slime, which, upon contact with the earth's soil, would give rise to the wolfsbane plants.

ALCOHOL CONTENT: 40% vol.

COLOR: dark coffee with green hues

BOUQUET: powerful nutmeg and chocolate notes on the nose

TASTE: warm and full, with aromatic orange and clove tips

AFTERTASTE: strong chocolate and walnut aftertaste

AMARO D'ERBE DEL FRATICELLO

Italiana Liquori e Natura
Ponte Nuovo di Torgiano, Perugia

Among his experiences, Ugo Natalini boasts a valuable collaboration with some Franciscan friars with whom he developed Amaro d'Erbe del Fraticello. It is a digestive with a bitterish taste, and it is based on medicinal herbs grown by the Franciscans in the area around Assisi.

ALCOHOL CONTENT: 16% vol.
COLOR: dark brown
BOUQUET: delicate and floral
TASTE: soft and vegetal
AFTERTASTE: caramel and chocolate notes stand out

AMARO FRANCESCANO

Francescano
Assisi, Perugia

Amaro Francescano is the result of an ancient 14th-century recipe found in a precious herbarium at the convent of Assisi, reinterpreted and adapted, since 1975, to contemporary taste. Among the botanicals used are gentian, angelica, rhubarb, eleutherococcus, horseradish, zedoary, ginseng, artichoke, sage, milk thistle, elderberry, chamomile, bitter orange, and centaury. In addition, it uses wheat germ, guarana, cardamom, quassia, tonka bean, soya, and myrrh.

ALCOHOL CONTENT: 28% vol.

COLOR: amber with golden highlights
BOUQUET: hints of licorice, rhubarb, and gentian
TASTE: harmonic, balanced, and vegetal
AFTERTASTE: full-bodied and persistent medicinal herbs

AMARO PAX

Italiana Liquori e Natura
Ponte Nuovo di Torgiano, Perugia

The world of amari never ceases to amaze with incredible botanicals and the use of herbs that until recently were unthinkable for any connoisseur. But above all, there are no limits to the creativity of producers, be they chemists, herbalists, or distillers. This was the case for Amaro Pax, the result of work started in the 1970s in Umbria, in Ponte Nuovo di Torgiano, where Ugo Natalini, with a degree in chemistry, decided to set up his own business and open a small factory. Here, in 2010, Ugo created Amaro Pax, which is based on olive leaves, selected from the best olive groves in the Assisi area, and lemon peel.

ALCOHOL CONTENT: 30% vol.
COLOR: hazelnut with orange reflections
BOUQUET: strong citrusy notes
TASTE: vegetal and citrusy notes stand out
AFTERTASTE: citrusy, good persistence

AMARO VALLENERA

Liquorificio M.C.P.
Terni

Maurizio Cappelletti and Rosaria De Angelis founded Liquorificio M.C.P. in Terni, in the green heart of Umbria, with the intention of offering ancient recipes from the Terni liqueur tradition. The pride and joy of the production is Amaro Vallenera, which is based on botanicals typical of Umbria and the valley of the Nera River where the splendid Marmore Falls reign. The territory, rich in beech, oak, and olive trees, offers numerous barks, flowers, and roots that are used in the preparation, among which the gentian in particular stands out.

ALCOHOL CONTENT: 21% vol.

COLOR: brown with copper reflections

BOUQUET: caramelized sugar and citrus notes

TASTE: balanced, slightly sweet

AFTERTASTE: bitter with predominance of gentian; long and persistent finish

AMARO VALLENERA AL TARTUFO NERO DI NORCIA

Liquorificio M.C.P.
Terni

Amaro Vallenera al Tartufo Nero di Norcia came about through the brilliant intuition of Maurizio Cappelletti, who was determined to put a product on the market in which the Norcia black truffle was the absolute protagonist of the sensory experience, even with the presence of other botanical components. It is

recommended to drink it neat or along with bitter chocolate.

ALCOHOL CONTENT: 28% vol.

COLOR: brown with emerald highlights

BOUQUET: intense and pleasant scent of truffle

TASTE: herbaceous and truffle notes stand out

AFTERTASTE: truffle

AMARO VIPARO

Morganti & C.
Terni

Amaro Viparo was created as a medicinal preparation in 1912 thanks to the apothecary Metello Morganti. The product, prescribed in drops, soon became a liqueur. Its name derives from the Latin words *vis* and *pario*, which together mean "I produce strength," precisely because of the invigorating character of the drink. Today Amaro Viparo is produced with the support of the Caffo company, following the original recipe that requires infusion in alcohol of herbs, roots, and aromatic woods and aging that can reach five years.

ALCOHOL CONTENT: 20.9% vol.

COLOR: brick red with orange nuances

BOUQUET: hints of citrus fruits and herbs

TASTE: soft, fresh, and sweet, with floral and citrus notes

AFTERTASTE: citrus fruit and good persistence

FRANCISCANUM

Francescano
Assisi, Perugia

Franciscanum is a mother tincture obtained from the solar maceration of 28 botanicals in a mixture of brandy at 70% vol. The absence of sugar and a careful aging process, first in steel containers and then in barriques, characterize this "absolute amaro" that is reserved for great lovers of the unique taste of medicinal herbs. Among the plant components of this amaro are juniper, gentian, angelica, mint, artichoke, rhubarb, licorice, cardamom, coriander, and burdock, the latter of which is rich in diuretic and digestive properties.

ALCOHOL CONTENT: 47% vol.

COLOR: brilliant gold

BOUQUET: embracing and elegant with notes of sherry and oriental spices

TASTE: warm and silky with hints of licorice and chocolate

AFTERTASTE: good persistence of mint, cocoa, and tobacco

HERBIO

Distilleria Morganti
Terni

The formula of the Herbio digestive tonic aperitif comes from the tradition of the Morganti family and uses five botanicals that include orange, quassia, wormwood, and gentian. The fifth plant element remains a secret ingredient. The characteristic packaging of Herbio is in a bottle that recalls the shape of the antique pharmacy bottles with a bitter orange peel attached.

ALCOHOL CONTENT: 20.9% vol.

COLOR: amber with gold reflections

BOUQUET: citrus notes prevail

TASTE: fresh, vegetal, and light

AFTERTASTE: slightly balsamic

L'ORVIETAN

L'Orvietan
Orvieto, Terni

L'Orvietan is a corroborating digestive stimulant amaro obtained from the maceration in a hydro-alcoholic solution of more than 25 botanicals including angelica, gentian, galanga, carlina, rhubarb, mallow, cinnamon, wormwood, myrrh, rue, and lavender that are pressed by hand with small presses and filtered by cloth. On June 9, 1603, Girolamo Ferranti, known as L'Orvietano, obtained a license from the Municipality of Orvieto to sell his product in the public square. The fame of L'Orvietan reached all the markets of Europe, conquering even Louis XIV, who was a habitual consumer. Quoted both in the first version of Alessandro Manzoni's *Promessi Sposi* (*The Betrothed*), and in Molière's opera *L'Amour medicine* (*Dr. Cupid*), L'Orvietan is now made using its original and secret formula with only 6 percent sugar per liter.

ALCOHOL CONTENT: 30% vol.

COLOR: straw yellow

BOUQUET: aromatic-vegetable profile

TASTE: dry and bitter, with distinct notes of gentian, angelica, and wormwood

AFTERTASTE: medium-length and spicy

Marche

AMARO DELL'ERBORISTA

Distilleria Varnelli
Muccia, Macerata

Amaro dell'Erborista comes from an old recipe in the Varnelli house dating back to the second half of the 19th century. It was discovered among the papers of the founder, Girolamo Varnelli. Its formula is an herbal-forward production, providing an immediate, unfiltered experience. Uncolored, the amaro looks like a botanical decoction made on a wood fire. The plant mix at the base of Amaro dell'Erborista includes yellow gentian, gentianella, orange bark, cinchona, cinnamon, and rhubarb, combined with the pleasantness of honey from the Sibillini Mountains.

ALCOHOL CONTENT: 21% vol.

COLOR: tobacco with brick shades, naturally opalescent thanks to the presence of honey

BOUQUET: scents of semi-cooked fruit and raisins with hints of gentian, rhubarb, sandalwood, honey, and spices

TASTE: dry and balanced, bitter and round, with pleasant notes of honey

AFTERTASTE: tannic and dry

AMARO MELETTI

Ditta Silvio Meletti
Ascoli Piceno

The company Ditta Silvio Meletti was founded in 1870 and has since been dedicated to the artisanal production of liqueurs from high-quality raw plant materials, many of which are cultivated in the lands adjacent to the company. Amaro Meletti, a rich and caramelized amaro, stands out among the product line. It is obtained by infusion in alcohol (with the addition of water and sugar) of botanicals that include bitter orange, cloves, gentian, and saffron from the Sibillini Mountains.

ALCOHOL CONTENT: 32% vol.

COLOR: chocolate hazelnut with orange highlights

BOUQUET: floral with hints of rose, lavender, and citrus fruits

TASTE: notes of Chantilly cream and bitter orange

AFTERTASTE: bitter and persistent

AMARO SIBILLA

Distilleria Varnelli
Muccia, Macerata

From the slopes of the Sibillini Mountains to the conquest of the world, the Varnelli brand has come a long way: Through four generations, it has reached over 150 years of uninterrupted family business. The company was founded in 1868 by Girolamo Varnelli, a great lover of aromatic herbs and medicinal plants, who was able to draw inspiration from nature, popular pastimes, and the products of Benedictine monks for a pleasant blend, Amaro Sibilla. This amaro was created as a "remedy" for the shepherds during times of transhumance, which is when livestock are moved between mountains and pasturelands. Today this amaro is still obtained from a decoction, made on a wood fire, having as its starting base a botanical blend that includes gentian, gentianella, orange peel, cinchona, and cinnamon. The sweetening with honey from the Sibillini Mountains is unique to the products of this distillery. The name of the amaro is inspired by the legendary figure of the Apennine Sibyl, of whom there is a representation on the label by symbolist painter Adolfo De Carolis from Marche.

ALCOHOL CONTENT: 34% vol.

COLOR: dark brown; consistent

BOUQUET: intense scents of bitter herbs, dried fruit, chestnuts, and walnut husk; on the bottom are recognizable hints of coffee and honey

TASTE: sweetness at the beginning due to the effect of honey, then a surprisingly intense and persistent bitter-tannic sensation that lasts

AFTERTASTE: delicate with chestnuts, honey, dried fruit, vanilla, and coffee

Lazio

AMARARTIS

**Free Spirit e Disperati
Andrea**
Rome

Amarartis was created in Rome based on an idea by Claudio and Andrea, one a pharmacy graduate who was fascinated by medicinal herbs and had a passion for liqueurs, the other an established bartender with a sophisticated palate and a lover of mixing. The manufacturing process for Amarartis involves 10 different alcohol macerations of which three are based on mixed ingredients and seven are carried out individually. Among the 24 botanicals used are star anise, wormwood, cinnamon, cardamom, cloves, gentian, and rhubarb.

ALCOHOL CONTENT: 30% vol.

COLOR: red-brown

BOUQUET: intoxicating and spicy scent

TASTE: velvety, warm, and embracing with hints of aniseed and a rhubarb finish with bitter notes

AFTERTASTE: chocolate and coffee

AMARIO

Alta Gradazione
Rome

Four and seven are the numbers that define a high alcohol content. Four are the young guys with a passion for good drinking who founded the Alta Gradazione brand; seven are their products, namely liqueurs. The latest addition to their range is called Amario. This spirit features a strong, dry, and markedly woody taste and is made by the synthesis of more than 20 roots and herbs, including rhubarb, gentian, wormwood, cardamom, and eucalyptus. An extra note is given by galangal, a sweet counterpoint to the pungent ginger. Partly replacing sugar with black molasses is unique but winning. Rich in minerals, the amaro has an exotic, slightly fruity flavor and a warm amber color reminiscent of caramel.

ALCOHOL CONTENT: 35% vol.

COLOR: hazelnut and brown highlights

BOUQUET: ginger and cardamom predominate

TASTE: pleasantly bitter with notes of wormwood and eucalyptus

AFTERTASTE: delicate citrus and spicy finish

AMARO 81

Earth Mother Project
Rome

ViviMoringa is the Earth Mother Project line of which Amaro 81 is part. The idea, conceived as a challenge, was developed by Sabrina Allegrini, the marketing manager of the company, who oversaw the graphics and the creative team with the aim of creating an original product of undisputed quality. The recipe for Amaro 81, prepared by an herbalist and distiller with many years of experience, includes a mix of botanicals that include gentian, cinchona, orange peel, mandarin, and Indian pepper. But its greatest peculiarity is represented by the use of the leaves of *Moringa oleifera*, the famous horseradish tree, whose medicinal properties make it one of the superfoods of the future.

ALCOHOL CONTENT: 30% vol.

COLOR: intense brown

BOUQUET: intoxicating, fresh, and spicy

TASTE: well-balanced with hints of gentian and cinchona

AFTERTASTE: citrusy and spicy with hints of Indian pepper and moringa

AMARO ADRIANO

Liquori di Tivoli
Tivoli, Rome

Amaro Adriano is a tribute to Publio Elio Traiano Adriano, or Hadrian, the Roman emperor who lived between the first and second century A.D. and who was also an architect, poet, writer, lover of beauty. Accordingly, this amaro is strong and powerful as well as sweet and sensitive. Amaro Adriano, with its captivating packaging,

expresses a delicate sweetness on the palate, reminiscent of the iconic Italian candy, Rossana, and is enriched with a hint of rum and diluted with citrus notes of lemon and bitter orange. The rest remains the secret of the recipe, jealously guarded by siblings Enrico and Simona, founders of Liquori di Tivoli, who continue their work with passion, dedication, sacrifice, and even a little bit of healthy madness.

ALCOHOL CONTENT: 38% vol.

COLOR: very dark, almost black

BOUQUET: vanilla and caramel scents prevail

TASTE: opens with notes of bitter orange

AFTERTASTE: long persistence reminiscent of custard

AMARO AL CARCIOFO

Agnoni
Cori, Latina

Respect for the land and its rhythms, genuine products, and flavors of the past are the cornerstones of Agnoni's production philosophy. The company was founded with a focus on the production of preserves, spreads, and extra virgin olive oil, and today also boasts a selection of typical liqueurs produced with dedication and great passion.

Amaro al Carciofo is obtained by selecting the best raw materials and patiently respecting a long production process that reflects the ancient heritage of Italian liqueurs.

ALCOHOL CONTENT: 16.9% vol.

COLOR: brown with copper reflections

BOUQUET: soft and vegetal

TASTE: round and enveloping with strong presence of artichoke

AFTERTASTE: good herbaceous persistence

AMARO ALL'OLIVO

Agnoni
Cori, Latina

In the 1960s, Neno and Nena Agnoni, a young married couple, bought the Podere Copellaro farm and mill in the Cori countryside. They had a strong desire to create something with their own hands that would endure, so they created what today corresponds to their family tradition: farm the land, grow its fruits, and preserve them while keeping the flavors intact. Today, Agnoni's range of products includes a small selection of

typical Italian liqueurs, including Amaro all'Olivo, produced from the infusion of fine olive leaves in top-quality alcohol.

ALCOHOL CONTENT: 28% vol.
COLOR: brown with golden reflections
BOUQUET: vegetable and citrus
TASTE: bitter with hints of olive leaves
AFTERTASTE: excellent herbaceous persistence with citrus hints

AMARO AL LUPPOLO

Antico Liquorificio Trappisti delle Tre Fontane
Rome

Amaro al Luppolo, made by Antico Liquorificio Trappisti delle Tre Fontane, was created from a group of botanicals including cinchona, rhubarb, and gentian. The botanicals, known for their strong digestive properties, are combined with a strictly artisan extraction of hops, the same used for the production of Tre Fontane beer. Three different macerations are necessary for the production of this amaro, and Sergio Daniele, lay manager of this Trappist liquor factory, personally and patiently follows the entire production process, before bottling and labeling by hand.

ALCOHOL CONTENT: 32% vol.
COLOR: amber with copper reflections
BOUQUET: intense scent of hops, rhubarb, and citrus fruits
TASTE: warm and embracing with distinct notes of hops and cinchona
AFTERTASTE: good aromatic and bitter persistence of gentian

AMARO AL TARTUFO PAGNANI

Pagnani Tartufi
Campoli Appennino, Frosinone

After about 30 years of experience in the research and marketing of fresh truffles, in 2002 the Pagnani family founded Pagnani Tartufi. The company's products represent a perfect combination of tradition and innovation, and their meticulous choice of truffles is combined with the careful selection of raw materials. Amaro al Tartufo Pagnani was developed based on the advice of an expert liquorist: Its recipe includes, in addition to the highly prized black truffle, the cold infusion of various botanicals including gentian, red cinchona, rhubarb, wormwood, cardamom, and cloves.

ALCOHOL CONTENT: 30% vol.
COLOR: intense straw yellow
BOUQUET: intoxicating scent of truffles and herbs
TASTE: strong hints of truffles combined with notes of gentian and rhubarb
AFTERTASTE: sweet, full, and aromatic

AMARO CIOCIARO

Paolucci Liquori
Sora, Frosinone

Paolucci Liquori was founded in Sora, in the province of Frosinone, at the beginning of the 20th century thanks to Vincenzo Paolucci's passion for medicinal plants, which are abundant near the national park of Abruzzo, Lazio, and Molise. Today, the most representative product of the company, led by Vincenzo's great-grandchildren Paola, Alessandro, and Francesco, is certainly Amaro Ciociaro. Its recipe, developed by Vincenzo himself and his son Donato, and proudly expressive of the territory, was readjusted to modern tastes in 1964. Its formula remains secret, but we know there are 16 botanicals used for the infusions that include gentian, cinnamon, rhubarb, cinchona, artichoke, sweet orange, and lemon. Amaro Ciociaro is particularly appreciated by mixologists around the world who choose it for the creation of cocktails with strong personality.

ALCOHOL CONTENT: 30% vol.

COLOR: deep brown

BOUQUET: hints of medicinal herbs accompanied by notes of cinchona and balsam

TASTE: full and well balanced with a citrusy nuance; the sugary note makes it slightly sweet

AFTERTASTE: cocoa flavor prevails

AMARO ERBES

Fratelli Izzi
Fondi, Latina

The Izzi family has been producing liqueurs since 1903, the year in which Vincenzo, a young confectioner from Fondi in the province of Latina, decided to make his passion for chemistry and herbalism a profession. He used herbs, seeds, and roots to make infusions with tonic and digestive properties. The fluid extracts of cinchona, rhubarb, gentian, and chamomile, suitably associated with other selected plant essences, represented the base of the final version of Amaro Eupeptico, created in 1927. After many national and international exhibitions and important awards received, Amaro Eupeptico changed its name first to Amaro Erbiz and finally to Amaro Erbes.

ALCOHOL CONTENT: 40% vol.

COLOR: coffee with emerald highlights

BOUQUET: enveloping hints of cream soda and peppermint

TASTE: balanced and dry, mentholated and fresh

AFTERTASTE: just bitter enough

AMARO ERBES GRAN RISERVA

Fratelli Izzi
Fondi, Latina

Today the Fratelli Izzi company, founded in 1903, is in the hands of the third generation, represented by Alessandro and Riccardo, who are constantly giving new life to the varied range of liqueurs. Amaro Erbes Gran Riserva, made in a limited series, sees the historic Amaro Erbes, whose formula is jealously guarded by the family, embellished by aging in fine Slavonian oak barrels and a slow filtration method. The result is an amaro with a unique and unmistakable taste, and with marked tonic and digestive properties.

ALCOHOL CONTENT: 40% vol.

COLOR: coffee with gold highlights

BOUQUET: coffee notes and balsamic nuances

TASTE: bitter, predominantly licorice

AFTERTASTE: mentholated

AMARO FORMIDABILE

Formidabile Liquori & Affini
Rome

Armando Bomba is co-owner and master herbalist of Formidabile Liquori & Affini of Rome and therefore the creator of the exclusive recipe of

Amaro Formidabile, which is made from the encounter of herbs, flowers, barks, roots, and fruit peels with concentration percentages much higher than normal. Among the botanicals used are red cinchona, nutmeg, pink burdock, Roman wormwood, gentian, Chinese rhubarb, sweet and bitter orange peel, kola nut, milk thistle, and star anise. Amaro Formidabile is produced by cold maceration in grain alcohol without any synthetic or natural additives, colorants, caramel, or flavorings.

ALCOHOL CONTENT: 33.5% vol.

COLOR: copper-bronze

BOUQUET: aromatic with hints of gentian

TASTE: warm with notes of gentian, rhubarb, and citrus fruits

AFTERTASTE: formidable persistence

AMARO NERI

Chinottissimo
Rome

Amaro Neri was conceived from an idea of Simone Neri, president of Chinottissimo and grandson of Pietro, inventor of Chin8Neri. Amaro Neri is produced from an infusion of chinotto to which are added 53 different extracts of wild herbs that grow at an altitude above 5,000 feet (1,500 m) in the national park of Abruzzo, Lazio, and Molise. Because it is a purely artisanal product, each bottle is rigorously numbered and dated.

ALCOHOL CONTENT: 35% vol.

COLOR: intense brown with warm orange reflections

BOUQUET: hints of plants and chinotto

TASTE: citrus notes prevail

AFTERTASTE: long and bitter

AMARO SAN MARCO

Sarandrea Marco & C.
Collepardo, Frosinone

Amaro San Marco was created around 1920, at the end of World War I, when the Capuchin friar Paolo Sarandrea, after leaving his military chaplain post, resumed his studies as an herbalist with the intention of enhancing the benefits of the medicinal plants of the Ernici Mountains through the production of medicinal liqueurs. Supported by his brother Marco, among his creations was the tonic and reconstituting liqueur Biosfero, known today as Amaro San Marco, which is made from botanicals infused

with high-quality alcohol and spring water.

ALCOHOL CONTENT: 30% vol.

COLOR: intense mahogany with orange reflections

BOUQUET: fresh and herbaceous with a predominance of rhubarb

TASTE: well balanced between sweet and bitter with notes of cinchona, rhubarb, and caramel

AFTERTASTE: fresh and spicy persistence

AMARO TONICO CON ERBE SVEDESI

Sarandrea Marco & C.
Collepardo, Frosinone

All the extracts used by Sarandrea Marco & C., founded in 1918, are obtained from the maceration of plants from the Ernici Mountains that are collected in an uncontaminated natural environment, in their own balsamic period, and placed in a hydro-alcoholic or hydroglycero-alcoholic solution immediately after collection. This is the case for Amaro Tonico con Erbe Svedesi, which is a liqueur based on an herbal infusion with a macerate of Swedish herbs that are famous all over the world for their tonic and highly digestive properties.

ALCOHOL CONTENT: 30% vol.

COLOR: amber with orange nuances

BOUQUET: hints of flowers and bitter herbs

TASTE: distinct flavor of lavender and rosemary

AFTERTASTE: excellent spicy and floral persistence with notes of gentian

AMARO TRE FONTANE

Antico Liquorificio Trappisti delle Tre Fontane
Rome

Antico Liquorificio Trappisti delle Tre Fontane is located inside the Tre Fontane abbey complex in Rome. Since 1873 they have been producing, with artisanal methods, liqueurs of the highest quality. The raw materials that do not come from the estate's crops are carefully selected by Sergio, lay manager of the liquor factory. Amaro Tre Fontane, a historic product of the abbey, comes to life thanks to the cold infusion of digestive botanicals in alcohol for about 30 days, including bitter orange, rhubarb, cinchona, licorice, gentian, coriander seeds, angelica roots, fennel seeds, cinnamon, and cloves.

ALCOHOL CONTENT: 27% vol.

COLOR: amber with copper highlights

BOUQUET: intense hints of rhubarb, cinchona, and orange

TASTE: soft and balanced with notes of licorice

AFTERTASTE: excellent balsamic persistence with a bitter gentian finish

AMARO VIRGILIO

Pallini
Rome

Pallini is one of the oldest and most representative Roman companies. Founded by Nicola Pallini in 1875 in Antrodoco (Rieti), it was moved to Rome by Virgilio Pallini in the 1920s where the plants are currently located. Virgilio, a man of great ideas and successes, inspired Amaro Virgilio, which is obtained from a mixture of botanicals including cinchona, rhubarb, sweet orange, and licorice.

ALCOHOL CONTENT: 30% vol.

COLOR: hazelnut with orange highlights

BOUQUET: hints of citrus fruits emerge

TASTE: clean and fresh, with notes of orange and rhubarb

AFTERTASTE: persistent licorice flavor

ARIMINUM

Leardini Liquori Produzione Artigianale
Affile, Rome

The company Leardini, in Affile, follows the ancient liquoristic tradition of using tools such as a bronze mortar in which herbs are crushed and mixed. In the range of Leardini's products, Ariminum is highly regarded. It is produced by a selected blend of botanicals including thyme, linden, basil, and rosemary. The choice of the name Ariminum recalls the Latin name of Rimini, the birthplace of the company's founder Domenico Leardini.

ALCOHOL CONTENT: 43% vol.

COLOR: amber with emerald reflections

BOUQUET: hints of herbs

TASTE: bitter, it opens with notes of rosemary, thyme, and linden

AFTERTASTE: delicate finish of chamomile

BARRUELL

Leardini Liquori Produzione Artigianale
Affile, Rome

Barruell is a bittersweet liqueur inspired by an old love of Domenico Leardini, founder of the Leardini liquor factory in Affile. During a winter in French-speaking Switzerland, the young shoemaker, Domenico, fell in love with a pretty blonde girl named Barruell, who often left a bottle of liqueur on her sweetheart's counter to help him fight off the effects of frosty weather. He brought the recipe back to Italy for the drink from which he later created Barruell, which is made from a mix of botanicals that include lemon balm, apricot seeds, and red tea.

ALCOHOL CONTENT: 34% vol.
COLOR: gianduja chocolate
BOUQUET: dry and vegetal
TASTE: bitter and mellow, rich in nuances of tea
AFTERTASTE: almond and chocolate notes prevail

FERRO CHINA BALIVA

Pallini
Rome

The recipe for Ferro China Baliva was developed in the late 19th century by Ernesto Baliva, a hospital doctor in Rome, who later asked Virgilio Pallini to produce his tonic on a large scale. The drink was immediately successful and was considered by consumers almost like a "miraculous tonic" with strong tonic, digestive, and antimalarial qualities; it was even exported to Asia and India where it was added to water as a purifying agent. Ferro China Baliva owes many of its benefits to ingredients such as cinchona bark (*china* in Italian) and iron citrate (which is why the product is reddish). Among the 13 other botanicals described in the recipe are cinnamon, quassia, calamus, bitter orange peel, gentian root, iris roots, and condurango.

ALCOHOL CONTENT: 21% vol.
COLOR: very dark brown, similar to coffee
BOUQUET: hints of citrus
TASTE: sweet and mellow with notes of cinnamon
AFTERTASTE: orange finish

NERONE

Italcoral
Ariccia, Rome

In the heart of the Castelli Romani, in Ariccia, stands Italcoral, a liquor factory that has been working since 1951 to transform medicinal plants, fruit, and carefully selected roots into amari, grappas, and liqueurs. In the company's range of products, Nerone, *l'amaro di Roma*, stands out. It was created with the intent to produce a spirit that was identifiable with the Roman territory and vice versa. Today, the Italcoral company is in the hands of Filippo, Andrea, and Franzo Caruso, grandsons of founder Franzo Caruso, who represent the third generation of a big family of liquorists of Sicilian descent.

ALCOHOL CONTENT: 25% vol.
COLOR: intensely dark, reminiscent of coffee
BOUQUET: intense vegetal and herbaceous scents, with very intense and embracing balsamic nuances
TASTE: very intense and embracing
AFTERTASTE: long balsamic persistence

VECCHIO AMARO CIOCIARIA

Sarandrea Marco & C.
Collepardo, Frosinone

In January 1948, the Certosa di Trisulti di Collepardo was closed and the Carthusian monks were succeeded by the Cistercians who continued the liquor business of their predecessors. They were flanked by the Sarandrea family who were able to preserve the research of the Carthusian monks, and who still keep the traditions of those places alive today in their Collepardo factory. Vecchio Amaro Ciociaria, made by the Sarandrea family, is a liqueur with a soft taste that is produced from an infusion of digestive, tonic, and aromatic

botanicals and include orange and mandarin peels.

ALCOHOL CONTENT: 30% vol.

COLOR: brown with reddish highlights

BOUQUET: distinct hints of citrus fruits and cinchona

TASTE: slightly sweet with a prevalence of orange and cinnamon

AFTERTASTE: sweet and fragrant with notes reminiscent of almonds

ZETHUS

Leardini Liquori
Produzione Artigianale
Affile, Rome

The small Leardini liquor factory operates thanks to the passion and tenacity of the Leardini family, who maintain and hand down the precious infusion recipes from generation to generation. It is said that around the middle of the 19th century, a priest passing through Rimini, after having had his shoes repaired by Domenico Leardini and not having enough money, paid the remaining part with the formula of the Zethus amaro, which falls into the category of a fernet. It is a liqueur that pulls at the heartstrings of enthusiasts, and is obtained by mixing as many as 43 botanicals, including gentian, galangal, and aloe. The recipe includes an extractive bath for each of the plant components used.

ALCOHOL CONTENT: 40% vol.

COLOR: amber with sapphire reflections

BOUQUET: exuberant and herbaceous

TASTE: pleasant, bitter, and overbearing, with embracing notes of licorice, gentian, and citrus fruits

AFTERTASTE: long persistence of mace and cloves

Abruzzo

AMARO ARTEMISIA

Artemisia Liquori
L'Aquila

Artemisia Liquori, founded in 1998, got its start from the enthusiasm of Cesare and Franco Farroni, united by passion and respect for the mountains of L'Aquila and its essences, values transmitted to the two brothers by their father Vincenzo. Amaro Artemisia, which has always been a part of the company's production, is obtained from selected Abruzzo plants and herbs. Through careful infusion methods, the aromatic and digestive principles of the botanicals are extracted and, only after having released all their properties into the alcohol, are separated from the infusion so that this amaro can continue its journey toward bottling.

ALCOHOL CONTENT: 25% vol.

COLOR: soft amber with orange reflections

BOUQUET: delicate herbaceous hints

TASTE: sweet with citrus and herbaceous notes among which gentian is recognizable

AFTERTASTE: sweet and vegetal persistence

AMARO D'ABRUZZO

Santo Spirito Liquori
Santo Spirito, Pescara

Santo Spirito Liquori takes its name from the hermitage of Santo Spirito, the largest and most famous in all of Maiella. The company still uses processing methods and recipes handed down by the friars who have inhabited the structure over the centuries. Amaro d'Abruzzo is obtained through ancient techniques of extraction of the active ingredients present in the plant mix. The original formula, which includes 29 basic botanicals, remains secret to this day.

ALCOHOL CONTENT: 30% vol.

COLOR: dark brown

BOUQUET: citrus scents prevail

TASTE: balanced with predominant notes of bitter orange

AFTERTASTE: citrusy finish with bitter persistence

AMARO D'ABRUZZO 77

Jannamico Michele & Figli
Lanciano, Chieti

The Jannamico Michele & Figli distillery, operated by four generations of liqueur makers, boasts more than a century of experience. From the time of its founding by Francesco Jannamico in 1888, their production philosophy was the careful choice of raw materials and suppliers. One of the outstanding products of the distillery is Amaro d'Abruzzo 77, created from the desire to rework the ancient recipe of Abruzzo Punch composed of orange, lemon, mandarin, black tea, and caramel with an alcoholic base of rum. Amaro D'Abruzzo 77 recalls the ancient punch that was formulated from rum, quality white sugar, and citrus peel that came mainly from the Gargano area.

ALCOHOL CONTENT: 30% vol.

COLOR: dark brown with orange reflections

BOUQUET: aromatic, fresh, and spicy

TASTE: semisweet with notes of orange, lemon, and caramel

AFTERTASTE: sweet persistence with hints of tea

AMARO DELLA LAGA

Scuppoz Liquori
Campovalano di Campli, Teramo

The Scuppoz Liquori company, founded in the late 1970s by Benito Cicconi, owes its Scuppoz name to an ancient dialectal term of Valle Castellana (Teramo) that indicated the festive tinkling of glasses full of wine. Amaro della Laga by Scuppoz Liquori is characterized by its distinct bitter notes, and its recipe features various botanicals, including dandelion, Roman wormwood, gentian, juniper, rhubarb, savory, and yarrow. The bottle recalls medicinal products of the 1930s, while the label, as a tribute to the territory, reflects the seasonal shepherding of flocks in Abruzzo.

ALCOHOL CONTENT: 30% vol.
COLOR: amber with gold reflections
BOUQUET: vegetal and gentian scents prevail
TASTE: strong and balanced with notes of gentian and rhubarb
AFTERTASTE: bitter finish of roots

AMARO GRAN SASSO

Fabbrica Liquori Paesani
Montorio al Vomano, Teramo

Established in 1961, Fabbrica Liquori Paesani is a successful artisan company whose quality-oriented production philosophy is based on the thoughtful selection of raw materials and the careful control of the entire production process. The factory is located in Montorio al Vomano in the small hamlet of Collevecchio and therefore close to the Gran Sasso d'Italia and Monti della Laga National Park. This territory of extraordinary beauty and the passion of the Paesani family are the inspiration for Amaro Gran Sasso, created by founder Ermanno Paesani and produced from 20 botanicals, including gentian, cinchona, rhubarb, cardamom, masterwort, vanilla, centaury, and orange. The plant components are subjected to cold maceration in alcohol and gently pressed by hand, following the same procedure used more than 50 years ago. In addition to the classic version, the stronger Amaro Gran Sasso Tipo Forte is produced. This amaro features a higher alcohol content of 40% vol., a more full-bodied structure, and a more intense taste. In addition there is Amaro Gran Sasso Riserva, an amaro that is left to age for 12 months in barriques that have first been in contact with Montepulciano grapes.

ALCOHOL CONTENT: 30% vol.
COLOR: brown with golden reflections
BOUQUET: delicate, with hints of spices and roots
TASTE: firm and full with the bitter notes of rhubarb and gentian that prevail over sweetness
AFTERTASTE: remnants of citrus and vanilla flavors

AMARO TORO

Enrico Toro Distilleria Casauria

Tocca da Casauria, Pescara

This distillery is located at the entrance of the Gole di Tremonti, which is nestled in the foothills of the Gran Sasso and Monte Morrone mountain peaks. The nature of the surrounding area has always been a source of inspiration for products of the Toro family, who for generations have been involved in creating spirits and liqueurs of excellent tradition. Amaro Toro is made from an ancient recipe inspired by the formula developed in 1817 by the apothecary Beniamino Toro della Centerba. The company's pride and joy, made with rhubarb, gentian, and wild mountain herbs contains all the flavors and scents of the beautiful Abruzzo region.

ALCOHOL CONTENT: 27% vol.

COLOR: bright mahogany with copper reflections

BOUQUET: hints of bitter wild herbs prevail

TASTE: herbaceous with notes of rhubarb and well balanced in sweetness

AFTERTASTE: soft and full with persistent notes of gentian and citrus fruits

ANTICO AMARO ABRUZZESE TORO

Enrico Toro Distilleria Casauria

Tocco da Casauria, Pescara

This type of amaro has very ancient origins in Abruzzo, in fact it is one of the typical specialties of the region and is produced by different companies that develop and customize the historic recipe. Enrico Toro's recipe combines the peculiar citrus notes of orange with those of the main botanicals of the historic Centerba liqueur, including the wild mint of Maiella. Rhubarb and gentian help to complete the plant mix, giving an aromatic and bitter touch to the Antico Amaro Abruzzese Toro. It remains loyal to the tradition of the territory, where amaro plays a leading role during the end of meals in the region.

ALCOHOL CONTENT: 25% vol.

COLOR: brown with red reflections

BOUQUET: distinct hints of orange with slight hints of caramel

TASTE: semisweet and citrusy with a prevalence of orange and herbaceous notes

AFTERTASTE: persistence of orange with light hints of rhubarb

CENTERBA 72

Enrico Toro Distilleria Casauria

Tocco da Casauria, Pescara

The Centerba (or Centerbe) is a typical liqueur product of many regions of Italy, but certainly the birthplace of this amaro is Abruzzo. It is the apothecaries of the religious orders who deserve the credit, more precisely those within the walls of the Abbey of San Clemente in Casauria. Over the years, the formula was perfected by the expert hands of the pharmacist Beniamino Toro, who in 1817 reworked the composition to treat patients suffering from cholera and plague. Centerba 72, which is dedicated to the year the company was founded by Roberto Toro and his son Enrico in 1972, is produced following Beniamino's secret recipe from 1817. Most of the nearly 100 herbs in the mix, including some varieties of wild mint, are still handpicked on the slopes of the Morrone and Maiella mountains and subjected to a long maceration in high-quality alcohol.

ALCOHOL CONTENT: 70% vol.

COLOR: emerald green

BOUQUET: intense hints of medicinal herbs

TASTE: intense and vegetal with distinct notes of fresh grass

AFTERTASTE: warm and intoxicating with long plant persistence

CENTERBA TORO FORTE

Enrico Toro Distilleria Casauria
Tocco da Casauria, Pescara

The ancient recipe of this amaro has been handed down for more than 200 years from generation to generation by the Toro family. Centerba Toro Forte comes from a skillful mix of wild herbs and precious spices that are handpicked in the mountains of the province of Pescara. Transported in special bags, the best parts of the herbs are dried on the farm while sheltered from changes in temperature and humidity. After skillful measuring, the ingredients are macerated in high-quality alcohol for a period that varies between two and four months depending on the climatic characteristics of the year of harvest. Without added sugar, Centerba Toro Forte brings to mind the unspoiled green valleys of Abruzzo.

ALCOHOL CONTENT: 70% vol.
COLOR: emerald green
BOUQUET: intense and intoxicating scent of wild herbs
TASTE: warm and overbearingly herbaceous
AFTERTASTE: pleasant, fresh, and clean with a long aromatic persistence

D'ABRUZZO

Artemisia Liquori
L'Aquila

"Fatigue makes artisans," says Franco Farroni, a partner together with his brother Cesare since 1998, of Artemisia Liquori whose products are strictly handmade in their workshop in L'Aquila. The strong passion and great commitment of this family business have allowed the Farroni brothers to acquire a deep know-how, and they feel it is their duty to pass it on to future generations, just as their father Vincenzo did with them. The exclusive recipe of D'Abruzzo contains herbs, roots, and mountain flowers, including Abruzzo gentian and the use of top-quality alcohol.

ALCOHOL CONTENT: 36% vol.
COLOR: soft amber with orange reflections
BOUQUET: mountain scents and bitter herbs
TASTE: bitter and aromatic with strong hints of gentian
AFTERTASTE: bitter persistence of gentian softened by vegetal tones

FERNET PAESANI

Fabbrica Liquori Paesani
Montorio al Vomano, Teramo

From an ancient recipe resulting from Ermanno Paesani's passion for botanicals and mixing herbs and roots, Fernet Paesani by Fabbrica Liquori Paesani was created. This amaro is made from plant components—including aloe, rhubarb, and cinchona—of the highest quality, carefully selected, and left to rest in a cold alcoholic infusion for about 60 days. The Paesani family also produces this spirit in a Fernet Menta version that is enriched with peppermint from a medicinal garden located in the province of Teramo, which gives the fernet an overwhelming freshness.

ALCOHOL CONTENT: 40% vol.
COLOR: brown with amber reflections
BOUQUET: spicy with strong bitter notes
TASTE: intense bitterness with hints of rhubarb and cinchona
AFTERTASTE: bitter and spicy persistence

JANNAMARO

Ival

Fara Filiorum Petri, Chieti

The actor Marcello Mastroianni was a great admirer of Jannamaro. He liked to have it mostly after meals, but also during breaks on his famed movie sets. The recipe for this historic product of the Ival company dates back to 1888, the year in which Francesco Iannamico began to produce it from a secret formula handed down from father to son for five generations, keeping the ingredients and processes in strict confidentiality. The aromatic bouquet of Jannamaro features a hint of citrus and notes of cinnamon, mace, allspice, carnations, and tea.

ALCOHOL CONTENT: 35% vol.

COLOR: dark brown

BOUQUET: soft scent of spices and citrus fruits

TASTE: balanced between sweet and bitter with hints of caramel and orange

AFTERTASTE: soft and warm, and embraces the palate with persistence of orange

Molise

AMARO DEL MOLISE

Liquorificio Artigianale Belmonte
Montenero di Bisaccia, Campobasso

The production of Amaro del Molise takes place in the artisan workshop of Liquorificio Artigianale Belmonte, owned by the Sparvieri family. The first phase of production of this traditional Molise amaro consists of a cold hydro-alcoholic infusion of secret botanicals that is left to soak for a few dozen days in large steel vats. The maceration is followed by filtration and the addition of the right amount of sugar and microfiltered water. Finally, the amaro is transferred into fine oak barrels for aging until it is ready to be bottled.

ALCOHOL CONTENT: 35% vol.

COLOR: amber with orange highlights

BOUQUET: prevailing herbaceous notes

TASTE: agreeable and well balanced between herbaceous and sugary notes

AFTERTASTE: soft and vegetal persistence

AMARO FERRAZANO

Saporicentroitalia
Campobasso

After the success of Root 13, Franco Passarelli from Saporicentroitalia decided to make a new product with no added sugar: Amaro Ferrazzano. This spirit is mainly produced with mountain herbs harvested in the countryside of Ferrazzano (Campobasso), an unspoiled area of Molise. The recipe uses more than 24 types of botanicals with digestive, antioxidant, toning, purifying, and detoxifying properties.

ALCOHOL CONTENT: 32% vol.

COLOR: brown with emerald highlights

BOUQUET: aromatic and light

TASTE: dry, bitter

AFTERTASTE: balsamic with long licorice finish

ROOT 13

Saporicentroitalia
Campobasso

"From the arid soils of the Molise hinterland, where temperature changes temper the plants, the air is clean, the water is clear, we search and select the best aromatic and medicinal herbs. We adopt an artisan production, which exalts old and new recipes." This is the production philosophy that inspires Franco Passarelli, owner of Saporicentroitalia, who inherited a series of uncultivated fields in Molise where he discovered an incredible variety of herbs that populated them. Hence the idea of creating a line of elixirs, liqueurs, and amari based on botanicals rich in beneficial properties and able to delight the palate. Among them is Amaro Root 13, an amaro that uses 13 herbs, all with digestive functions, which grow wild on the company's properties. The name *Root* refers to the Molise roots of the amaro as well as to the sound that—according to popular tradition—is emitted to express satisfaction after a meal.

ALCOHOL CONTENT: 32% vol.

COLOR: straw yellow, clear, and clean

BOUQUET: fresh and light scents with hints of dandelion and fennel

TASTE: slightly sweet; the bitterness is mitigated by herbaceous flavors

AFTERTASTE: balsamic

Campania

AMADIVO

H. Domus
Naples

An idea of Pasquale Damiano, former barman and current liquorist, led to the conception of a project called Amadivo, an *AMAricante aperitIVO* (bitter aperitif). Amadivo is an amaro that brings back to life a product category that has fallen into disuse: bitter wine. In 2016, Pasquale, inspired by an ancient recipe from Abruzzo, developed the recipe for this spirit that includes selected infusions of bitter botanicals and the addition of Trebbiano wine. In compliance with legislative dictates, the main ingredient of Amadivo is gentian, which is accompanied, in the botanical mix, by 15 other plant elements, including elecampane, chamomile, myrtle, grapefruit, elderberry, damiana, quassia, and columbo.

ALCOHOL CONTENT: 15% vol.
COLOR: straw yellow
BOUQUET: intense vinous and spicy scent with sweetish and vegetal notes
TASTE: fresh opening with false sweetness, immediately bitter with dominance of gentian
AFTERTASTE: dry and bitter

AMAPIPERNA

Amarischia
Caivano, Naples

Piperna, better known as wild thyme, grows wild on the volcanic island of Ischia, both in the high areas and those closer to the sea. Besides its strong aromatizing power, piperna also has important appetite-inducing, digestive, and detoxifying properties. Amapiperna is a full-bodied and well-structured liqueur with a strong and marked taste that is obtained from the infusion of several typical island herbs, including piperna.

ALCOHOL CONTENT: 30% vol.
COLOR: brown with copper shades
BOUQUET: herbaceous with hints hints of wild thyme and orange
TASTE: balanced and robust; citrus notes emerge
AFTERTASTE: aromatic, complex, and persistent with predominance of wild thyme

AMARÈ

Antica Distilleria Petrone
Mondragone, Caserta

Amarè is an amaro obtained from the infusion of herbs and plants coming from the "Royal English Garden" of the Royal Palace of Caserta, the precious 18th-century garden wanted by Queen Maria Carolina, consort of the Bourbon King Ferdinand IV. Its recipe was created in 1858 by Don Domenico Petrone, founder of the Antica Distilleria Petrone, for the Royal House.

ALCOHOL CONTENT: 33% vol.
COLOR: dark brown
BOUQUET: herbaceous and spicy notes prevail
TASTE: well-balanced between sweet and bitter
AFTERTASTE: bitter finish; herbaceous persistence

AMARISCHIA

Amarischia
Caviano, Naples

Since 1920, the Cola family, originally from Ottaviano in the heart of Vesuvius National Park, has been producing typical liqueurs of the Campania tradition such as Nocillo and Limoncello. Among the flagship products of the company is the amaro Amarischia, whose creation is thanks to Cavalier Arcangelo Cola, an exponent of the second generation of

Vesuvian liquorists, who left for Ischia on the trail of an ancient recipe developed in the second half of the 18th century by a friar belonging to the Franciscan order. The latter, experts in herbal infusions and present on the island since 1225, were forced to leave the convent by the Napoleonic government established in the Kingdom of Naples in 1805. Once the precious formula was recovered, at the end of the 1960s, Arcangelo created an amaro capable of releasing the most authentic flavors and aromas of Ischia, obtained from botanicals that grow naturally on the island, such as aloe, gentian, calamus, Breckland thyme, and arugula.

ALCOHOL CONTENT: 30% vol.
COLOR: coffee with emerald reflections, good clarity
BOUQUET: sober hints of natural herbs
TASTE: pleasant and aromatic; sweetly bitter
AFTERTASTE: cocoa

AMARO 31

Martino Liquori
Naples

Amaro 31 is considered the flagship product of Martino Liquori. A proud expression of the Neapolitan territory, this drink was created from 31 botanicals that are typical of the Vesuvian area. The original recipe remains a well-kept secret.

ALCOHOL CONTENT: 34% vol.
COLOR: dark amber
BOUQUET: very spicy
TASTE: agreeable, with notes of ginger
AFTERTASTE: bitter persistence

AMARO 40 MAURIZIO RUSSO

Liquorificio Maurizio Russo
Cava de' Tirreni, Salerno

Liquorificio Maurizio Russo was founded back in 1899, making it one of the first distilleries in the whole of Campania. Today the company is run by Gianluca and Massimiliano Russo, authentic guardians of the secret family recipes. One of the most popular products of the distillery is Amaro 40 Maurizio Russo, which boasts among its botanicals cinnamon, cloves, nutmeg, cinchona bark, and walnut husk.

ALCOHOL CONTENT: 40% vol.
COLOR: very dark brown

BOUQUET: intense aroma of herbs and spices with a predominance of cinnamon and walnut husk
TASTE: pungent and well balanced, with marked clove and walnut flavors
AFTERTASTE: bitter finish with hints of walnut husk

AMARO BENEDUCE

Il Beneduce
Sant'Antimo, Naples

Founded in 1970, Il Beneduce is a liquor factory that has always favored handcrafted production. In order to meet an increasingly multifaceted and demanding market, over time the company has undergone structural changes and embraced innovation, without ever degrading the quality and authenticity of its products. Amaro Beneduce, made following an ancient recipe, is a digestive amaro based on wormwood, rhubarb, gentian, sweet orange, and bitter orange.

ALCOHOL CONTENT: 32% vol.
COLOR: dark brown
BOUQUET: herbaceous and citrusy hints of orange emerge
TASTE: well balanced between sweet and bitter with notes of rhubarb and wormwood
AFTERTASTE: citrusy persistence of orange

AMARO DEL ROSSO

Alambicco Rosso
San Marco Evangelista, Caserta

Amaro del Rosso is inspired by Grandpa Vincenzo, called Rosso, because of the color of his hair and his smoldering temperament. During card games with his equally "agitated" friends, there was always a bottle of amaro that Vincenzo had learned to produce himself: A small glass was useful to restore harmony in case of quarrels and arguments. The original recipe, which involves the use of 24 botanical herbs and spices, remains a well-kept secret.

ALCOHOL CONTENT: 35% vol.

COLOR: dark amber

BOUQUET: herbaceous hints prevail

TASTE: sweet and bitter, well balanced

AFTERTASTE: long bitter persistence

AMARO DI SAN CONSTANZO

Distilleria Nastro d'Oro
Massa Lubrense, Naples

The artisanal distillery Nastro d'Oro is situated on the slopes of Mount San Costanzo, the highest hill in the territory of Massa Lubrense, which takes its name from the patron saint of the small hamlet of Termini, the last outpost of the Sorrento Peninsula, overlooking the sea. On the path that, starting from the factory, leads to the chapel of San Costanzo that dominates the panorama, you can recognize the main botanicals that give life to the Amaro di San Costanzo: mint, arugula, anise, and fennel.

ALCOHOL CONTENT: 30% vol.

COLOR: dark brown

BOUQUET: menthol with notes of arugula

TASTE: well balanced between sweet and bitter

AFTERTASTE: mentholated persistence

AMARO DON CARLO

Gargiulo Coloniali
Eboli, Salerno

Amaro Don Carlo, produced by Gargiulo Coloniali, is made from only natural ingredients. Among the botanicals used are artichoke, cinnamon, cloves, licorice, and 60 percent walnut husk. This amaro, made by Angela Caliendo, is one of the company's flagship products and represents a sort of creative evolution of the traditional Nocino.

ALCOHOL CONTENT: 25% vol.

COLOR: dark amber

BOUQUET: herbaceous hints prevail with notes of walnut

TASTE: well balanced between sweet and bitter with notes of licorice and cloves

AFTERTASTE: distinct nuances of walnut husk

AMARO ERBISE

Il Beneduce
Sant'Antimo, Naples

The company Il Beneduce from Sant'Antimo has always aimed for high-quality production based on the selection of raw materials, respect for processing times, and meticulous control of production processes. In the company's range of liqueurs and distillates, Amaro Erbise stands out. It is a digestif amaro obtained from an ancient recipe developed by expert pharmacists that involves the use of various botanicals including cinchona, chamomile, mint, rhubarb, and licorice.

ALCOHOL CONTENT: 38% vol.

COLOR: dark brown

BOUQUET: hints of licorice and cinchona prevail

TASTE: well balanced between sweet and bitter

AFTERTASTE: bitter persistence with licorice finish

AMARO ITALYCO

Il Beneduce
Sant'Antimo, Naples

Il Beneduce, a company that has specialized in the production of liqueurs and distillates for over 40 years, today combines technical and productive innovation while maintaining an artisan approach to processing and absolute attention to the choice of quality raw materials. In the range of products there is Amaro Italyco, with marked digestive properties that is composed of cinchona, sweet orange, bitter orange, rhubarb, wormwood, cloves, and chamomile.

ALCOHOL CONTENT: 35% vol.

COLOR: amber

BOUQUET: distinct hints of cinchona and orange

TASTE: agreeable with notes of cloves and rhubarb

AFTERTASTE: bitter persistence with hints of chamomile

AMARO PENNA

Ditta Alfonso Penna
Sassano, Salerno

Amaro Penna was created more than a hundred years ago during an evening of bad weather, when Alfonso Penna, founder of the company of the same name, was forced to stay with a pharmacist friend of his in the back of his shop. There, mixing popular knowledge, tradition, and the experience of the apothecary, the original recipe for this amaro with marked digestive properties was developed.

ALCOHOL CONTENT: 27% vol.

COLOR: amber

BOUQUET: prevalent herbaceous hints

TASTE: bitter

AFTERTASTE: sweet with a persistent herbaceous finish

AMARO SANSEVERINO

Distilleria Russo
Salerno

Distilleria Russo has been producing liqueurs, distillates, and syrups since 1936, always paying great attention to finding quality materials linked to the territory. The company, with artisanal inspiration, today makes use of innovative production structures and processes oriented to the best enhancement of the final product. Amaro Sanseverino was created from a secret recipe that uses botanicals that include cinnamon, cinchona, and walnut husk.

ALCOHOL CONTENT: 30% vol.

COLOR: intense brown

BOUQUET: hints of walnut husk

TASTE: well balanced between sweet and bitter

AFTERTASTE: persistence of walnut husk

AMARO SIANO

Bellingusto
Naples

Amaro Siano is a creation from the slopes of Vesuvius, the land of origin of the Siano family who wanted as much as possible to express the unmistakable scents and flavors of the area of provenance in this amaro. The original recipe includes the use of different botanicals including gentian, yarrow, and vanilla.

ALCOHOL CONTENT: 25% vol.

COLOR: light brown

BOUQUET: herbaceous note of gentian

TASTE: well balanced between sweet and bitter

AFTERTASTE: vanilla finish with bitter persistence

AMARO TEGGIANO

Gaetano Tropiano
Teggiano, Salerno

Amaro Teggiano was created in the early 1990s by Gaetano Tropiano, owner of a small food shop in the heart of Teggiano. However, production was suspended due to numerous work and family duties. In 2014, Gaetano's dream came true again thanks to his daughters Anna and Vincenza, who, with the support of Enzo Sorbo and the Penna family, reworked the formula of the drink, making it less decisive and more elegant to the taste. Amaro Teggiano is obtained from aromatic and medicinal herbs without the addition of preservatives and stabilizers. Among the botanicals used in the secret recipe, only two are known: orange blossom and laurel.

ALCOHOL CONTENT: 30% vol.

COLOR: dark amber

BOUQUET: herbaceous and floral notes prevail

TASTE: lovely, well balanced between sweet and bitter

AFTERTASTE: persistence of orange blossom

AMARO VILLA DELLE GINESTRE

Distilleria Amato
Striano, Naples

Founded in 1881, the Distilleria Amato boasts generations of skilled and passionate liquorists. In 1997, the company decided to restore an old copper still that had belonged to the founder Gaetano, and it remains in operation today. The product line from this distillery includes Amaro Villa delle Ginestre, which is produced from more than 20 botanical herbs and spices that are combined with infusions of citrus fruits from the Sorrento Peninsula. Among the ingredients are angelica, peppermint, ginger, cardamom, carnation flowers, and star anise, suitably dried and pounded in a stone mortar and then subjected to maceration in alcohol for over a month.

ALCOHOL CONTENT: 33% vol.

COLOR: dark brown

BOUQUET: herbaceous and mentholated notes emerge

TASTE: well balanced between sweet and bitter with spicy notes of ginger

AFTERTASTE: bitter persistence

AMARUCOLA

Amarischia
Caivano, Naples

From 1920 to the present day, the Cola family, owner of the Amarischia brand, has shown great entrepreneurial ability: They are the second great Italian power in the production of candies, sweets, and chewing gum. They have also shown knowledge and passion for the world of liquor and for the island of Ischia, whose perfumes and flavors are present in every spirit they produce.

Amarucola, a liqueur obtained from the alcohol infusion of local arugula leaves, is inspired by ancient Neapolitan recipes.

ALCOHOL CONTENT: 35% vol.

COLOR: rust with orange nuances

BOUQUET: Chantilly cream and citrus fruits prevail

TASTE: more sweet than bitter; decisive and creamy entrance

AFTERTASTE: continuation of arugula and citrus fruits with a very long bitter finish

IL GREEN DEL FALERIO

Agrocetus
Cetara, Salerno

Agrocetus was conceived in the heart of the Amalfi Peninsula, a territory of extraordinary beauty also known for its centuries-old lemon groves. The company from Cetara is part of the Consorzio di Tutela "Limone d'Amalfi" (Amalfi Lemon Consortium), and it is from this king of Mediterranean citrus fruits that it derives most of its liqueurs. Il Green del Falerio is obtained by artisan methods, which is done through traditional drying and maceration of multiple herbs collected in the mountainous

regions of Cetara in the Monti Lattari park area.

ALCOHOL CONTENT: 30% vol.
COLOR: dark brown
BOUQUET: penetrating herbaceous scents
TASTE: bitter with hints of fennel
AFTERTASTE: balanced between sweet and bitter

ROBORIS

Mavidrink
Naples

Mavidrink, a modern liqueur factory based in Naples, has products that range from the most traditional liqueurs to the most famous Italian and international spirits. Among the strengths of the company are the careful selection of raw materials and the careful management of their highly automated production processes. Roboris is an amaro that comes from the reworking of an ancient recipe, very secret and jealously guarded.

ALCOHOL CONTENT: 30% vol.
COLOR: amber
BOUQUET: herbaceous and citrus scents prevail
TASTE: well balanced between sweet and bitter
AFTERTASTE: herbaceous finish with floral notes

SIGNORE DI DIANO

Gaetano Tropiano
Teggiano, Salerno

Signore Di Diano by the Gaetano Tropiano company is dedicated to a historical character of Teggiano: Antonello Sanseverino, Prince of Salerno, Count of Marsico, Great Admiral of the Kingdom of Naples, and Lord of Diano, who lived in the second half of the 15th century. For the creation of this amaro, the basic herbs of Amaro Teggiano have been used, with the addition of rhubarb that provides a strong bitter boost.

ALCOHOL CONTENT: 35% vol.
COLOR: hazelnut
BOUQUET: intense herbaceous hints
TASTE: robust with notes of rhubarb
AFTERTASTE: very persistent bitter finish

Puglia

AMARO 63 LUCERA

La Rusticana
Lucera, Foggia

The creator of Amaro 63 Lucera is Sergio La Cava. After 20 years of experience in the restaurant industry, in 2019, Sergio decided to produce an amaro to be recommended after meals. This is how Amaro 63 Lucera was conceived. It is dedicated with love to his wife, having chosen to put the year of her birth on the label: 1963. This very young amaro contains all the typical flavors and aromas of the Apulian territory, more precisely of the Lucera area, in the province of Foggia. Some botanicals present in the mix of this product are licorice, cinnamon, oregano, and mallow.

ALCOHOL CONTENT: 25% vol.

COLOR: amber with caramel reflections

BOUQUET: intoxicating scent of spices and herbs

TASTE: bitter and spicy with notes of licorice and oregano

AFTERTASTE: persistent spicy and vegetal note; balanced sweetness

AMARO DEI TRULLI

Merak Spirits & Drinks
Putignano, Bari

Merak Spirits & Drinks of Putignano represents an evolution of the historical company Beltion of the Giannandrea family, specializing in the artisan production of almond milk and liqueurs. Today Francesco, Angelo, and Roberto continue the family tradition, focusing on innovative technological systems and modern workshops for production development with the aim of creating an increasingly varied offer that is attentive to customer needs while respecting quality and the environment. Amaro dei Trulli is an amaro with herbaceous and citrus scents whose recipe is kept secret.

ALCOHOL CONTENT: 30% vol.

COLOR: dark brown

BOUQUET: prevailing hints of citrus

TASTE: balanced with citrus notes of orange

AFTERTASTE: soft with hints of licorice

AMARO GARÌGA DI MURGIA

Amari e Rosoli
Gravina in Puglia, Bari

Amaro Garìga di Murgia is made from 43 botanicals, many of which come from the vast territories of the Alta Murgia and other neighboring areas. The herbs that grow wild here are harvested by hand from early spring until early summer, in their balsamic period. Among the main components of Amaro Garìga di Murgia are thyme, thistle, and artichoke.

ALCOHOL CONTENT: 28% vol.

COLOR: amber

BOUQUET: very rich, with hints of wild thyme and mountain savory

TASTE: well balanced between sweet and bitter with clear notes of thyme

AFTERTASTE: bitter persistence

AMARO IMPERATORE

Terre da Bere
Lucera, Foggia

Amaro Imperatore was created in 2017 thanks to the discovery by Salvatore Marchetti of an old recipe developed by his grandfather Giuseppe, a great lover and expert of wild herbs of the Lucerino countryside. The name Imperatore is a tribute to Frederick II of Swabia, who in medieval times gave prestige to the territory of Daunia and the city of Lucera where the family is originally from. Amaro Imperatore is made with the use of different botanicals, including lampascione, arugula, chamomile, mallow, laurel, carob, and pomegranate.

ALCOHOL CONTENT: 25% vol.
COLOR: amber
BOUQUET: herbaceous hints of laurel prevail
TASTE: balanced, with notes of almond and chamomile
AFTERTASTE: bitter persistence

AMARO LIMOLIVO

Carlucci Food
Torremaggiore, Foggia

Carlucci Food was founded in 2014 thanks to the passion of a group of friends for the Apulian territory and for its main product, extra virgin olive oil.

The company's range of products includes Amaro Limolivo, obtained from the infusion of olive leaves in alcohol. These leaves are pleasant to the taste and naturally rich in polyphenols, which are powerful antioxidants with multiple benefits. Orange and lemon peels are added to the botanical mix.

ALCOHOL CONTENT: 28% vol.
COLOR: dark brown
BOUQUET: persistent hint of olive leaves
TASTE: bitter with orange and lemon flavors
AFTERTASTE: persistence of olive leaves

AMARO MAFFEI

Licor s.r.l.
Gravina in Puglia, Bari

Amaro Maffei is produced in Gravina in Puglia by Gaspare Maffei and Vincenzo Carlucci, founders of Licor, with the intent to enhance the products and the unmistakable scents of the territory. From an old Maffei house recipe comes this amaro, with detoxifying and digestive properties, made from a slow maceration in alcohol (about 30 days) of wild fennel from the Murgia Barese, harvested between the months of December and March.

ALCOHOL CONTENT: 42% vol.
COLOR: emerald green
BOUQUET: vegetal, fresh, and herbaceous scents predominate
TASTE: intense and persistent taste of wild fennel
AFTERTASTE: persistent herbaceous aromas

AMARO MEDITERRANEO

Beltion
Putignano, Bari

Merak Spirits & Drinks is located in Putignano, and today the company includes in its offer the products of the historic Beltion liquor factory whose history began in 1885, when Francesco and Maria Concetta Giannandrea opened a café where they served almond milk prepared with a stone mortar still kept on the farm. Amaro Mediterraneo comes from an ancient recipe of the Giannandrea family that includes the infusion of herbs, spices, barks, berries, and aromatic roots, among which the typically Mediterranean flavors stand out.

ALCOHOL CONTENT: 30% vol.

COLOR: dark brown

BOUQUET: herbaceous hints prevail

TASTE: well balanced between sweet and bitter

AFTERTASTE: persistent citrus finish

AMARO PUGLIESE

Fiume
Putignano, Bari

Amaro Pugliese is the result of the passion for amari of Vittorio Fiume, founder in the early 1960s of the Fiume brand that specialized in the production of liqueurs and almond milk. This amaro with marked digestive, tonic, and detoxifying properties contains the typical scents of the Apulian Murgia and is obtained from 40 botanicals—including cinchona, rhubarb, wormwood, mint, and aloe, as well as orange, saffron, sage, artichoke, and valerian—left to macerate for about three months in a hydro-alcoholic solution.

ALCOHOL CONTENT: 30% vol.

COLOR: dark brown

BOUQUET: fresh and balsamic scents of aromatic herbs

TASTE: pleasant bitterness, with menthol and floral notes

AFTERTASTE: bitter persistence of cinchona and rhubarb

AMARO SALENTO

Amaro Salento s.r.l.
Veglie, Lecce

In Salento, around the middle of the 20th century, homemade production of liqueurs and rosolios was still widespread, while in bars you could find handmade spirits, often added to coffee. Amaro Salento resulted from the Mazzotta family's desire to retrace local traditions through a modern version of amaro that was pleasant and harmonious to the palate by reworking ancient Salentino recipes. Over 45 botanicals are used for its production. Among them are cinchona, gentian, bitter and sweet orange, Roman wormwood, chamomile, columbo, quassia, aloe vera, and calamus. In addition, this amaro features rue, elderberry, fennel, angelica, sandalwood, tonka bean, cinnamon, cloves, clary sage, nutmeg, oregano, thyme, basil, coriander, and cardamom. Today on the market there is also an Amarissimo version of Amaro Salento, for those who prefer their amari old school.

ALCOHOL CONTENT: 30% vol.

COLOR: brown with emerald highlights

BOUQUET: herbaceous and delicate

TASTE: sweetly bitter, complex, and persistent with hints of plants and roots

AFTERTASTE: coffee notes

AMARO ZENZEN

Infuso Natura
Cocumola, Lecce

Infuso Natura is a small family-run, artisanal business that has been operating in the liquor industry since 1995. Their production philosophy is guided by the absolute search for quality, the selection of raw materials, and the full exploitation of the territory. Their offerings include Amaro Zenzen, which is produced from the infusion of ginger alcohol, mint, and botanicals that contribute to making it a good end-of-meal digestif with a fresh and bitter taste.

ALCOHOL CONTENT: 35% vol.
COLOR: light brown
BOUQUET: penetrating mentholated scents
TASTE: balanced between sweet and bitter with a spicy note of ginger
AFTERTASTE: mint and ginger persistence

AMARUM

Fiume
Putignano, Bari

Amarum by Fiume, founded in the early 1960s by Vittorio Fiume, is produced from a mixture of aromatic herbs from Puglia and the Orient, walnuts, and Jamaican rum. The recipe contains more than 30 botanicals, including rhubarb, cinchona, cinnamon, wormwood, cloves, mint, quassia, cascarilla, chamomile, gentian, and cardamom, which are left to macerate in a hydro-alcoholic solution for about three months. Maceration of the walnut husks is about one month in a solution of alcohol, water, and spices.

ALCOHOL CONTENT: 28% vol.
COLOR: amber with sapphire highlights
BOUQUET: penetrating and spicy scents with notes of rum, herbs, and nuts
TASTE: pleasantly bitter, complex, persistent and soft
AFTERTASTE: persistence of nuts and cloves

BILIQ

Fiume
Putignano, Bari

Biliq, an amaro produced by the Fiume company, includes in its formula the use of multiple botanicals, including cinchona, gentian, wormwood, rhubarb, angelica, sweet and bitter orange, lemon, licorice, ginger, coriander, and juniper that are left to macerate in a hydro-alcoholic solution for three months, followed by compression in a wooden press,

according to ancient artisan methods.

ALCOHOL CONTENT: 32% vol.
COLOR: dark brown
BOUQUET: intense and complex with hints of aromatic herbs and citrus peels
TASTE: bitter aromatic with hints of rhubarb, cinchona, and ginger
AFTERTASTE: citrusy persistence with spicy notes

BORSCI ELISIR SAN MARZANO

Caffo
San Marzano di San Giuseppe, Taranto

The Borsci family, originally from the Caucasus, moved from Albania to Puglia during the Middle Ages, following their national hero Giorgio Castriota Scanderbeg. In 1840, Giuseppe Borsci, reworking an ancient recipe that belonged to his ancestors, created the Borsci Elisir San Marzano. Marketed as an "oriental specialty," it represents the oldest liqueur of southern Italy still on the market today.

ALCOHOL CONTENT: 38% vol.
COLOR: dark brown
BOUQUET: bitter hints are very present
TASTE: well balanced between sweet and bitter
AFTERTASTE: herbaceous finish

Basilicata

AMARO LUCANO

Amaro Lucano s.p.a.
Pisticci Scalo, Matera

The history of Amaro Lucano begins in Pisticci, in the province of Matera, where Pasquale Vena was born in 1871. Once an adult, Pasquale and his brothers went to Naples, ready to leave for America in search of fortune. Once in America he worked making pastries. However, he eventually decided pastry making was not right for him. As is known, you can take a Lucanian out of Lucania, but you cannot take Lucania out of a Lucanian: He missed the colors and scents of Pisticci, and so he returned to open a cookie factory. Pasquale Vena also cultivated a passion for herbalism: He tried and tried again different mixtures of herbs, in search of the perfect liqueur. In 1894, after several attempts, he finally found the ideal blend for what was to become Amaro Lucano, destined to become famous all over the world. This amaro is made from 30 different botanicals including bitter orange, wormwood, gentian, muscatel sage, aloe ferox, cnicus, Muscat yarrow, Roman wormwood, angelica, elderflower, and rue.

ALCOHOL CONTENT: 28% vol.

COLOR: intense golden

BOUQUET: hints of quince, cinchona, orange peel, wormwood, and exotic spices

TASTE: complete and complex aromatic bouquet, floral, citrusy, spicy, and herbal notes

AFTERTASTE: bitter and balsamic

L'AMARO DI BARAGIANO

Giuseppe Russo
Baragiano, Potenza

L'Amaro di Baragiano was conceived in 2015 from an idea by Giuseppe Russo, who was motivated by the desire to create an amaro inspired by the unmistakable scents of an herbal tea that his grandfather Nicola prepared to cure all ailments. Among the basic ingredients of the precious recipe are wild chicory and common sow thistle.

ALCOHOL CONTENT: 30% vol.

COLOR: variable, according to the chicory harvest

BOUQUET: very aromatic; hints of wild arugula predominate

TASTE: sweet

AFTERTASTE: soft; chicory finish with bitter persistence

AMARO LUCANO ANNIVERSARIO

Lucano 1894 s.r.l.
Pisticci Scalo, Matera

Amaro Lucano was created in 1894 in Pisticci, in the back shop of the cookie factory of Cavalier Pasquale Vena who, as a lover of herbal medicine, created a special herbal blend characterized by citrus and floral aromas that was soon destined to enter the hearts of Italians. To celebrate 120 years of Lucano 1894, a more robust and bitter version of Amaro Lucano was created, inspired by an ancient recipe by Pasquale Vena. For Amaro Lucano Anniversario, the same botanicals as Amaro Lucano are used for the bitter base—more than 30, including wormwood, holy thistle, and gentian—but dosed differently.

ALCOHOL CONTENT: 34% vol.

COLOR: dark brown

BOUQUET: herbaceous hints prevail

TASTE: well-balanced between sweet and bitter

AFTERTASTE: persistence of bitter herbs

CRITHMUM

Giaskett di Liberatore Gianpaolo & C. sas
Maratea, Potenza

In 2015, Gianpaolo Liberatore and Biagio Schettino founded the Giaskett company in Maratea with the intent to enhance the essences and scents of a territory waiting to be discovered. In search of ancient recipes, the two discovered that on the Tyrrhenian coast of Basilicata, as well as in nearby Cilento, it was customary to eat the succulent leaves of *critini* in salads, a dialectal term that unites two plants that colonize the same coastal areas: sea fennel (*Crithmum maritimum*) and golden samphire (*Limbarda crithmoides*). Both are used for the creation of the amaro Crithmum.

ALCOHOL CONTENT: 32% vol.

COLOR: greenish amber

BOUQUET: intense and balsamic, recalls the typical smell of the Mediterranean shorelines

TASTE: delicate and at the same time pungent, with notes of chamomile that sweeten the marine flavor

AFTERTASTE: intense and persistent

Calabria

AMARO BIZANTINO

Perla di Calabria
Cosenza

Amaro Bizantino is produced by the artisan liquor factory Perla di Calabria from wild herbs that grow in the territories of Corigliano and Rossano, in the province of Cosenza. Among the cornerstones of the company's philosophy are the careful selection of raw materials and the use of traditional processes carried out following ancient recipes, without the use of preservatives or coloring agents of any kind.

ALCOHOL CONTENT: 30% vol.
COLOR: bright brown
BOUQUET: intense hints of aromatic herbs
TASTE: bitter and bursting
AFTERTASTE: bitter and balsamic persistence

AMARO BRETHIUM

Calabro Liquori
Cariati Marina, Cosenza

Calabro Liquori was conceived from an idea by Roberto Maiorano, who is passionate about herbs and good drinking. After graduating in veterinary medicine in Milan, Roberto continued his studies in agriculture at prestigious international universities before returning to his native Calabria and taking over the reins of his family's citrus grove located in Cariati. Here the young man started a 35-acre farm that included citrus groves, olive groves, and arable land. To complete the project, a distillery was made where liqueurs are produced from local raw materials, without the addition of flavors and colorants. These liqueurs include Amaro Brethium whose original recipe was created at the beginning of the 20th century by Donna Rachele, Roberto's great-grandmother. The plant mix necessary for the preparation includes 16 botanicals, including gentian, chicory, bergamot, bitter orange, angelica, arugula, chamomile, peppermint, rhubarb, and wild fennel. The name on the label is inspired by the ancient Brettii (or Bruzi) people who lived in the territory of Cariati between the fourth and third centuries B.C., where the herbs that give life to Brethium are collected.

ALCOHOL CONTENT: 30% vol.
COLOR: amber with green reflections
BOUQUET: vegetal aroma with notes of chicory and fennel
TASTE: bitter to the right point, balsamic and fresh
AFTERTASTE: bitter gentian aroma

AMARO DELL'ABATE

Sapori Silani
San Giovanni in Fiore, Cosenza

The Sapori Silani company of Alessio Antonello is located in San Giovanni in Fiore (Cosenza), in the heart of Sila, and their aim is to enhance the flavors and products of the territory. Their varied offerings include Amaro dell'Abate, inspired by the liquoristic tradition of Florentine monks and obtained from a mixture of herbs. Many of these herbs come from the Silan territory, including cloves, yarrow, juniper, and common centaury that are macerated in distilled water and pure alcohol.

ALCOHOL CONTENT: 35% vol.

COLOR: intense amber

BOUQUET: delicate scents of mountain herbs

TASTE: decisive and aromatic

AFTERTASTE: rich finish with fresh and aromatic notes

AMARO SILANO

Bosco Liquori
Reggio Calabria

Bosco Liquori, founded in 1864 by Raffaello Bosco, was inspired by a family tradition that consisted of the homemade preparation of liqueurs based on Mediterranean herbs. With unchanged passion, Amaro Silano is obtained through slow maceration of botanicals typical of the mountainous Sila plateau region.

ALCOHOL CONTENT: 30% vol.

COLOR: dark amber

BOUQUET: the herbaceous part is very present

TASTE: full-bodied and aromatic

AFTERTASTE: bitter persistence

CEDRAMARO

Officine dei Cedri
Santa Maria del Cedro, Cosenza

Officine dei Cedri was founded in 2012 by Salvatore and Angela with the intent to make known and give luster to the unique flavors of their land of origin. Cedramaro was in fact created to enhance the cedro, the main product of the Riviera dei Cedri, which extends along the Tyrrhenian coast of Calabria. In the recipe for this citrus-flavored amaro, in addition to citron peel, there are also herbs such as dandelion, purslane, edible canna, sage, and laurel, which are cold macerated in ethyl alcohol.

ALCOHOL CONTENT: 28% vol.

COLOR: light brown

BOUQUET: fruity and citrusy scents of cedro predominate

TASTE: soft and well balanced between sweet and bitter

AFTERTASTE: citrusy persistence of citron

FRACK

Vecchio Magazzino Doganale
Cosenza

Frack, "an undisciplined amaro from birth," created by Vecchio Magazzino Doganale, comes from a secret recipe that includes separate infusions and the union of three blends, each with its own character: bitter, round, and spicy. Among the botanicals used are bitter orange, sweet orange, bergamot, rosemary, oregano, gentian, rhubarb, and lemon.

ALCOHOL CONTENT: 24% vol.

COLOR: amber

BOUQUET: herbaceous part very present

TASTE: well balanced, with strong citrusy hints of bergamot and orange

AFTERTASTE: bitter persistence

JEFFERSON

Vecchio Magazzino Doganale
Cosenza

Jefferson, the "important" amaro of Vecchio Magazzino Doganale, is obtained from a mixture of spices and selected aromatic herbs from throughout the Calabrian territory. Among the main botanicals in the recipe are bergamot, bitter orange and sweet orange, rosemary, and oregano. Vecchio Magazzino Doganale is a brand founded by the young Ivano Trombino with the aim of producing "rural liqueurs" that are made as in the past, through single and

separate infusions, freshly processed herbs, and in full respect of the rhythms of nature.

ALCOHOL CONTENT: 30% vol.

COLOR: bronze with copper reflections

BOUQUET: citrus fruits and vanilla predominate

TASTE: citrusy flavors of lemon and grapefruit intertwine with bitter notes of wormwood and gentian

AFTERTASTE: soft with fresh, citrusy returns

VECCHIO AMARO DEL CAPO

Caffo

Limbadi, Vibo Valentia

Vecchio Amaro del Capo, the result of an ancient recipe improved by the experience acquired by four generations of the Caffo family, is a symbolic product of the well-known Calabrian company. Among the 29 botanicals used for the preparation include some with tonic-digestive properties like bitter orange, sweet orange, licorice, mandarin, chamomile, and juniper.

ALCOHOL CONTENT: 35% vol.

COLOR: bronze with copper reflections

BOUQUET: notes of medicinal herbs, orange, and bitter juniper berries

TASTE: very pleasant bitterness with citrus notes

AFTERTASTE: flavors of candied fruit, cinnamon, licorice, and vanilla

VECCHIO AMARO DEL CAPO RISERVA DEL CENTENARIO

Caffo

Limbadi, Vibo Valentia

The history of the Calabrian company Caffo has its roots in the last decade of the 19th century when Giuseppe Caffo, a master distiller, began distilling pomace on the slopes of Mount Etna before taking over an old distillery in Santa Venerina (Catania) in 1915. Vecchio Amaro del Capo Riserva del Centenario was created to celebrate the 100th anniversary (1915–2015) of the historic brand, and it is obtained from the artisan workmanship of many local botanicals and the use of fine brandies aged for a long time in Slavonian oak barrels. The blend obtained is in turn refined in oak barrels to achieve a maximum harmony of taste.

ALCOHOL CONTENT: 37.5% vol.

COLOR: bronze with copper reflections

BOUQUET: medicinal herbs, orange, and juniper berries

TASTE: very pleasant bitterness with citrus notes

AFTERTASTE: candied fruit, cinnamon, licorice, and vanilla

Sicily

AMACARDO BLACK

Amacardo Sicily
Catania

Amacardo Sicily is a young company founded in 2015 by Maurizio Belfiore, a graduate of economics and commerce, to satisfy his great passion for the world of liqueurs and spirits. The idea of creating two amari, Amacardo Black and Amacardo Red, both made with wild artichoke from Etna, was conceived by Maurizio together with Angelo Romeo, a dear friend and great connoisseur of wild plants, who, since he was a young boy, enjoyed collecting small thistle in the hilly terrain around Etna. Amacardo Black is prepared with an infusion of artichoke is blended with other botanicals after only a few months. The Amacardo Black label represents the thistles of the artichoke with its typical colors.

ALCOHOL CONTENT: 30% vol.
COLOR: coffee, slightly viscous
BOUQUET: fresh and herbaceous
TASTE: hints of green tea and artichoke
AFTERTASTE: persistent notes of artichoke

AMACARDO RED

Amacardo Sicily
Catania

With their botanicals, the Amacardo amari (Amacardo Red and Amacardo Black) represent a perfect balance with the surrounding territory. The aromas and essential oils are extracted naturally from the wild artichoke that grows along the slopes of Etna and from the botanicals belonging to the territory, without the use of additives or artificial colors. The infusion of blood oranges from the Catania plain embraces the wild artichoke in a balanced, harmonious, and lively flavor. The labels of both amari were created by a young Sicilian artist, Valerio Contiguglia; the Amacardo Red label abstractly represents a festive tribal dance.

ALCOHOL CONTENT: 30% vol.
COLOR: brown with gold highlights
BOUQUET: highly citrus
TASTE: prevalence of orange with hints of artichoke
AFTERTASTE: long plant and citrus fruit persistence

AMALIME

Giardini di Sicilia
Catania

Since the early 1950s, Giardini di Sicilia has been known in the territory for the production of citrus fruits. Subsequently, the property added a tropical citrus fruit to its production of classic Sicilian citrus fruits, the lime, bringing innovation and new productions. The company is today led by Salvatore Caruso, proud to market Giardini di Sicilia as the first establishment to produce Sicilian lime with which Amalime, the first and only lime amaro of Sicily, was created. The name represents, in a certain sense, in its etymology, the love for one's own land, Sicily. Amalime takes its cue from an old recipe, jealously preserved by Salvatore's grandmother, and its production includes cold maceration of different botanical blends, represented by lime, gentian, rhubarb, sweet orange, bitter orange, juniper, mint, star anise, cumin, and lime leaves that are mixed and stabilized in alcohol before bottling.

ALCOHOL CONTENT: 30% vol.

COLOR: lime green

BOUQUET: notes of fresh lemonade

TASTE: strong and aromatic with an unmistakable scent of Sicilian lime

AFTERTASTE: long aromatic persistence with notes of citrus and spices

AMARA

Rossa Sicily
Misterbianco, Catania

In a farm with a millstone surrounded by acres of citrus groves that embrace a gently hilly landscape in the Catania Plain, between Etna and the Mediterranean, stands the facilities of Rossa Sicily where Amara amaro is produced using PGI-certified blood oranges of Sicily. The production process is totally artisanal and follows unique methods and a secret recipe. After the picking and selection of the oranges, the pulp with which to make marmalade is collected, while the peels are put into alcohol for a certain period. The same procedure is repeated with the selected herbs. Then everything is assembled in a blend, adding water and sugar. Amara amaro needs six months to be ready to drink. The packaging is very simple but captivating, and the beautiful cap sealed with red wax recalls the old preparations of the past.

ALCOHOL CONTENT: 30% vol.

COLOR: amber with gold reflections

BOUQUET: citrusy

TASTE: adequate sweetness, strongly orange

AFTERTASTE: prevailing and persistent note of orange

AMARO 21

Sixilya–Liquor Division
Marsala, Trapani

Amaro 21 is produced by a small artisan company owned by Vincenzo Maggio and Francesco Martinico, respectively a designer and an oenologist. Production takes place in Marsala, the extreme tip of western Sicily, home of the oldest Italian D.O.C. and, above all, the cradle of "splendid civilizations." Obviously, the production of this amaro is managed by Francesco, who carefully mixes the maceration of the 21 botanical elements and follows its production until bottling. The recipe is inspired by an ancient recipe for a decoction made with herbs, roots, and citrus fruits, including aloe, rhubarb, cardamom, cloves, mint, and rosemary. The botanical ingredients that make up this amaro are all of native origin, an absolute guarantee of the Sicilian character of Amaro 21.

ALCOHOL CONTENT: 30% vol.

COLOR: amber with copper reflections

BOUQUET: citrusy, strongly orange

TASTE: agreeable and delicate

AFTERTASTE: bitter and vegetal

AMARO AMURI

Amuri Cose di Sicilia
Campobello di Mazara, Trapani

Friends since childhood, they found each other after a long time: Giacomo, a successful entrepreneur whose occupation ranges from pastry making to catering in the tourism sector, and Antonio and Andrea, who live and work in northern Italy where they import food products of Sicilian excellence. Their love for Sicily is united and translated into the production of amaro liqueurs, the first of which, Amaro Amuri, shares the name of their company. From the right balance of the island's indigenous herbs comes a smooth and brilliant digestive liqueur with herbaceous and floral aromatic notes. This amaro is one of a kind, thanks to the strong presence of wild fennel, a guarantee of aromaticity.

ALCOHOL CONTENT: 32% vol.
COLOR: amber with emerald highlights
BOUQUET: balsamic
TASTE: herbaceous and balsamic
AFTERTASTE: vegetal and long persistence

AMARO AVERNA

Gruppo Campari
Caltanissetta

Around the world, Amaro Averna represents the authentic digestive liqueur, the result of a secret recipe kept in the Benedictine abbey of Caltanissetta and handed down from four generations. The first factory was built in the summer family house in Xiboli (Caltanissetta), which is still operational today. Amaro Averna's success in the world is due in part to Salvatore's son, Francesco, who began to promote amari in Italy and abroad. In 1895, King Umberto I paid tribute to Francesco with a golden brooch with the emblem of the House of Savoy, and in 1912 Vittorio Emanuele III authorized the affixing of the royal coat of arms on the label. In 2014, the Averna Group was acquired by Gruppo Campari. All ingredients of Amaro Averna, including essential oils of lemon peel and bitter orange, pomegranate, herbs, and fruits are carefully selected, painstakingly blended, and infused with pure alcohol.

ALCOHOL CONTENT: 29% vol.
COLOR: brown with ruby shades
BOUQUET: opens with notes of citrus fruits, mixed with the scent of Mediterranean herbs such as myrtle, juniper, rosemary, sage, and aromatic resins

TASTE: orange notes balanced with licorice and Mediterranean herbs
AFTERTASTE: velvety and round

AMARO AVERNA RISERVA DON SALVATORE

Gruppo Campari
Caltanissetta

On the occasion of its 150 years of operation, Gruppo Campari launched a special edition of Amaro Averna. This edition is entirely dedicated to Don Salvatore Averna, founder of this company in 1868. That is the year when he received a handwritten note from Fra Girolamo, monk of the Abbey of the Holy Spirit in Caltanissetta, with the precious recipe of a bitter elixir that is known throughout the world as Amaro Averna. Amaro Averna Riserva Don Salvatore is, in terms of composition and production method, an Amaro Averna in every way, but with an additional 18 months of aging in small oak barrels, which deepen the aromas of Mediterranean scrub and dried fruit, making the drink incredibly soft. This premium amaro is presented in an elegant and refined package.

ALCOHOL CONTENT: 34% vol.

COLOR: coffee, slightly viscous

BOUQUET: honey, rosemary, oregano, and bitter orange

TASTE: citrus fruit and licorice

AFTERTASTE: spicy and persistent

AMARO BAROCCO

Amuri Cose di Sicilia
Campobello di Mazara, Trapano

Amaro Barocco is slightly lower in alcohol content than other amari. It is a product in which the combination of Ribera orange peel and the famous bottled Modica chocolate dominate the final taste. This is another product from Amuri Cose di Sicilia, a company that with the right commercial experience pays particular attention to the packaging of each product. This time the detail of the baroque design on the label captures attention for its beauty and elegance.

ALCOHOL CONTENT: 28% vol.

COLOR: brown with emerald reflections

BOUQUET: orange

TASTE: perfectly balanced between sweet and bitter, hints of citrus fruits

AFTERTASTE: notes of chocolate

AMARO DEL BOSS

Simone Calogero
Favara, Agrigento

This amaro symbolizes the new generation of Sicilian liqueurs that, while respecting ancient and artisanal methods, operates with innovation and progress. This tonic and digestive amaro is created through a skillful infusion of aromatic herbs that requires a long period of maceration. Its alcohol base is a wine brandy aged in Slavonian oak barrels. Numerous Sicilian herbs, flowers, and fruits are immersed in it to obtain the best balance of aromatic peaks. The recipe has been extrapolated from an ancient manuscript belonging to the ancestors of the Simone family, producers of the amaro. It can be considered an amaro for meditation.

ALCOHOL CONTENT: 30% vol.

COLOR: light red

BOUQUET: floral and citrusy, notes of sage and mint

TASTE: alcoholic, fresh, and persistent

AFTERTASTE: sweetish

AMARO DELL'ETNA

Agrosan
Agnone Bagni, Syracuse

"The energy that nature expresses is the most disruptive force that exists, and all this for us must be transferred into one drink." This is the thinking of Fabio Parziano, owner together with Alfio Caramagno of Agrosan, a company that has been producing Amaro dell'Etna since 2000. This amaro, which is different from classic Sicilian amari, bursts on the palate, is sharp in its tenderness, but is very drinkable and "real" like old-time amari. The production philosophy of Agrosan is based on the enhancement of the concept of the "phytocomplex" and everything that a plant can express in terms of energy. Therefore, in the example of the bitter orange, grown in the company's citrus groves, both the peel and the orange blossom are used in such a way that the plant can best express all its "organoleptic" and energetic characteristics. And Etna has botanicals with incredible energy to offer, the same that we find in this amaro that is attained from multiple components (many of which are local), including bitter orange, orange blossom, licorice, wormwood, aloe, gentian, quassia, cinchona, saffron, rhubarb, angelica,

gentianella, myrrh, vanilla, and cinnamon.

ALCOHOL CONTENT: 29% vol.

COLOR: brown with golden highlights; very limpid

BOUQUET: herbaceous hints with notes of orange and vanilla

TASTE: the right bitterness, mitigated by nuances of cinnamon and orange

AFTERTASTE: cocoa

AMARO DEL PRINCIPE

Principe di Corleone-Pollara
Monreale, Palermo

Among the hills of Corleone, in the Malvello and Patria districts, in the heart of the Monreale DOC, one can see the rows of vines grown by Pippo, Vincenzo, and Lea Pollara, siblings who have turned their love for grapes into a passionate trade. This passion is demonstrated by the continuous attention to the evolution and enhancement of the classic wines of Sicily, including production of an amaro: Amaro del Principe. This liqueur is from a secret recipe, and it is produced through cold maceration with medicinal herbs, roots, fruits, flowers, citrus peel, and Sicilian spices that help digestion and present a delicate sensation of pleasure.

ALCOHOL CONTENT: 30% vol.

COLOR: brown with emerald highlights

BOUQUET: citrus fruits and licorice

TASTE: aromatic and slightly balsamic

AFTERTASTE: long, persistent, and spicy

AMARO DI SICILIA

Distillerie dell'Etna dei Fratelli Russo
Santa Venerina, Catania

Distillerie dell'Etna dei Fratelli Russo, whose origins date as far back as 1870, is the only one currently active in eastern Sicily. The brothers, Salvatore and Giuseppe Russo, now in their 80s, can now also count on the valuable support of their children, who have contributed with their creative and innovative spirit and their ambition, while fully respecting tradition, to making the company increasingly competitive and at the forefront of Italian and foreign markets. Although the Russo family is a family of fine distillers, the great-grandparents of the current owners decided to start production of the most difficult liqueur: amaro. They chose the most characteristic herbs and roots of Etna's botanical heritage, and they reached perfection with the addition of an infusion of

oranges and lemons to complete the botanicals already present: laurel, cinnamon, cinchona, cloves, coriander, gentian, licorice, mint, nutmeg, rosemary, and elderberry.

ALCOHOL CONTENT: 32% vol.

COLOR: brown with copper highlights

BOUQUET: citrus fruits and balsamic notes

TASTE: delicate and fresh with citrus and aromatic herbs and spicy notes

AFTERTASTE: honey and peppermint

AMARO FLORIO

Duca di Salaparuta
Marsala, Trapani

This company was founded in Marsala in 1833 by the entrepreneur Vincenzo Florio who bought a piece of land on a stretch of beach located between the rural farms of Ingham-Whitaker and Woodhouse to build a plant for the production of Marsala wine. The first years of the winery were very difficult, with little income and few prospects, but the entrepreneur did not give up and continued to work by diversifying his business and investing in transport and maritime activities. Marsala wine began to establish itself 20 years later, which was the time necessary to refine it and make it better and more balanced, using barrels of American oak. Florio thus became one of Italy's iconic companies, and it was visited by Giuseppe Garibaldi in 1860. The Company's Florio Elisir—Florio's elisir—amaro was created from a secret recipe made up of 13 different botanicals left to improve in barrels for 18 months. This amaro was referred to as "the Company's" because for many years it was reserved for Florio's fleet, which transported colonial foodstuffs and spices from the Far East.

ALCOHOL CONTENT: 32% vol.

COLOR: hazelnut with copper reflections

BOUQUET: citrus fruits

TASTE: soft and balanced, orange dominates the palate

AFTERTASTE: pleasant bitter notes

AMARO GERLANDO

Gerlando Group
Caltagirone, Catania

The name of this Sicilian amaro was conceived to honor the knight Beato Gerlando D'Alemagna, one of the last soldiers of the Order of the Knight's Templar, who has always been surrounded by a halo of mystery that feeds myths and legends. When Pope Clement V decreed the closure of the Order in 1314 and Philip the Handsome, King of France, had the last Grand Master burned at the stake, Gerlando took up residence in the small church of Our Lady of the Temple of Caltagirone, of which he became the guardian and protector of the weakest. Devotion to him was so deeply felt that, in 1327, his remains were transferred to the Basilica of San Giacomo Maggiore in Caltagirone. Amaro Gerlando comes to life from a process of cold maceration of fresh herbs and spices, among which we can recognize allspice, cinnamon, and star anise.

ALCOHOL CONTENT: 34% vol.

COLOR: amber with honey reflections

BOUQUET: fresh and citrusy

TASTE: herbaceous and spicy

AFTERTASTE: long vegetal persistence

AMARO HENNÀ

Amuri Cose di Sicilia
Campobello di Mazara, Trapani

Giacomo, Andrea, and Antonio, in producing their amaro liqueurs, have created a line of flavors that does not leave out any of the wonderful and characteristic scents of Sicily. Amaro Hennà could not do otherwise than to have the almond of Agrigento in its blend of botanicals and plants that are endemic to the territory, in a winning combination with the fragrant oranges of Ribera. Every sip is like a bite into one of the delicious almond paste cookies typical of Sicilian confectionery culture.

ALCOHOL CONTENT: 28% vol.

COLOR: amber

BOUQUET: irrepressible almond

TASTE: almond takes over

AFTERTASTE: mainly citrus fruit

AMARO INDIGENO

Malìa65
Catania

Amaro Indigeno is produced by Malìa65, a company founded by two women: Agata Di Fede, born in 1965, a cooking teacher for foreigners, and Rita Cocuzza, a journalist and writer. Raised on the sounds of the famous Italian TV show *Carosello*, with Ernesto Calindri and Gino Cervi, both founders were passionate about botanicals and Etnean cuisine, and both were tired of the wear and tear of everyday life with three children each. They decided together to shake up their lives and unleash their skills and imagination, thus creating the bitter kiss of the volcano, the first pomegranate amaro from Sicily. Amaro Indigeno is produced through cold maceration, using a mix of 11 different botanicals. The fruity note is composed of Sicilian pomegranate juice, a fundamental and peculiar element of the product, contained in a higher percentage than the infusions of carob and sweet orange peel. The name chosen for this amaro exalts the spirit of the place and suggests the autochthonous origin of the elements that compose it.

ALCOHOL CONTENT: 32% vol.
COLOR: brownish amber
BOUQUET: citrusy
TASTE: fruity, thanks to pomegranate combined with orange peel and carob
AFTERTASTE: bitter and fresh from the wild herbs of Etna

AMARO K1

Perollo–Food & Beverage International
Sciacca, Agrigento

Amaro K1 is the brainchild of a team of experienced entrepreneurs in the food industry, Food & Beverage International, who have joined together to create a line of high-quality products that are made with respect for centuries-old traditions and are strictly *Made in Italy*. The group's passion for excellence led to the creation of the Perollo line of products that includes Amaro K1. Conceived at the foot of Mount Kronio, aka Mount San Calogero, Amaro K1 is a digestive liqueur based on herbs and citrus fruits, produced according to an ancient Sicilian recipe, including sweet and bitter orange peel, aloe vera, mint, rhubarb, and gentian. Although bitter, it can be very versatile in mixing drinks.

ALCOHOL CONTENT: 30% vol.
COLOR: deep mahogany
BOUQUET: citrus fruits, mint, and rhubarb
TASTE: persistent, soft, and embracing
AFTERTASTE: bitter, yet warm and persistent

AMARO MÈNNULA

Mènnula
Valverde, Catania

Preparing an amaro is a rather simple operation, but creating a fine amaro with character requires ambition and intuition! You need to know how to recognize quality ingredients, search for union, and connect with their essence. Giovanni Samperi, creator of Amaro Mènnula, knows this well. Giovanni, as a restaurateur, has thought well to create an amaro with almonds that grow around his restaurant. This is an all-Sicilian amaro, just like its name *mènnula*, which means almond in the Sicilian dialect. In its composition, Amaro Mènnula also includes orange peel, wormwood, and gentian (planted on farmland on the slopes of Etna). Amaro Mènnula is inspired by the love between two young people recounted in a Greek legend: Phyllis, the princess of Thrace, and Acamas, son of Theseus. It is a poignant love story shattered by the sudden death of the beautiful princess. The goddess Athena turned Phyllis into a perennial almond tree. Acamas, upon his return, learned of the transformation of his beloved and abandoned himself among the "herbs" in an eternal embrace: "Mènnula."

ALCOHOL CONTENT: 30% vol.
COLOR: amber, with brick-red reflections
BOUQUET: intense herbaceous and balsamic scents with the addition of Sicilian almond
TASTE: the palate is warm and pleasantly bitter
AFTERTASTE: full-bodied and characterized by good persistence back on the nose

AMARO MIDÒ

Midò
Syracuse

Amaro Midò, a Sicilian amaro, is the brainchild of Francesco Midolo, from which it also takes its name. It is an amaro that uses the energy of the Mediterranean sun, which is symbolized in the blend of PGI-designated oranges from the Conca d'Oro, carob collected from wild plants and rich in healing properties, and aromatic herbs. It is an amaro with digestive properties that is also good as an aperitif. It is produced through the blend of different infusions of carob and orange peels with the macerations of medicinal herbs. After a rest period that establishes balance and equilibrium,

it is bottled after filtration. The recipe is jealously kept secret.

ALCOHOL CONTENT: 30% vol.
COLOR: hazelnut with gold highlights
BOUQUET: herbaceous and bright
TASTE: the carob immediately takes the palate with notes of chocolate
AFTERTASTE: balsamic

AMARO MONTE POLIZO

Alicia Liquori
Salemi, Trapano

Alicia Liquori, an artisanal company founded in 2003, was born from the passion of winemaker Vincenzo Distefano, and is today carried on with great pride and dedication by his loved ones. The oenologist, driven by the desire to create a product with a unique and inimitable taste, containing all the flavors and aromas of his beloved land, created Amaro Monte Polizo, an exclusive blend of 30 herbs and spices, including cinnamon, peppermint, sweet oranges from Sicily, clary sage, star anise, and cardamom. Alicia Liquori's guiding philosophy is to limit the production of every single product to the exclusive advantage of excellence and high quality, creating a genuine product with unique flavor while maintaining the good taste of things made with love.

ALCOHOL CONTENT: 30% vol.
COLOR: mahogany
BOUQUET: fresh and citrusy
TASTE: well-balanced between sweet and bitter with distinct notes of citrus fruits
AFTERTASTE: clean and herbaceous with fresh hints of mint

AMARO NEBROS

La Casa della Natura
Sinagra, Messina

La Casa della Natura is a young artisanal liquor company founded in 2012. Their master herbalist is Attilio Faranda, who runs the business with his two daughters Rossana and Sonia. Amaro Nebros brings together the characteristics of the surrounding area, and "exploits" the raw materials that are abundant in the Nebrodi Mountains. Its recipe has been perfected following the manuscripts of Father Bernardino of Ucria, a great botanist who lived from 1739 to 1796, and founder of the botanical garden of Palermo. The main ingredient of Nebros is *centaurea minore* (minor centaury), an herb rich in digestive and bittering properties. The other botanicals in this amaro are helichrysum, nepitella, cinnamon, peppermint, orange peel, wild fennel, and cloves.

ALCOHOL CONTENT: 25% vol.

COLOR: amber with emerald highlights

BOUQUET: herbaceous and rooty

TASTE: bitter and dry

AFTERTASTE: mentholated with very long persistence

AMARO NEPÈTA

Nepèta

Syracuse

The Nepèta project was conceived in Syracuse in 2017 by Federico and Andrea. Their commitment is aimed at reclaiming a Sicilian herb unknown to most people: nepitella (*Calamintha nepeta*), or lesser calamint. It is a perennial aromatic plant similar in aroma to mint, growing at 1,600 feet (500 m) on the rocky plateaus of the Hyblaean Mountains. Their first production with nepitella was an amaro and then a chocolate. For the production of Amaro Nepèta, Federico and Andrea have farmed nepitella in certified organic fields. After harvesting, it is infused in top-quality alcohol for a week and then combined with a blend of Syracuse PGI-designated lemons and Sicilian bittering herbs.

ALCOHOL CONTENT: 28% vol.

COLOR: clear, slightly amber

BOUQUET: herbaceous

TASTE: mentholated and dry, thanks to citrus fruits

AFTERTASTE: fresh persistence that somehow recalls the taste of an excellent Cuban mojito

AMARO NOSTRUM

Primoti

Santa Venerina, Catania

Amaro Nostrum is the fruit of an ancient recipe handed down from generation to generation by a family of excellent distillers. The fact that the recipe's main ingredient is seaweed makes the production of Amaro Nostrum very precious. The mix of prestigious Sicilian oranges, aloe, cinchona, and of course seaweed, together with other botanicals of the Sicilian territory, gives life to one of the most interesting amari in Sicily. It represents a journey through time and taste, research, history, tradition, and mythology.

ALCOHOL CONTENT: 32% vol.

COLOR: amber with gold highlights

BOUQUET: citrus fruits accompanied by a vegetal scent

TASTE: full and spicy flavor where orange dominates

AFTERTASTE: persistent spicy and vegetal note

AMARO PUNICO

Punico Liquori

Marsala, Trapani

A splendid Sicilian amaro produced in Marsala, kingdom of the eponymous liqueur. Here the three Maltese brothers met to set up a company totally focused on this amaro, the flagship product of the Punico Liquori company, which has grown exponentially throughout the country over the years. This amaro was the brainchild of their father, an important Sicilian liqueurist, Vito Maltese, who created the recipe on commission of a friend who was a producer of dessert wines. Amaro Punico is made with 30 different botanicals with a single cold maceration involving herbs such as wild fennel, mint, sage, laurel, rosemary, and oregano, and spices such as cinnamon, cloves, star anise, coriander, licorice, and cinchona roots. Amaro Punico contains no artificial colors: the only sweetener used is burned sugar.

ALCOHOL CONTENT: 30% vol.

COLOR: brown with ruby reflections

BOUQUET: balanced with citrus notes

TASTE: agreeable and balanced

AFTERTASTE: bitter and vegetal

AMARO SHURHUQ

I Due Mori di Roberta Giangrande
Palermo

Amaro Shurhuq is produced with a high percentage (28 percent) of pure Sicilian pomegranate juice. The word *shurhuq* means sirocco, a warm wind from the southeast, just like the pomegranate fruit. The pomegranate juice is mixed with an infusion of Sicilian orange peel and another of wild fennel. The pomegranate juice is produced by pressing the fresh fruit to maintain the nutritional values of vitamins, antioxidants, and natural minerals. The label on the bottle shows a Moor in a turban with a pomegranate at the apex.

ALCOHOL CONTENT: 30% vol.
COLOR: rosé
BOUQUET: the pomegranate releases its irrepressible scent
TASTE: fruity, bitter, and sour to just the right degree
AFTERTASTE: pomegranate juice accompanies a pleasant, almost summery finish

AMARO TERRAMARA

Amuri Cose di Sicilia
Campobello di Mazara, Trapani

This amaro breaks the mold of Amuri products because it exploits the strong scent typical of the Sicilian lemon and the aroma of the laurel of the Belice Valley in its botanical blend. The name of this amaro (roughly, "bitter land") reminds us that, as beautiful as it is, Sicily has often been a place of unpleasant events, the result of deep-rooted problems that have accompanied it for hundreds of years. This amaro encapsulates the true and strong flavors of a Sicily rich in flavor and tradition. In every Amuri product you can breathe the love for the Sicilian land that the three young producers know how to transfer into each of their creations in a different way, but always wonderful and impeccable.

ALCOHOL CONTENT: 28% vol.
COLOR: straw yellow
BOUQUET: citrus fruits
TASTE: aromatic and citrusy
AFTERTASTE: long citrus persistence

AMARU SABBENERICA

Amari Siciliani
Santa Flavia, Palermo

The adventure of the Amari Siciliani company began, almost by accident, in 2014. In the Carmuco family restaurant in Bagheria, in the province of Palermo, they serve a house amaro that is made using an old family recipe. The customers of the restaurant loved this amaro and began asking about buying it, and thus the Amaru Sabbenerica was born. Its name refers to an ancient greeting used until the 1950s that literally means "be blessed." The label depicting a man with a typical Sicilian *coppola* cap was drawn by hand by one of the company's four partners, Massimo. The recipe includes an alcohol infusion of several secret botanicals among which we can identify as artichoke, laurel, lemon, ginger, gentian, and juniper.

ALCOHOL CONTENT: 28% vol.
COLOR: amber with orange highlights
BOUQUET: recognizable nuances of herbs and citrus fruits
TASTE: embracing and citrusy with notes of gentian
AFTERTASTE: persistent hints of lemon and fresh sensations of juniper

AMARU UNNIMAFFISSU

Beverage Distribution
San Giovanni La Punta, Catania

In the Sicilian dialect, *unnimaffissu* means a mania, an obsession. Behind Amaro Unnimaffissu is the obstinacy and initiative of a young entrepreneur in the Sicilian catering sector. In 2013, after developing a unique combination of prickly pear, carob, and orange juice infusions, a mixture of herbs was added, turning a rosolio into an amaro. Importantly, the ingredients and products are all natural from the territory, including carob, coming from the Consortium of Modica.

ALCOHOL CONTENT: 26% vol.

COLOR: brown with emerald highlights

BOUQUET: citrus and vegetal

TASTE: sweet; you can taste the prickly pear and orange

AFTERTASTE: bitter finish with hints of carob

ARÀNCIU

Magiantosa
Paternò, Catania

Matteo, Gianfranco, Antonio aka Tonio, and Santi, with the steady support of grandmother Sara, the owner of the Fiorini pharmacy and accidental master herbalist, made another attempt at creating an amaro and, in 2018, put Arànciu on the market. It is an amaro that uses the same botanicals used for Lumìa, produced in 2016, and it is left to macerate for 60 days. For Arànciu, like for Lumìa, at the end of the maceration period the peels of oranges (that were picked at the foot of Etna) are added to the mix of herbs. It is bottled and sealed by hand with a shellac seal, an unmistakable characteristic of Magiantosa artisanal production. Magiantosa liqueurs are the result of pharmaceutical research handed down to preserve the scents of Sicily from the past. The whole process is done manually, and every single fruit is the result of an autochthonous cultivation with everything *Made in Italy*.

ALCOHOL CONTENT: 30% vol.

COLOR: very light orange

BOUQUET: citrus fruits

TASTE: orange pervades the palate

AFTERTASTE: persistent bitterness of orange essential oils

BATÒ

Carlo Pellegrino & C.
Marsala, Trapani

The historic Sicilian brand, Cantine Pellegrino, presents the new label of Batò, an amaro made according to an ancient recipe that is still jealously guarded today. The name Batò derives from the Italianization of the word *bateau* (boat in French). At the end of the 18th century, the French liquorist Oscar Despagne, who had been purposely called by Paolo Pellegrino, came to the island to avail himself of his proven technical skills. Despagne created an amaro inspired by the great French liqueur tradition, but it was characterized by the warm and embracing notes that are typical of the Mediterranean. This amaro is obtained by slow and long maceration in alcohol of a selection of medicinal herbs and essences.

ALCOHOL CONTENT: 33% vol.

COLOR: deep brown

BOUQUET: balsamic and aromatic scents typical of the Mediterranean maquis with evident notes of bitter oranges, mint, cocoa, licorice, and roasted coffee

TASTE: balanced, mainly bitter, soft, and round

AFTERTASTE: sweet notes but not cloying

L'AMARO LIMONIO

Limonio
Partinico, Palermo

Limonio was founded in the early 1990s as the brilliant brainchild of Vincenzo Russo. The family farm, which has been producing citrus fruits, mulberries, prickly pears, olives, and wine grapes for at least two centuries, had never experimented with the production, bottling, and marketing of liqueurs based on fruit and spices, even though it possessed the raw material and the perfect recipe had been handed down through the Russo family for years. In Partinico, where the company is located, in addition to fruit liqueurs and aromatic plants, they produce a very good amaro, created with medicinal herbs and fruit from the hills around Palermo. The care of the packaging is in the hands of Giusy Russo, current standard-bearer of the new generation of liqueur makers.

ALCOHOL CONTENT: 30% vol.
COLOR: intense orange with gold reflections
BOUQUET: intense citrus fragrance
TASTE: soft and sweet; Sicilian orange predominates
AFTERTASTE: vegetal

LUMÌA

Magiantosa
Paternò, Catania

Behind the Magiantosa brand there are four young partners who, using a prescription prepared by their pharmacist grandmother, created their first product in 2016: Lumìa. It is a handmade lemon amaro with a fresh and delicate character obtained through the selection of 20 dry botanicals placed inside a silo for 60 days with pure alcohol. Afterward, dried peels of Fior di Sicilia lemons are added, picked one by one at the foot of Etna. After about 24 hours, Lumìa is bottled and hermetically and manually sealed with shellac. *Lumìa* means lemon in the Paternò dialect. The softness and the presence of citrus fruits makes this amaro an excellent element for mixing, and for the creation of great classics or beautiful twists.

ALCOHOL CONTENT: 30% vol.
COLOR: clear gold
BOUQUET: citrusy and fresh
TASTE: full and fresh lemon notes
AFTERTASTE: persistent citrus note combined with herbaceous scents

ROSSO AMARO

Rosso Sicilia
Syracuse

Rosso Amaro is the only amaro produced with Nero d'Avola—the prince of Sicilian grape varieties for red wine—and a mix of herbs and plants typical of the Sicilian countryside, from laurel to thyme and carob, and, of course, bitter orange and lemon peel. The first production phase begins in the cellar, with the infusion of some herbs in the Nero d'Avola. The second is typical of the production of amari: infusion of plants and herbs in alcohol. The process ends with the mixing of the two infusions and the addition of sugar. The recipe does not use water.

ALCOHOL CONTENT: 28% vol.
COLOR: intense and lively ruby red
BOUQUET: embracing and intense, with distinct notes of juniper, licorice, and aromatic herbs, from thyme to laurel, mixed with the aroma of morello cherry and orange peel
TASTE: full and deep
AFTERTASTE: pleasantly bitter and balanced, very persistent

Sardinia

AMARO ARISTOCRATICO

Marco Pistone
Olbia, Olbia-Tempio, Sassari

Amaro Aristocratico was conceived in 2019, the brainchild of Marco Pistone, to celebrate the unmistakable fragrances of Sardinia, like those you can breathe just outside Olbia airport. The characteristic botanical mix includes helichrysum, white fennel, white myrtle leaves, orange peel, cinchona, and gentian.

ALCOHOL CONTENT: 28% vol.
COLOR: deep brown
BOUQUET: balsamic and floral
TASTE: pleasant sweetness with strong balsamic notes
AFTERTASTE: spicy and citrusy with hints of chinotto

AMARO BÀTTORO

Bàttoro Liquori di Sardegna
Silius, Cagliari

The Bàttoro brand was founded in 2008 and takes its name from a word in the Sardinian dialect of Logudorese that means "four." Like the four Moors depicted on the Sardinian flag and the four main components of Amaro Bàttoro, including lemon, walnut, and

myrtle—plus "an idea" of putting together botanicals belonging to different genres and collected at different times of the year.

ALCOHOL CONTENT: 31% vol.
COLOR: dark brown
BOUQUET: delicate and vanilla
TASTE: bitter but pleasant with hints of walnut and vanilla
AFTERTASTE: persistence of vanilla, walnut, and lemon

AMARO DEI SARDI

Distilleria Mario Pacini
Elmas, Cagliari

The history of Distilleria Mario Pacini has its roots in the years of World War II when Bruno Pacini decided to begin his adventure in the world of spirits. Since then, there have been three generations of liquorists who have worked in full respect of family traditions. Among the company's flagship products is Amaro dei Sardi, of which only a few of the botanicals used are known: cinchona, laurel, gentian, and myrtle leaves.

ALCOHOL CONTENT: 30% vol.

COLOR: caramelish amber

BOUQUET: distinct hints of myrtle leaves and gentian

TASTE: firm and round with notes of the Mediterranean maquis

AFTERTASTE: agreeable with a bitter finish

AMARO MONTANARU

Arbisos
Desulo, Nuoro

Alberto Casula is the sole owner of the Arbisos company located in Desulo (Nuoro) where women continue to wear the old traditional clothes, in the mountains of Gennargentu ruled by *Ierru, Eranu, Istade, Atognu*: winter, spring, summer, autumn. Among the outstanding products of the Arbisos company is Amaro Montanaru, which is made from a mix of typical botanicals from the area, including caraway, thyme, helichrysum, thistle, peppermint, laurel, yarrow, gentian, and blackberry bramble. The aromatic bouquet is enriched by an infusion of old-fashioned Sardinian apples.

ALCOHOL CONTENT: 25% vol.

COLOR: light brown

BOUQUET: very present herbaceous scents

TASTE: balanced with notes of Sardinian apple

AFTERTASTE: bitter finish

AMARO MONTE NIEDDU

Distilleria Mario Pacini
Elmas, Cagliari

The Pacini liquor factory is a family-run business that has been producing syrups, traditional Sardinian liqueurs, and Italian liqueurs since 1944. Amaro Monte Nieddu is one of the flagship products of the Elmas-based company, whose recipe has always remained secret.

ALCOHOL CONTENT: 24% vol.

COLOR: amber

BOUQUET: the grassy element is very present

TASTE: well balanced between sweet and bitter

AFTERTASTE: rather soft finish

CARCIO'

Saint Martino
Cagliari

The San Martino company was founded in 1987 by Maria Antonietta and Alesssandro, and over the years it has been able to establish itself as a production company thanks to the wide range of liqueurs whose labels are all hand-drawn. The Carcio' amaro is made from the combination of thistle and Sardinian artichoke, harvested and defoliated in February, and then put into an infusion for a period of three weeks.

ALCOHOL CONTENT: 23% vol.

COLOR: deep green

BOUQUET: penetrating wild scents prevail

TASTE: robust and austere, bitter but pleasant

AFTERTASTE: herbaceous finish with notes of thistle and artichoke

CHRYSOS

Silvio Carta s.r.l.
Zeddiani, Oristano

Chrysos is produced by the Silvio Carta company, founded in the early 1950s and one of the most prestigious businesses in the area. At the head of the company today is Elio, the founder's son, who carries on the family tradition in close connection with the nature that surrounds him. Chrysos is an amaro made from a high-quality alcohol infusion of helichrysum, a plant whose flowers are characterized by an intense golden yellow color; in fact, helichrysum derives its name from the combination of two Greek words *hélios* (sun) and *chrysós* (gold).

ALCOHOL CONTENT: 23% vol.

COLOR: dark brown

BOUQUET: marine and maquis scents prevail

TASTE: pleasantly aromatic

AFTERTASTE: persistence of Sardinian helichrysum

MIRTAMARO

Bresca Dorada
Località Cann'è Frau,
Muravera, Cagliari

In 1986, Paolo Melis and Enrico Diana founded Bresca Dorada, a company located in an oasis of Mediterranean maquis in the heart of Agro di Muravera, where excellent honey was initially produced. A few years later, they developed a unique liqueur made with honey mixed with myrtle, which became the company's flagship product. The desire to bring the authentic scents of Sardinia to the table continued to inspire Paolo and Emilio, who, after many tests and experiments, in search of the difficult balance between bitter, balsamic, spicy, and citrus notes, developed Mirtamaro. Mirtamaro is obtained from an infusion of ripe myrtle berries that is combined with a series of infusions of herbs and aromatic plants gathered from the mountains of Gennargentu to the eastern coasts of Sardinia. Among the botanicals used are helichrysum, rosemary, arbutus, mastic, juniper, lavender, phillyrea, heather, eucalyptus, and mallow. For the production of this amaro, which features an intense taste and wild character, there is no use of colorants, flavors, or stabilizers; it is therefore a totally natural product.

ALCOHOL CONTENT: 30% vol.

COLOR: rust, slightly opaque

BOUQUET: bursting with hints of myrtle and mauve

TASTE: pleasantly bitter with a balsamic and embracing finish

AFTERTASTE: mentholated

Amari from Europe

Wʜᴇɴ traveling around Europe it is easy to notice the numerous convents, monasteries, and abbeys that dot the landscape. It doesn't matter whether they are in France, Spain, Switzerland, Germany, Hungary, or the Czech Republic: In each of them, the day was marked by the same moments, from waking up to evening vespers, from activities in the orchard to tending the botanical garden. In short, the hours were divided between prayer and work, according to one rule that the Benedictines expressed succinctly as *Ora et labora*. All of this is to remind us that historically, in the monastic sphere, the preparation of lotions, infusions, alcohols, and tinctures with healthy and medicinal purposes was not just an "Italian Job." Everything started, it is true, from the Medical School of Salerno, but from then on, first thanks to the Franciscan order, then to that of the Jesuits, this knowledge reached every single convent or abbey on the European continent. We will therefore now take off together for a short trip to the most secret and hidden places in Europe where, still today, amari are produced in the old way, the result of the work of the new evangelists of amaro, scholars and enthusiasts who have gone back through the centuries looking to reproduce the flavors of yesteryear. How? By reinterpreting recipes of ecclesiastical origin with the hope of converting their fellow citizens to the ancient pleasures of the spirits of the old school and distracting them for a moment from all the distillates from all over the world that have nearly led to their extinction.

AMER GENTIANE

France

This type of French bitter liqueur in some way represents the "category" in France. It is nice to dwell on Amer Gentiane because of the great passion behind this bitter liqueur produced by Distillerie de Grandmont. Behind Amer Gentiane's project lies the name of Matt Sabbagh, who, a few years ago, while he was the international director for Pernod-Ricard, was commissioned to revive old brands of French culture, partly forgotten because of new products arriving from all over the world. The first step for Matt was to revalorize absinthe, a historic mugwort liqueur, through the reopening of a new factory in Thuir in the South of France. Here he met Karim Karoum, a collector of bottles of ancient spirits and liquors, with whom he began a collaboration that soon turned into friendship. The two of them later decided to found a company, the Distillerie de Grandmont, in order to give new life to the "ancient" spirits characterized by the flavors of the past. Amer Gentiane is the product that most resembles the Suze from more than a century ago, a recipe with a high concentration of gentian. It is an amaro produced through the

maceration process of various herbs and types of gentian from Aubrac, a town in the Massif Central, with the addition of a distillate of gentian.

ALCOHOL CONTENT: 32% vol.
COLOR: dark goldish yellow
BOUQUET: floral with notes of berries
TASTE: round and full, the bitter part envelops the palate; strong persistence of gentian and angelica
AFTERTASTE: aromatic and floral; elegant citrus finale

APPENZELLER ALPENBITTER

Switzerland

In Appenzel, immersed in the beautiful Swiss mountains, and where you can still vote by a show of hands, the Appenzeller Alpenbitter AG liquor company, producer of an amaro of the same name, was founded. The business was started by Emil Ebneter who opened a liquor store in 1902. In 1908, together with his brother-in-law Beat Kölbener, Emil founded Emil Ebneter & Co. AG, which continued until 2006. The company is still family-run today. It is run by the third and fourth generation of liquorists, including Beat Kölbener and Walter Regli, the only two people who have the secret recipe for the Appenzeller Alpenbitter, which was first produced in 1908 as a medicinal remedy to stimulate digestive activities and to treat gastrointestinal problems.

Since then, it has been produced with 100 percent natural ingredients, without chemical additives, following the original formula, so much so that it is considered by many to be the Swiss national drink. Appenzeller Alpenbitter is produced from 42 botanicals, including herbs, barks, roots, leaves, fruits, tubers, and seeds, many of which come from the surrounding area. The bottle label features an image of L'Äscher-Wildkirchli, an Alpine restaurant famous for its unusual location in the mountains.

ALCOHOL CONTENT: 29% vol.
COLOR: amber with emerald highlights
BOUQUET: balsamic and licorice notes
TASTE: moderately sweet, gentle, and quite pleasant; the bitter part comes later without disturbing the balance
AFTERTASTE: mint and licorice

BECHEROVKA

Czech Republic

Becherovka was created more than 200 years ago in Karlovy Vary, West Bohemia. The mayor of this town was, back in 1805, Josef Vitus Becher, a pharmacist with a passion for herbs, who was always involved in the production of medicinal alcoholic potions and who experimented in a workshop just outside the town. One day, Josef received a visit from Count Maxmilian Friedrich von Plettenberg-Wittem-Mietingen accompanied by four of his servants and his personal physician, Dr. Frobrig, an Englishman who was also passionate about herb maceration in alcohol. After a series of exchanges and discussions on the subject, the English doctor released a "miraculous" formula that Josef took two years to codify and then gave birth to the English bitter—to be taken in drops to aid digestion—later called Becherovka. Even today the production of Becherovka is still marked by the same timing: Wednesday was and still is the day of the weighing of the 32 secret botanicals for which the palate can recognize cinnamon, lemon balm, and cloves. There are only two copies of the original recipe: one is locked in the safe of the company headquarters in Karlovy Vary, the other is in the Parisian vault of the French group that now owns the brand, Pernod Ricard.

ALCOHOL CONTENT: 38% vol.
COLOR: straw-yellow; clear and clean
BOUQUET: herbaceous with hints of cinnamon
TASTE: moderately sweet, fruity, slightly mentholated, and bitterish
AFTERTASTE: herbaceous and slightly spicy

BORGMANN 1772
Germany

The Borgmann family was part of the body of pharmacists at the court of the Duke of Brunswick, as confirmed in a letter signed by the Duke himself dated June 6, 1772, which included their activity among the privileged pharmacies of the kingdom so as not to confuse it with the many "wild" pharmacies found around the area. The Borgmann 1772 amaro was created in the same year by Wolfgang Borgmann, after a long period of laboratory tests, thanks to his knowledge of the therapeutic effects of local herbs. Over the generations, the formula remained unchanged, only to be adapted to the times in 1976. The production process takes about 10 days and the most important botanicals that make up the mixture are cinnamon, cloves, bitter orange, galanga, gentian, and cinchona bark. Since 2005, this amaro has been experiencing a period of rebirth thanks to the commitment and passion of two brothers, Hendrik and Jan Borgmann, who, together with their old friend Jörn Clausen, decided to make Borgmann 1772 more youthful and accessible, starting with a redesign of the label.

ALCOHOL CONTENT: 39% vol.
COLOR: amber with bronze reflections
BOUQUET: balsamic hints of eucalyptus, mint, and licorice prevail
TASTE: initially sweet, but quickly balanced by strong herbaceous notes, hints of cinchona, and mountain pine
AFTERTASTE: warm and full of cinnamon, licorice, and cloves

FERNET DEL FRATE
Switzerland

Tempus Fugit Spirits is a company that aims to give life to new spirits that unleash the fragrances and flavors of the past by revisiting historical recipes such as the Fernet del Frate. This product, which is the result of extensive research, originates from an ancient formula attributable to a monk, Friar Angelico Fernet, who, according to some investigations, was responsible for the creation of many herbal elixirs and tonics. This fernet was created for medicinal purposes to counter the effects of cholera and malaria, and later was used as a universal remedy, a laxative, or a hangover cure. According to tradition, Tempus Fugit's Fernet del Frate is obtained through a mixture of botanical elements that include aloe, cinchona, gentian, anise, angelica, mint, and myrrh. The

latter ingredient along with saffron are the decisive elements for the success of the best fernet.

ALCOHOL CONTENT: 44% vol.

COLOR: almost black with golden reflections

BOUQUET: balsamic with hints of licorice

TASTE: very bitter, but pleasantly balanced by a mentholated note

AFTERTASTE: licorice predominates; long persistence

GOTLAND'S BITTAR

Sweden

Gotland's Bittar was created on a large island, Gotland, in the Baltic Sea, where the largest town is Visby, home of the impressive Sankta Maria Cathedral and the remains of the ancient churches of Sankt Nicolai and Sankta Katarina, just outside the city. Since 1995, this island has also hosted a modern brewery, Gotlands Bryggeri, which, after changing the concept of beer drinking in Sweden, created and marketed in 2009 a wonderful amaro called Gotland's Bittar, produced using 30 different botanicals, many of them native. The aim of creating this amaro was to concentrate the flavors and fragrances of an ideal garden full of aromatic herbs from the Baltic Sea in a bottle—herbs that have been used for thousands of years by local people as medicines with beneficial effects for the heart and for digestion. A particularity that distinguishes

Gotland's Bittar and that fully identifies the producer is the addition to the blend of a beer distillate aged in French oak barrels for 12 months.

ALCOHOL CONTENT: 38% vol.

COLOR: coffee, similar to a licorice liqueur

BOUQUET: hints of licorice predominate

TASTE: rich, with balsamic, mentholated, and rooty notes

AFTERTASTE: kaffir lime and winter spices

KAMM & SONS

Great Britain

Kamm & Sons is a British amaro-aperitif, distilled in London and marketed for the first time in 2011. Although it does not have the classic characteristics of an amaro as we know it in Italy or Germany, Kamm & Sons represents in Great Britain, where it was created, the alcoholic form closest to the concept of Italian amaro. The creator, Alex Kammerling, has worked in the beverage industry for more than 25 years, making drinks for royalty, rock stars, and world-class actors, and inventing hundreds of recipes, many of which can be found in his book on cocktails. In 2011, Alex launched his brand, which was inspired by the classic Italian brands Aperol and Campari, and the English tradition of gin.

Kamm & Sons is produced from 45 botanicals, including ginseng, fresh grapefruit peel, juniper berries, goji berries, echinacea, elderflowers, fennel seeds, gentian, wormwood, and annatto with the addition of manuka honey. The production methods are similar to those of gin.

ALCOHOL CONTENT: 33% vol.

COLOR: amber with golden reflections; clean

BOUQUET: hints of juniper and citrus fruits dominate

TASTE: spicy and herbaceous with a strong bite of honey

AFTERTASTE: bitterly herbaceous

MEYER BITTER

Germany

This German amaro is named after its inventor, Georg-Ernst Eduard Meyer, who, in 1825, in his early 20s, decided to start a vinegar factory in Stadthagen, in contrast to his family, which had always been engaged in commercial activities. Some time later, the young man decided to expand his business by opening a liquor factory whose first label, created in 1852, was Meyer's 52er. The following year, the company created a new product, an "amaro" made from a mixture of herbs from the Bernese Alps to which medicinal properties were attributed. The label had the slogan: "An amaro that makes you healthy." The recipe for Meyer Bitter is still today a jealously guarded secret: There are 40 botanicals used in all and come from a careful selection and processing that has remained unchanged over time. Since 1999, the trademark has been owned by Schwarze & Schlichte GmbH & Co. KG, based in Oelde, Westphalia.

ALCOHOL CONTENT: 35% vol.

COLOR: golden brown

BOUQUET: complex with herbaceous scents

TASTE: balsamic with predominance of mint and licorice

AFTERTASTE: complex and persistent in the finish with notes of star anise

SALMIAKKI DALA

Iceland

Anyone who decides to take a trip to the Scandinavian countries, including Sweden, Iceland, and Finland, will discover simple and popular licorice candies called "Salmiak." They are bitter candies with a unique taste, enriched by the presence of ammonia salt that gives a pleasant savory aftertaste. Among the locals there was also the custom of making a homemade drink based on vodka or brandy and then melting these goodies in it. So Dala

Spirits thought it best to create an amaro that had the same aromatic profile as Salmiak candies, starting with a classic fernet, a familiar liqueur much loved by Scandinavian people. The recipe for Salmiakki Dala uses 10 botanical products, including a pinch of saffron and a massive dose of aloe to give the right degree of bitterness. The mix also includes licorice root, aniseed, chicory, and ammonia salt. The sweetness is brought out with beet sugar and caramel, which helps to give the classic brown color to the amaro.

ALCOHOL CONTENT: 38% vol.

COLOR: coffee

BOUQUET: hints of licorice predominate

TASTE: very bitter and sapid; licorice root prevails

AFTERTASTE: the savory note envelops the tongue in a persistent way

UNDERBERG

Germany

The Underberg amaro was first introduced in Germany by Hubert Underberg in 1846 and is produced from a mix of 43 secret herbs from all over the world to help digestion and to strengthen the spirit after a demanding meal. Nowadays, every botanical in this amaro is subjected to careful analysis and selection by members of

the fourth and fifth generations of the Underberg family of liquorists. After a phase of hot maceration in distilled water and neutral alcohol, the blend then undergoes a long period of maturation in oak barrels. This amaro only achieved success after World War II, thanks to the introduction of small single-portion bottles wrapped in straw paper—an idea suggested by Emil Underberg, Hubert's grandson. Despite the secrecy of its elements, when sipping Underberg, it is easy to distinguish the intense flavors of herbs and spices such as aniseed, wormwood, and cloves. In legislative terms, Underberg is considered to be an aromatic bitter and is categorized as a nondrinking product, which means that the product is not subject to liquor laws. It is on the market only in the 2 cl (about 7 oz.) format.

ALCOHOL CONTENT: 44% vol.

COLOR: brown with gold highlights

BOUQUET: herbaceous with notes of cinnamon, ginger, and licorice

TASTE: medicinal and balsamic with nuances of chocolate and citrus fruits

AFTERTASTE: strongly bitter with persistence of licorice

Amari from Around the World

In this historical period, the United States represents the new Mecca of amaro. Yes, I said the United States because Americans have first learned to drink amari and then, slowly, to produce their own, often with very positive and surprising results, as happened in Brooklyn, Chicago, Philadelphia, and outside the big cities in places like Brekenridge, Colorado, and Milwaukee, Wisconsin. But as you may know, the Italian immigrant has always been like parsley: you find him everywhere, with his suitcase and his bottle of amaro to offer to new friends to remember and celebrate his territorial roots. We will therefore discover new and incredible places in the world where amari are starting to find themselves at home, created with the most diverse and unknown botanicals—in Australia, Mexico, Brazil, Iceland . . . on with your backpack and off we go!

AMARO CINPATRAZZO

Chicago, USA

Produced in Chicago, Illinois, and introduced on the market in 2016, Amaro Cinpatrazzo is the result of Pat Magner and his wife Cindy Tegtmeyer's great passion for amari. It all began when Pat, an architecture student in Florence in the 1970s, fell madly in love with the Italian amaro, making every journey an opportunity to discover a new product. This love was so deep that he put aside his career as an architect to devote himself to the production of spirits. Behind the Cinpatrazzo brand is therefore a beautiful couple, Pat and Cindy, who, inspired by an amaro bought in a trullo in Alberobello, set to work to develop a recipe for their own amaro that brings to mind southern Italy. Amaro Cinpatrazzo is made from 19 botanicals, most of them organic, including Seville orange peels from Coachella (California), arugula, sage, mint, elderflower, coffee, vanilla, cardamom, and hazelnuts. The sweetening is brought about with the addition of Midwest honey. The name Cinpatrazzo comes from the combination of the names Cindy and Pat and the Italian word *razzo* (rocket), another way to refer to arugula, the main ingredient of this amaro, which mingles with sage and mint from a hydroponic farm in Chicago.

ALCOHOL CONTENT: 21.5% vol.

COLOR: brown with golden highlights

BOUQUET: hints of espresso coffee and chocolate predominate

TASTE: strongly balsamic with notes of licorice

AFTERTASTE: clean with memories of chocolate pudding

AMARO DI ANGOSTURA

Trinidad-Tobago

Everything that House of Angostura has achieved over the years is due to Dr. Johann Siegert, who left Prussia to join the liberation army of Simón Bolivar, founder of the State of Venezuela, as a military doctor. Siegert took care of the soldiers through medical preparations for the treatment of fever and intestinal disorders. In 1824, after much experience in the field, and thanks to the knowledge acquired on the medicinal properties of various tropical botanicals, Siegert developed a very concentrated amaro to help the soldiers' digestion and appetite. Thus, was born Angostura Bitter, from the name of the Venezuelan city where Siegert lived, renamed Ciudad Bòlivar in 1846. That bitter has come a long way, and since 2014, on the occasion of the company's 190th anniversary, it has become the basis for a new product, obtained through the maceration of other botanical components and the addition of neutral alcohol: Amaro di Angostura. The amaro, after its 2015 presentation at Tales of the Cocktail, the annual American event dedicated to the international beverage, was awarded the most prizes, making it the most awarded product in the world.

ALCOHOL CONTENT: 35% vol.

COLOR: brown with ruby highlights

BOUQUET: spicy hints of cinnamon, cola, and cardamom

TASTE: dry with the right sweetness; cloves, cinnamon, and licorice predominate

AFTERTASTE: notes of honey, spices, and a bit of gingerbread prevail

BRASILBERG

Brazil

Brasilberg amaro represents the Brazilian cousin of the very famous German amaro Underberg, which began to be exported to Brazil in 1884. After World War I, the production of Underberg unfortunately suffered a setback and the makers had to break off relations with the important Rio market. History recounts that Dr. Paul Underberg, cousin of the founder Hubert, a great travel enthusiast, in 1932 during an excursion in the Brazilian Amazon rainforest was fascinated by the halo of magic that enveloped the culture of the locals who were able to cure themselves with only the use of herbs and roots that grew wild in those territories. Paul, after learning and studying local botanicals together with the native peoples, used them to develop a recipe inspired by the original family recipe. Underberg do Brazil, or Brasilberg, was thus created. Its creation allowed the company to overcome the import/export crisis by producing an amaro directly in Brazil. The taste captured Brazilian society, along with German and Italian immigrants. One of the national cocktails of Brazil, the Rio Negro, features Brasilberg as the main ingredient, together with tonic water.

ALCOHOL CONTENT: 42% vol.

COLOR: brown with emerald highlights

BOUQUET: herbaceous, complex, and slightly fruity

TASTE: moderately bitter, aromatic; strong and persistent herbaceous notes

AFTERTASTE: slightly sweet and fruity; long and complex finish

BRECKENRIDGE BITTER

Colorado, USA

Breckenridge Bitter is produced in the "highest" distillery in the world and can confidently call itself the first and only American mountain amaro. Breckenridge Distillery was founded in 2008, the brainchild of Brian Nolte, in the small town of Breckenridge, Colorado, which lies at an altitude of more than 9,000 feet (2,750 m). It all began during a trip to Scotland when Brian, a medical radiologist, was struck by the activity of the Glenmorangie distillery in Tain, and he became a convert to the "whiskey god." The first products from the factory he founded were bourbon whiskeys and American vodkas, then the decision to make a mountain amaro along the lines of a European Génépy. In fact Breckenridge Bitter includes among its ingredients genepy plants, belonging to the wormwood family, with a very bitter and herbaceous taste. It is produced with meticulously selected and handpicked herbs together with ancient roots, spices, and dried fruit and is processed according to medieval-style production methods.

ALCOHOL CONTENT: 36% vol.

COLOR: amber with gold highlights

BOUQUET: herbaceous and aromatic

TASTE: complex, bitter, and vegetal notes embrace the palate

AFTERTASTE: dry and citrusy, similar to the pink grapefruit peel

FERNET VALLET

Mexico

History tells us that Monsieur Henri Vallet emigrated from France to Mexico during the brief reign of Maximilian I, the unfortunate Habsburg monarch who was deposed by Mexican nationalists three years after his rise as emperor of Mexico in 1864. Like other French emigrants of the time, Monsieur Vallet chose to remain in his adopted homeland and in 1880, thanks to his skills and past herbalist studies, he became the main distiller of liqueurs and elixirs in Mexico

City, including Fernet Vallet and Amargo-Vallet, which continue to be made according to the original formulas. Fernet Vallet was discovered by an importer from San Francisco during a trip to Mexico: It was easy to find it in many bars in the capital where it was used in drops like a bitter. The beverage was created more than 150 years ago and its real function was that of an antibacterial and disinfectant bitter for the human body. Unlike other fernets, Fernet Vallet is less mentholated and balsamic, denser in consistency, and is produced through the maceration of botanicals that include cinnamon, cloves, quassia, gentian root, cardamom, rhubarb, and mint.

ALCOHOL CONTENT: 70% vol.

COLOR: very dark red, almost brown

BOUQUET: hints of cardamom and mace

TASTE: very bitter, mentholated, and balsamic

AFTERTASTE: notes of gentian and cinchona predominate

HEIRLOOM PINEAPPLE AMARO

Milwaukee, USA

In 2016, the Heirloom brand was conceived as a branch of the mighty Bittercube tree, a leading American company in the production of flavored bitters, with the aim of creating vibrant spirits produced only with natural botanicals. The founders of Heirloom are the same as Bittercube, Nick Kosevich and Ira Koplowitz, together with Brandon Reyes, a former Bittercube employee. Heirloom Pineapple Amaro is the result of the combination of the Italian amaro tradition, Brandon's Caribbean roots, and his experiences in Wisconsin. Heirloom Pineapple Amaro's essential ingredient is Queen Victoria pineapple, an aromatic and flavorful variety that is macerated in rum, combined with Jamaican quassia bark and Wisconsin ginseng root. Other botanicals that complete the mixture are gentian root, sacred bark, wild cherry bark, cinnamon, Jamaica pepper, vanilla, cardamom, raisins, lemongrass, and citrus peel. The sweetening is entrusted to burnt and muscovado sugars.

ALCOHOL CONTENT: 30% vol.

COLOR: copper with gold highlights

BOUQUET: warm hints of cinnamon, caramel, and vanilla prevail; hints of cherry cola fill the nose

TASTE: light, rich, and sophisticated with succulent

nuances of tropical fruit and baked goods

AFTERTASTE: deliciously bitter; woody and earthy finish

MARSEILLE AMARO

Brooklyn, USA

Marseille Amaro was created in 2017 in a microdistillery, Forthave Spirits, in the heart of Brooklyn, on the sixth floor of an industrial building, bordering Williamsburg and Bed-Stuy. Behind the project: two friends, Daniel de la Nuez, former film and television producer, and Aaron Fox, his collaborator and designer. The journey began one night when Daniel drank a glass of herbal liqueur that he discovered Aaron made. The two of them began to experiment with new spirits and soon decided to become master distillers. Daniel and Aaron created their Marseille Amaro on the basis of a secret recipe of medieval origin developed by a certain Richard Forthave, who, according to legend, had developed an herbal tonic for four thieves in order to protect them from the plague, with a view to robbing a ship ravaged by the disease that had traveled from Tripoli to Marseille. Its mixture actually had medicinal properties, but it certainly did not give immunity to the plague. The four scoundrels were arrested anyway, and in exchange for clemency they offered the judge the secret formula of their "miraculous medicine." Eucalyptus, mint, cinnamon, dried lemon peel, dried tea leaves, and honey dominate the botanical mix at the base of the Marseille Amaro, which is sweetened with raw honey.

ALCOHOL CONTENT: 36% vol.

COLOR: brown with emerald highlights

BOUQUET: balsamic scents predominate

TASTE: honey and menthol notes prevail

AFTERTASTE: vanilla and lemon

ØKAR

Australia

Brendan and his wife Laura started creating the Økar bitter in 2015 as the best way to show and share with the world the unique and extraordinary flavors of the Australian territory. From the beginning, the great variety of botanicals that the earth offered pushed them to invest in the most "botanical" spirits on the market: gin and of course amaro. Brendan and Laura have never tried to reproduce an Italian amaro, but rather they tried to create a 100 percent Australian amaro, an "island amaro" that is far removed from our concept of amaro. Økar has a bitterish

character that crosses, with its characteristics, Italian, Asian, Polynesian, and obviously Australian cultures, through the use of ingredients typical of the ancient coastal rainforests of Australia. Økar's recipe contains 16 different botanicals, 8 of which come from and can only be found on the Australian continent, and they include riberries (a type of berry native to the continent), Davidson's plums, eucalyptus piperita, wild thyme, finger lime, and local currants. The botanicals are macerated in alcohol for about four weeks before being mixed and left to rest prior to bottling.

ALCOHOL CONTENT: 24% vol.

COLOR: ruby red

BOUQUET: herbaceous with balsamic hints

TASTE: fruity and fresh thanks to the riberries and the balsamic notes of eucalyptus; just bitter enough with good acidity thanks to the Davidson's plums

ST. AGRESTIS

Brooklyn, USA

St. Agrestis was created in 2014 as the brainchild of two former sommeliers of the Batali & Bastianich Hospitality Group, who left for a journey of three months in Italy to learn the secrets of amaro production. The identity of this

amaro is closely linked to that of the Brooklyn area and its surroundings. For example, it is aged in barrels used for bourbon from a local artisanal distillery, which in turn purchases corn and rye from a farm in upstate New York. In 2017, the St. Agrestis estate passed into the hands of Louis Catizone and Steven De Angelo, and was later joined by Louis's brother Matthew. The three of them updated some details of the recipe and production so that today the recipe of St. Agrestis amaro consists of 20 different, completely organic botanicals. These include citrus fruits, seeds, herbs, roots, and spices that undergo separate maceration in hydroalcoholic solution for up to six weeks. Then the blend is aged in American oak bourbon barrels for 16 weeks. Once filtered, water and organic cane sugar are added to the blend, and then it is bottled.

ALCOHOL CONTENT: 30% vol.

COLOR: deep brownish red

BOUQUET: warm notes of cinnamon, nutmeg, and rhubarb prevail

TASTE: structured and refreshing; aromas of bark, vanilla extract, and cream soda emerge

AFTERTASTE: powerful hints of green mint

VIGO AMARO

Philadelphia, USA

The Philadelphia Distilling company is a magnificent distillery located in Philadelphia, a center of Italian immigration for centuries. The first arrivals here would convert a few yards of earth into lush gardens with fruits, vegetables, and medicinal herbs that they often turned into liqueurs, served with Italian pride to family and visitors as part of the evening ritual. This concept of hospitality is what inspired Philadelphia Distilling to create Vigo Amaro, an amaro that proudly expresses the Italian spirit of the city of Philadelphia. This amaro takes its name from Francis Vigo, a revolutionary Italian financier who supported the colonial cause of independence, and it includes the following botanicals in its mix: California prunes, nutmeg, rose, elderflower, cinnamon, cinchona, cola nut, and gentian. The real secret of Vigo Amaro is the American white oak aging barrels that the company's gin are made in, which in this case is treated as a botanical (pre-roasted) macerated in alcohol.

ALCOHOL CONTENT: 25% vol.

COLOR: copper bronze

BOUQUET: hints of sweet and sour nuts emerge with hints of cinnamon, nutmeg, and aromatic woods

TASTE: sweetish and balanced by a bitter note; flavors of strudel and winter fruit

AFTERTASTE: caramel and a touch of dry woodiness

TEN THINGS YOU DIDN'T KNOW ABOUT AMARO

1

In Italian, the word *amaro* means "bitter." Despite the similarity in the ingredients, the main difference between an **AMARO** and an **AROMATIC BITTER** is that an amaro is intended to be consumed neat, and an aromatic bitter is more suitable as a flavoring agent, applied in drops and dashes.

2

HERBAL INFUSIONS were conceived as curatives, and they remained as such until the 15th and 16th centuries. To treat smallpox, for example, it was customary to give a patient an infusion of pine nuts, watermelon roots, rose petals, and honey. For the treatment of intestinal worms, a decoction of rosemary and sage was recommended. For revitalization, a suitable liqueur was based on mint, saffron, aloe, cloves, and nutmeg.

3

The first fernet in history was **FERNET VITTONE**, produced in Milan in 1842, three years before the appearance of the more familiar and well-known Fernet-Branca.

4

The writer and poet **GABRIELE D'ANNUNZIO**, who lived at the turn of the 19th and 20th centuries, was also a great advertising art director; in this regard, he had the opportunity to engage with the Italian liquor industry to provide his intellectual and artistic contribution. His engagement extended to products such as Aurum liqueur (whose name he invented) and Amaro Montenegro for which he coined the famous slogan *"Liquore delle Virtudi"* (Liqueur of the Virtues). He also rebranded the Luxardo Cherry Liqueur with the curious name of Luxardo Sangue Morlacco (Morlacco's Blood).

5

Cynar was created in 1952 by the Venetian **ANGELO DALLE MOLLE**, starting with 13 botanicals, including artichoke leaves. It was launched with the slogan "Cynar, against the wear and tear of modern life," but its creator had anything but a modest existence. Considered an authentic Italian playboy, he was always animated by a progressive and visionary spirit that led him to support studies and research related to artificial intelligence and to be involved in the invention of the electric car. Dalle Molle had six children with six different women. He died at the age of 90 and left his entire fortune to his secretary.

6

In **ARGENTINA,** the national cocktail is the **FERNANDITO,** made with fernet and Coca-Cola. Fernet arrived in Argentina from overseas thanks to Italian emigrants. In fact, Fratelli Branca Distillerie opened a factory in Buenos Aires in 1941, and it is still more than active today. In 1980, the Fernandito was all the rage on university campuses when students boycotted British whisky in protest of the Falklands War. *Viva la revolución!*

7

AMARO CORA appeared in some commercials of the famous Italian TV show *Carosello*, in which the actors Gaia Germani and Giulio Bosetti played spouses who, at the end of every quarrel, were reconciled by drinking the well-known amaro produced by the Bosca di Canelli company. In the background, the notes of *"Amorevole"* ("Lovingly") were sung by Nicola Arigliano with the first word changed to *"Amarevole"* ("Bitterly"), which also represented the advertising slogan.

FERNET reached the height of its popularity in the United States for its particular balsamic taste and bitter character, but also thanks to the many appearances on the legendary set of TV series, *The Sopranos*.

The creator of Amaro Montenegro was **STANISLAO COBIANCHI,** a young man predestined by his family for an ecclesiastical career. From his hometown, Bologna, he decided to run away against his father's wishes to undertake a trip around the world that led him to the discovery of unusual botanical specialties. Back in Italy, he dedicated himself to the preparation of liqueurs and in 1885 he created the Elisir Lungavita. Eleven years later, on the occasion of Vittorio Emanuele III's marriage to Elena di Montenegro, in honor of the latter, Stanislao decided to change the name to Amaro Montenegro.

10

JUSTIN SEVERINO, owner and executive chef of Cure, the award-winning restaurant in Pittsburgh, Pennsylvania, which closed in 2019 after operating for seven years, was among the first to promote the use of amaro in cooking. His Negroni salami flavored with amaro, vermouth, and juniper as well as lamb and pork salami flavored with olives and fernet were famous. One of his his best-selling dishes was a very expensive cut of salmon left to marinate for 30 hours in a mixture of two different types of orange juice, beets, hibiscus flowers, and lots of Fernet-Branca. The salmon was then served sliced and decorated with almonds, beets, cucumber, green apple, dry fennel, and flower petals.

Recipes

Mixology

Il Formidabile

I was in Paris in 2012, invited as a guest at the famous Maria Loca. It was a moment of great excitement for European mixes, and even the City of Light saw the birth of new dedicated venues, many of which would hold a prominent place in the World's 50 Best Bars, such as Sherry Butt and Candelaria. As soon as I arrived, my friend and co-owner Michael Landart welcomed me with a nice French-style aperitif based on gentian from beyond the Alps. I was so impressed that I tried to reproduce its goodness using local ingredients. With this cocktail, The Formidable, I think I succeeded.

INGREDIENTS

1⅔ ounces Amaro Formidabile

¾ ounce Amaro Aurora Carciofo Setino

1 ounce lime juice

Tonic water to taste

GLASS: highball
GARNISH: 3 lime wheels + highball ice spears
METHOD: shake & double strain

Pour all the ingredients except the tonic water into the shaker. Add plenty of ice and shake vigorously. Pour into a highball glass full of ice and top with tonic water.

MILK AMARO
CLARIFIED PUNCH

The year 2016 was the year of the clarified cocktail boom in New York. In every bar in the Big Apple the menus were filled with themed preparations: clarified lemon juice, clarified Bloody Mary, or clarified milk punch. The same thing happened in the prestigious Betony restaurant, temple of Eamon Rockey, the former barman and manager at Eleven Madison Park and reference point for bartenders at the time. I wanted to pay homage to Eamon with a personal recipe of my own, the Milk Amaro Clarified Punch, obviously with an amaro base. For those who don't know it, clarification is a (not simple) process based on a natural reaction called rennet.

INGREDIENTS

2½ ounces Milk Punch Mix
(recipe follows)

1 ounce Amaro Maffei

¼ ounce sugar syrup (1:1)

3 drops of orange bitters

GLASS: old fashioned
GARNISH: lemon zest & large ice cubes
METHOD: stir & strain

Combine all the ingredients in a mixing glass, add plenty of ice and mix with a barspoon. Once the mixture has cooled, pour into an old fashioned glass.

MILK PUNCH MIX

6¼ cups pineapple extract

2 cups Granny Smith
apple extract

2 cups vanilla black tea

2 cups lemon juice

4 cups milk

Combine the juices (pineapple and apple) and black tea in a bowl. Bring the milk to a boil in a large pot and add the lemon juice. Pour the juices into the pot with the milk, turn off the heat, and let it cool. Filter the mixture at least four times through a filter bag, until it is completely clear.

MI QUERIDA SOLEDAD

This drink bears the signature of a young bartender, Martina Proietti, an integral part and fulcrum of the Amaro Obsession project, who is endowed with great imagination, intelligence, and originality that she always conveys in her drinks. Martina is a great fan of music, of all music. The cocktail Mi Querida Soledad was conceived while listening to the album *La Cantina* by Mexican singer-songwriter Lila Downs and, more specifically, from a verse of the song "La Cumbia del Mole": "*Cuentan que en Oaxaca se toma el mezcal con café*" ("It is said that in Oaxaca that mezcal is drunk with coffee") are the first words that Lila sings in this song that refers to the tradition of the Mexican mole, a sauce prepared with different chilies, herbs, and spices. Martina therefore thought of combining these Latin American flavors with the taste of the Italian-style aperitif.

INGREDIENTS

1 ounce mezcal

1 ounce Pasubio Vino Amaro

1 ounce Martini Bitter Riserva

1 barspoon of coffee

2 dashes of chocolate bitters

Velvet Top of Ancho Reyes Verde (recipe follows)

GLASS: Nick & Nora
GARNISH: coffee powder
METHOD: stir & strain

Pour all the ingredients into a mixing glass except the Velvet Top of Ancho Reyes Verde. Add ice cubes and mix with a barspoon until the mixture cools. Pour it all into a Nick & Nora glass and complete with the Ancho Reyes Verde velvet.

VELVET TOP OF ANCHO REYES VERDE

1 ounce water

4 ounces Ancho Reyes Verde liqueur

Pinch of sucrose ester

Add water, Ancho Reyes Verde, and sucrose ester and whip everything with a whisk.

THE GOLDEN MAI TAI

In 2011, I was lucky enough to win the national competition to participate in the Bacardi Legacy Cocktail Competition global finals in Puerto Rico, a competition that established me as an international bartender and gave me the opportunity to grow a lot over the years and to live wonderful and unimaginable experiences. In Puerto Rico, I brought a drink inspired by the tiki cocktail, but with more elegance: The Golden Mai Tai. The original recipe called for Martini Gold vermouth with its blend of saffron, myrrh, and ginger. Unfortunately this vermouth had been taken out of production by the Martini & Rossi company, so to reproduce The Golden Mai Tai, I replaced the Martini Gold vermouth with an amaro with a strong ginger component, Amaro 33.

1 ounce Bacardi
Carta Blanca

½ ounce Amaro 33

½ ounce lime juice

½ ounce Falernum #12
(recipe follows)

½ ounce orgeat syrup

2 drops of cardamom bitters

Bacardi Carta Negra
to taste

2 absinthe
vaporizations

GLASS: Nick & Nora
GARNISH: grated tonka beans + ice chunks
METHOD: throwing

Put all the ingredients in a shaker except the Bacardi Carta Negra and the
absinthe. Add ice and mix the drink with the throwing technique that allows
good oxygenation of the cocktail and low dilution from the ice. Pour in the glass
and proceed with a float in suspension of Bacardi Carta Negra and flame with
absinthe with a vaporizer.

FALERNUM #12

2 tablespoons peeled
almonds

40 whole cloves

3 star anises

3 Ceylon cinnamon sticks

15 cardamom seeds

¼ cup freshly peeled and
chopped ginger

¾ cup overproof white rum

Zest of 9 limes without pulp

3 teaspoons almond
extract (almond essence
for desserts)

1 cup + 3 tablespoons agave
or honey

5¼ cups fresh lime juice

In a saucepan, toast all the almonds and spices except the ginger. Pour the
spices, almonds, rum, lime zest, and ginger into a sealed jar to preserve,
leaving the mixture to macerate for 24 hours. The next day, filter well with
a moistened cheesecloth. Add the almond extract, agave or honey, and
lime juice. Keep the mixture in the bottle and stir occasionally for the next
24 hours. Keep in the fridge.

TRUFFLE FASHIONED

As a good Italian and a lover of good food, I have a weakness for truffles. So, over the years, I tried to develop a cocktail that reproduces the same pleasant sensations that tease the palate like a good dish of risotto or tagliolini with fresh truffles. This is how the Truffle Fashioned was born, using a fat-washing technique with truffle butter.

INGREDIENTS

1½ ounces Fat Washed Truffle Rye Whiskey (recipe follows)

¾ ounce Amaro al Tartufo Vallenera

¼ ounce of white truffle honey

5 drops of Angostura bitters

2 drops of chocolate bitters

Absinthe to taste

GLASS: old fashioned
GARNISH: truffle chip + large ice cubes
METHOD: stir & strain

Pour all the ingredients, except the absinthe, into a mixing glass; add plenty of ice and mix with a barspoon. Pour everything into an old fashioned glass previously vaporized on the inside with plenty of absinthe.

FAT WASHED TRUFFLE RYE WHISKEY

4 cups rye whiskey

¼ cup truffle butter

In a saucepan, simmer the rye whiskey and the truffle butter over low heat until completely melted. Pour the mixture into a preserving jar and leave in the freezer for 24 hours. The next day, remove the fat from the solidified butter, filter the liquid part with the help of a very finely woven cloth, and bottle it.

ALASKA

The Alaska cocktail is mentioned in Harry Craddock's famous *The Savoy Cocktail Book* from 1930 and, even before that, in Jacques Straub's famous *Straub's Manual of Mixed Drinks* from 1913. But these recipes are just starting points: It is almost impossible to find a cocktail recipe that hasn't undergone changes and modifications. The Alaska cocktail—probably originally from South Carolina—over time has undergone some changes in the use of the main spirit, going from Old Tom Gin to London Dry gin, even though the official 1961 IBA (International Bartenders Association) recipe calls for the use of three-quarters gin and one-quarter yellow Chartreuse. The bartender Andrea Cardinale decided to give the Alaska cocktail an all-Italian character, replacing the Chartreuse with a product from Italy that is very similar to it: Centerba Toro, a liqueur from Abruzzo, which is made from the infusion of 100 medicinal herbs and has a higher alcohol content.

INGREDIENTS

2 ounces Gin Bombay Sapphire

½ ounce Centerba Toro Forte

2 drops of orange bitters

GLASS: Nick & Nora
GARNISH: very thin lemon twist
METHOD: stir & strain

**Pour the ingredients into a mixing glass and mix until completely cooled.
Serve in a Nick & Nora glass.**

FRA' BASTIANO

I created this drink in honor of Sasha Nathan Petraske, the legendary founder of the New York cocktail bar Milk & Honey, who unfortunately passed away a few months after my arrival in the Big Apple. On the Milk & Honey menu there was a drink created by bartender T. J. Siegal, the Gold Rush, which was amazing in its simplicity, using a perfect mix of bourbon whiskey, honey, and lemon: an incredible sour. Over time, a portion of ginger liqueur was added to the mix and the cocktail turned its name into the Ginger Gold Rush, a drink brilliantly revamped in the bar Sweet Polly in Brooklyn (Park Slope), where I had the pleasure of being behind the counter several times and from which I drew inspiration.

INGREDIENTS

1½ ounces bourbon whiskey

¾ ounce Amaro Montenegro

¾ ounce fresh lemon juice

*¾ ounce Honey Syrup
(80:20; recipe follows)*

¼ ounce ginger extract

*20 drops of Angostura bitters
to top off*

GLASS: old fashioned
GARNISH: large ice cubes
METHOD: shake & double strain

Pour all the ingredients except the Angostura into a shaker with lots of ice. Shake briskly with a double filtration and pour into an old fashioned glass with ice. Top off with the 20 drops of Angostura.

HONEY SYRUP

2 cups millefiori honey

¼ cup hot water

Pour the honey and hot water into a saucepan, heat over low-medium heat and stir with a spoon until the mixture becomes liquid.

GASPERINO'S MARGARITA

This drink is inspired by a drink called Tommy's Margarita, invented by the owner of Tommy's Restaurant in San Francisco, Julio Bermejo, who in 1990 decided to replace the classic triple cec in the margarita recipe with agave syrup. The success was enormous and word spread throughout the United States. My Gasperino's Margarita, first created for Ammazzacaffè, an amaro bar in Brooklyn, and used also for Il Marchese in Rome, exploits the aromaticity of hibiscus flowers in the agave syrup and in the mix of Amaro Stilla by Lombardi and Visconti.

INGREDIENTS

1⅓ ounces tequila

¾ ounce Amaro Stilla

¾ ounce Agave Syrup and Hibiscus Flowers (recipe follows)

¾ ounce fresh lime juice

GLASS: old fashioned
GARNISH: Tajín Clásico + large ice cube
METHOD: shake & double strain

Pour the ingredients into a shaker and shake energetically. Pour into an old fashioned glass garnished with a crust of Tajin seasoning and add a large ice cube.

AGAVE SYRUP AND HIBISCUS FLOWERS

4 cups water

4 cups agave syrup

⅞ cup dried hibiscus flowers

Pour the ingredients into a pressure cooker and cook at 150°F for 1 hour.
Once the mixture has cooled, filter and seal.

THE MOCKAMARO SOUR

Speaking of amaro, I couldn't help but mention my version of the ultimate amaro-based cocktail: the amaro sour. In preparing it I was inspired by the new trends in mixed drinks, meeting the needs of those who want to enjoy nonalcoholic drinks without sacrificing the taste and aromatic complexity of alcoholic drinks. With this in mind, a revolutionary product came to my rescue, The Bitter Note, an amaro without alcohol characterized by seven notes of flavor that give the drink herbaceous, spicy, citrusy, and balsamic nuances collected in a pleasant bitterness. Together with my team, I also decided to replace the classic sugar syrup with a fructose syrup, characterized by a lower glycemic index to give even more "wellness value" to the cocktail.

INGREDIENTS

2 ounces The Bitter Note	*¾ ounce fructose syrup (1:1)*
1 ounce fresh lemon juice	*1 egg white*

GLASS: sour coupette
GARNISH: Angostura & Peychaud bitters drops
METHOD: shake & double strain

Pour the ingredients into a shaker and shake without ice (dry shake), so that the albumen can mount well. Add ice and shake further until cooled. Pour the mixture into a sour coupette.

POOR'S BREAD

Poor's Bread is a drink with an exquisitely wintry flavor in which chestnut, Sicilian almond, and American whiskey meet in a warm and flavorful mix that is best savored slowly, maybe in front of a fireplace with a burning fire. The main character of this cocktail is Amaro Ménnula d'Erbe, which is Sicilian and produced with completely local botanicals, including almond, gentian, and citrus fruits harvested directly by the producer.

INGREDIENTS

1⅔ ounces Knob Creek
Straight Bourbon

⅔ ounce fresh lemon juice

½ ounce Amaro Ménnula

⅓ ounce Roasted Chestnut
Syrup (recipe follows)

Salt to taste

GLASS: Nick & Nora
GARNISH: steamed chestnut
METHOD: shake & strain

Pour all the ingredients into a shaker and add ice. Shake vigorously and pour into a Nick & Nora glass.

ROASTED CHESTNUT SYRUP

1 cup chestnuts

1¼ cups raw sugar

1 cup boiling water

Peel of 2 oranges

1 vanilla pod

¼ cup dark rum
(e.g., Bacardi Carta Negra)

After cutting the chestnut shells with a knife, place the whole chestnuts in an oven preheated to 350°F for about 45 minutes, then let them cool. Remove the shell and the skin surrounding the chestnuts while they are still warm. Prepare the syrup by dissolving the sugar in the boiling water, adding the orange peel and the seeds extracted from the vanilla pod. When the sugar has dissolved and the syrup has thickened, remove the orange peel. Using a heavy knife, lightly press the chestnuts with the side of the blade until they break open. Place the lightly pressed roasted chestnuts, the rum, and the sugar-vanilla-orange syrup in a preserving jar. Place everything in the refrigerator and leave it to rest for about 7 days; after filtrating it, the syrup will be ready to be used.

Cooking with Amaro

PRAWNS WITH CERBERUS AMARO

⋯ • • • ⋯

GIANFRANCO VISSANI

Casa Vissani, Cannitello, Baschi (Treviso)

—— SERVES 4 ——

2 eggplants	*2 cinnamon sticks*	*EVO oil to taste*
1 cup caster sugar	*1 pound fresh red prawns*	*Amaro Cerberus*
2 star anise	*Salt and pepper to taste*	

Boil the eggplants in water in a large pan until the skin is tender. Once cooked, drain them, rinse them under cold water, and put them in a large nonstick pan with a little water, the sugar, star anise, and cinnamon sticks. Dissolve the sugar, stirring continuously, then blend everything in the pan with an immersion blender and cook until the consistency of the mixture is more or less that of jam. Clean the prawns well, removing their heads and intestines, and place them between a sheet of lightly oiled parchment paper and plastic wrap. At this point, with a meat tenderizer, beat the prawns until you have four discs equal in both circumference and thickness. Place the discs in the freezer until they have hardened and, once ready, transfer them to a flat plate. Season with a little salt, pepper, and olive oil. Finish off the dish with a dab of eggplant jam and a few drops of Amaro Cerberus.

Seared Cuttlefish with Amaro Tenace and Vignarola

FEDERICO DELMONTE

Acciuga, Rome

SERVES 4

8 small-medium fresh cuttlefish

EVO oil

Salt and pepper

2 tablespoons lemon juice

4 teaspoons Amaro Tenace

Vignarola (recipe follows)

Onion Puree (recipe follows)

2 sprigs of marjoram

Wild oregano to taste

Basil leaves to taste

Celery heart leaves to taste

1 dried lemon peel

Breadcrumbs (recipe follows)

Clean the cuttlefish, sear it very quickly on the grill, and cut it into thin slices to be seasoned with olive oil, salt, pepper, lemon juice, and Amaro Tenace. Place the cuttlefish at the bottom of a large serving dish, placing the Vignarola on top. Add the onion puree together with marjoram, oregano, basil leaves, celery heart leaves, and dried lemon peel. Finish the dish by adding the breadcrumbs and a drizzle of olive oil.

FOR THE VIGNAROLA

2 pounds fresh fava beans	EVO oil to taste	Few drops of Amaro Tenace
1 pound peas	Salt and pepper to taste	
½ bunch of asparagus	Vinegar to taste	Cumin to taste

Wash and clean the fava beans and peas, placing them in a large container. Cut off the tough bottom parts of the asparagus, wash the tops, and cut them into ¾-inch slices, leaving the tip intact. Blanch the asparagus in a medium pan in boiling water for 15 seconds. Dress the Vignarola with the olive oil, salt, pepper, vinegar, few drops of Amaro Tenace, and a small amount of cumin.

FOR THE ONION PUREE

3 medium onions	Salt and pepper to taste
1⅔ cups Amaro Tenace	

Finely slice the onions, roast them on the grill, and then stew them slowly in a large pan over medium-high heat until they become light brown. Take off the stove and add the Amaro Tenace, blend the mixture, then add salt and pepper.

FOR THE BREADCRUMBS

5 slices of stale bread	EVO oil to taste
	Salt to taste

Finely grate the slices of stale bread, then fry them in a medium pan over medium-high heat with the oil to make them crunchy, and season lightly with salt.

Sweetbreads of Calves' Throat, Lampascioni, and Amaro Imperatore

ARCANGELO DANDINI

The Archangel, Rome

— SERVES 4 —

½ cup chopped celery

½ cup chopped carrot

½ cup chopped onion

1 pound sweetbreads of calves' throat, cleaned and cut

8 pistils of Castelluccio saffron

6 tablespoons of butter

⅜ cup all-purpose fine flour

¼ cup Vintage Port

½ cup Amaro Imperatore

8 lampascioni, preserved in oil

Salt to taste

In a large saucepan, prepare a light broth with celery, carrot, and onion. Simmer and add the sweetbreads. After about 15 minutes turn off the flame, add the saffron pistils, cover, and let it rest. Melt the butter in a medium pan over medium heat and add the flour to make a roux. After 15 minutes, pour a tablespoon of the broth, the Vintage Port, the Amaro Imparatore, and the lampascioni into the mixture. Cook everything slowly, stirring consistently over medium heat. Finally, dip the sweetbreads in the roux and serve them doused with their sauce.

RISOTTO WITH FAVA BEANS, GOAT CHEESE, AND AMARO GRINTA GEL

GIUSEPPE DI IORIO

Aroma Restaurant in Palazzo Manfredi, Rome

SERVES 4

1½ cups rice

3½ tablespoons extra virgin olive oil

2 ounces Amaro Grinta

3 to 4 cups vegetable broth as needed

¼ cup whole fava beans

Fava Bean Puree (recipe follows)

Salt and pepper to taste

Pecorino to taste

Parmesan to taste

Fava Bean Crumble (recipe follows)

Grated aged goat cheese to taste

Amaro Grinta Gel (recipe follows)

In a large saucepan with high edges, toast the rice with a little oil. Blend in the Amaro Grinta; let the liquid evaporate and add 3 cups of the broth, adding more if needed to create a creamy consistency. After 5 to 10 minutes, add the whole fava beans. When almost cooked, add the fava bean puree, salt and pepper, pecorino, and Parmesan. Plate the risotto and garnish with the fava bean crumble, goat cheese, and amaro gel tips.

FOR FAVA BEAN PUREE

¼ cup whole fava beans

EVO oil to taste

Salt and pepper to taste

Blanch the fava beans in a small pan and remove the skins, set aside most (leaving some), and blend the rest with oil, salt, and pepper. Sieve to get a smooth puree.

FOR THE FAVA BEAN CRUMBLE

½ cup flour	*2 teaspoons salt*
½ cup butter	*¼ cup almond flour*
½ cup sugar	*½ cup fava bean puree*

Knead the flour with the butter, sugar, salt, almond flour, and bean puree. Spread the mixture on a baking tray with parchment paper and bake at 250°F for 35 to 40 minutes. Once cooked, let it cool and then turn it into powder using a pastry cutter.

FOR THE AMARO GRINTA GEL

2 cups Amaro Grinta	*Agar-agar to taste*

Bring the Amaro Grinta and the agar-agar to a boil. Let it cool until it becomes solid. Then blend everything and sieve until you have a smooth and homogeneous gel.

✦ *The* BIG BOOK *of* AMARO ✦

GNOCCHI, CUTTLEFISH, ARTICHOKE, AND MINT

DANIELE USAI

Il Tino, Fiumicino (Rome)

SERVES 4

1 pound Gnocchi
(recipe follows)

Oil for frying

Amaro Nepéta

2 pounds very fresh
cuttlefish*

Maldon Sea Salt to taste

Cuttlefish Eggs

Artichoke Cream
(recipe follows)

Cuttlefish Base

Mint Oil (recipe follows)

Fresh mint to taste

*Cuttlefish will be used
for the Raw Cuttlefish
Sheets, Cuttlefish Eggs,
and Cuttlefish Base
(all recipes to follow)

Boil the gnocchi in a medium pot until cooked, 2 to 3 minutes. Drain, dry, and fry them in a large pan with a little oil on the side with the cross-shaped incision until golden. Add a little Amaro Nepéta. Place the gnocchi on a baking sheet and line them with the Raw Cuttlefish Sheets (instructions follow). Season each gnocchi with the sea salt and garnish with Cuttlefish Eggs. On the bottom of a large dish, arrange the Artichoke Cream and dressed gnocchi, then spoon some Cuttlefish Base, which has been foamed with a blender. Season with Mint Oil and fresh mint leaves.

FOR THE GNOCCHI

1 pound old red
potatoes, unpeeled

2½ cups coarse salt

4 egg yolks

All-purpose flour as needed
(as little as possible)

(CONTINUED)

Cook the unpeeled potatoes in 2 quarts of water, with all the salt, until completely cooked. Cooking the potatoes with their skins on in heavily salted water removes much of the moisture from the pulp of the potato, allowing for less flour in the recipe and making for a better consistency of the gnocchi, eliminating the "flouriness" that can occur.

Remove the peels and drain the potatoes. Add the egg yolks and the flour (it is not possible to determine the amount of the flour as it depends on the amount of water in the potatoes. However, it is advisable to add very little flour at a time and do some cooking tests). Proceed by forming large, flat gnocchi and make a crosscut on one of the two sides.

FOR THE RAW CUTTLEFISH SHEETS

⅔ pound of cuttlefish tubes

Thoroughly clean the cuttlefish, using the tubes—that is the white part—cutting it into ½-ounce pieces that will be finely beaten between two sheets of parchment paper. One flattened sheet of cuttlefish will be used to stuff each gnocchi.

FOR THE CUTTLEFISH EGGS

Cuttlefish eggs from one cuttlefish	*Coarse salt, same amount as the eggs*	*Sugar, half the amount of the eggs*

Marinate the cuttlefish eggs in the salt and sugar for at least 4 hours. Then rinse the eggs under water, dry, and store in a hermetically sealed container with as little air inside as possible for up to a week.

FOR THE ARTICHOKE CREAM

4 Roman artichokes	*¼ cup artichoke amaro*	*Salt and pepper to taste*
¼ cup shallots, julienned	*EVO oil as needed*	

Clean the artichokes, cut them as finely as possible, and brown them in a large saucepan with a drizzle of oil and the shallots. Douse with the amaro, allow it to evaporate, cover with water, and cook until the fibers have completely disintegrated, about 10 minutes. Blend the mixture finely and season with salt and pepper. If necessary, sieve the cream.

FOR THE CUTTLEFISH BASE

All the tentacles, arms, and remaining parts of the cuttlefish, cut into small but coarse pieces

EVO oil as needed

¼ cup shallots

Thyme, wild fennel, basil, and mint to taste

Black pepper, aniseed, and fennel seeds to taste

¼ cup artichoke amaro

Stew the cuttlefish in a large pot over medium heat, taking care to turn them over every minute for at least 40 minutes, adding oil as necessary. Every part of the cuttlefish should be golden brown and caramelized. Add the shallots and herbs and brown for another 2 minutes. Douse with the amaro, evaporate, and cover with water and ice. Simmer at 185°F for at least 3 hours. Add water if necessary. Filter through cheesecloth and reduce by 50 percent over low heat.

FOR MINT OIL

½ cup light EVO oil

¼ cup fresh mint leaves

Add the oil and mint leaves to a small pan and bring to 210°F. As soon as the temperature is reached, blend and drain into a steel bowl immersed in a larger one filled with water and ice. This will allow the oil to cool instantly, maintaining aroma, color, and flavor.

PIGEON, PUFFED BULGUR, SMOKED ROASTED CHESTNUTS, 5 SPICES, AMARO 81

• • •

STELLA SHI

Cu_Cina, Rome

SERVES 4

2 Tuscan pigeons, skin on

¼ cup bulgur

Sunflower seed oil as needed

1½ cups whole chestnuts

Flour as needed

1 egg for breading

Panko to taste

Brown pigeon stock

2½ teaspoons 5-spice powder

Amaro 81 to taste

Gut the pigeons, separating the thighs, wings, and the lower part of the carcass. The breast must remain whole, attached to the bone structure. Debone the thighs, mince the meat, and form jambonettes using the thigh bones as a support. Overcook the bulgur in a small pan in salted water for 2 hours, bake in the oven for 3 hours at 150°F, and then fry in plenty of sunflower oil at 350°F so that it becomes puffy. Bake the chestnuts whole at 570°F for 20 minutes until roasted. Once they are roasted, remove them from the oven and peel when cool enough to touch. Once peeled, place them in a bowl, add ½ cup of water, and blend until a homogeneous sauce is obtained. Cold-smoke for 30 minutes with chestnut wood. Cook the whole pigeon breast for 7 minutes in a steam oven at 190°F and then let rest. Bread the pigeon jambonettes in flour, egg, and panko, repeating the procedure twice and frying at 350°F until golden brown. In a separate small pan, reduce the brown pigeon stock to make a glaze and add the 5-spice powder. Place the roasted chestnut sauce, the spicy brown base,

and the two fried jambonettes on the bottom of a serving plate. Then place the two boneless pigeon breasts and the bulgur on the pigeon skin—previously glazed—to re-create the crunchiness of the browned skin. Finish the dish with drops of Amaro 81.

Chianina Hamburger with Amaro Sfumato Cappelletti Sorbet

SIMONE BONINI

Carapina, Florence

SERVES 4

2½ cups Amaro Sfumato Cappelletti

1 cup cane sugar

1 teaspoon inulin (plant fiber)

¾ cup boiling water

Zest of ½ orange, no pith

4 Chianina beef hamburgers

Fresh seasonal vegetables, julienned

Pour the Amaro Sfumato Cappelletti, the sugar, and the inulin into a large bowl and blend everything at high speed with an immersion mixer. Pour the water into a bowl and add the orange zest to make an infusion. After 30 minutes, filter the infusion water and pour it into the bowl together with the amaro preparation. Mix again at high speed, pour the mixture into an ice cream maker, and stir. Store the sorbet in the freezer until ready to use. Cook the burgers on a grill and serve them, each accompanied by a scoop of sorbet and seasonal vegetables.

Amaramente (Whipped Dekopon Ganache with Amaro Maffei Gel)

DANIELE DE SANTI

Aroma Restaurant in Palazzo Manfredi, Rome

MAKES 1½ CUPS

FOR THE GANACHE (PREPARATION TIME: 2 DAYS)

1 cup cream

Zest of 1 dekopon

¼ cup invert sugar

5 ounces white chocolate

*Cocoa Sablée
(recipe follows)*

*Hazelnut Maltodextrin
(recipe follows)*

*Amaro Maffei Gel
(recipe follows)*

Edible flowers

Dark chocolate branches

Place ½ cup of the cream and the dekopon zest in a bowl and leave overnight in the fridge, making a note of the weight. The next day, filter and return to the initial weight by adding the invert sugar. Place the infused cream in a small pan and bring to a boil. Add the white chocolate. Emulsify with a handheld immersion blender and add the remaining ½ cup cream. Leave to rest overnight. Whip in a stand mixer and, with a sac à poche, pipe the whipped ganache onto a serving plate. Continue by adding the Cocoa Sablée and the Hazelnut Maltodextrin to the edges. With a second sac à poche, with a fine tip, create small tips of Amaro Maffei Gel. Garnish with edible flowers and dark chocolate branches.

FOR THE COCOA SABLÉE

3 tablespoons butter

2 tablespoons icing sugar

2 tablespoons hard-boiled
egg yolk, pushed through
a fine-mesh sieve

2 tablespoons almond flour

2 tablespoons flour

1 teaspoon cocoa

Combine the butter and icing sugar in a stand mixer, add the sieved egg yolk,
then complete the dough with the almond flour, flour, and cocoa.

FOR THE HAZELNUT MALTODEXTRIN

2½ teaspoons hazelnut paste

5 teaspoons maltodextrin

Emulsify the hazelnut paste and maltodextrin in a thermomix, taking care not to
overheat the mixture.

FOR THE AMARO MAFFEI GEL

½ cup simple syrup (1:1 water
and granulated sugar)

½ cup Amaro Maffei

1 teaspoon agar-agar

Add the simple syrup to the Amaro Maffei and add the agar-agar. Bring to a boil,
pour into a container, and let the agar-agar do its work. Finally, blend everything
with a handheld immersion blender to obtain a typical gel consistency.

FORMIDABLE PIZZA

• • •

PIER DANIELE SEU

Seu Pizza Illuminati, Rome

MAKES 4 PIZZAS

6⅓ cups water

⅓ teaspoon dry yeast

4¼ cups all-purpose fine flour

1 cup cake flour

2½ teaspoons salt

1 tablespoon EVO oil

Artichoke Cream (recipe follows)

Artichokes, grilled

Pecorino Cheese Fondue (recipe follows)

Amaro Formidabile Gel (recipe follows)

Grated pecorino cheese

Mint leaves

In a large bowl, combine the yeast and water. In a separate bowl, combine the flours and salt. Once the yeast is activated, about 5 minutes, add the oil and then pour in the flour mixture. Combine to form a dough and knead for about 10 minutes. Place in a lightly oiled covered bowl somewhere warm to proof until volume is doubled. Divide the dough into four balls and cover again until risen, another hour or so. Roll out the already-leavened dough until it reaches a diameter of about 12 inches. Spread the Artichoke Cream on the dough and bake in a wood-fired oven at 800°F for 90 seconds. After baking, place the grilled artichokes cut in two on the pizza. With a sac à poche, alternate the tips for the Pecorino Cheese Fondue and the tips for the Amaro Formidabile Gel. Garnish with grated pecorino cheese and mint leaves.

FOR THE ROMAN-STYLE ARTICHOKES AND ARTICHOKE CREAM

2 cloves of garlic

3 anchovies

Parsley stalks, plus parsley leaves to taste

12 artichokes, trimmed and prepared

1 cup white wine

2 cups water

Salt to taste

Mint leaves to taste

Fry the garlic, anchovies, and parsley stalks in a saucepan. Add the artichokes— upside down, then the wine, water, salt, mint, and parsley leaves. Cover with a

lid and simmer until artichokes are cooked to desired consistency. Then cut the artichokes in two. Blend 6 artichokes until creamy, adding the necessary water. Pound the remaining 6 artichokes.

FOR THE PECORINO FONDUE

½ cup water	*1⅔ cups pecorino cheese*
¼ cup milk	*Pepper to taste*

In a saucepan, add the water and milk and bring them to a temperature of 175°F. Remove from heat and add the pecorino cheese and pepper. Blend with an immersion blender until a fairly thick cream is obtained. Season with pepper.

FOR THE AMARO FORMIDABILE GEL

¼ cup Amaro Formidabile	*¼ teaspoon agar-agar*
7 teaspoons water	

Dilute the Amaro Formidabile with the water in a small saucepan on the stove, bringing it to a boil. Add the agar-agar. Leave to cool on a baking tray, and then blend until a smooth, transparent gel is obtained.

ZETHUS BITTER SANDWICH

VITTORIO RAELE

I Gastronauti-Instant Kitchen, Ostia (Rome)

SERVES 4

1 bunch of asparagus

1 untreated lemon

1 cup Amaro Zethus

¼ cup brown sugar

1¼ teaspoon agar-agar

⅔ cup sunflower oil

2 eggs

Salt to taste

½ cup rice flour

¾ cup plus 1 teaspoon cold sparkling water

2 artichokes (purple variety)

8½ cups peanut oil

⅔ pound codfish fillet

½ cup panko

8 slices of rye bread, decrusted

EVO oil as needed

White pepper to taste

Peel the asparagus and barely blanch them in a medium pot in boiling salted water, then let them cool quickly. Cut the lemon rind into julienne and blanch for a few seconds in boiling water, repeating this three times. Prepare a syrup with Amaro Zethus and sugar, bringing it to a boil for a few seconds. Place the lemon rind in the syrup for about 10 minutes, then remove the rind pieces and cool them on a sheet of parchment paper. Prepare an Amaro Zethus mostarda by adding the agar-agar to the syrup, stirring well and letting it warm for 30 seconds. Let the mixture cool in the refrigerator and, once it has reached a gelatinous consistency, cut it into coarse pieces, place it in a glass, and blend it with an immersion blender. Make a mayonnaise by pouring the sunflower oil, 2 teaspoons lemon juice, 1 of the eggs, a pinch of salt, and 1 teaspoon of the Amaro Zethus in the container, and blend with an immersion blender. Store in the fridge until ready to use. Prepare a batter with the rice flour, iced sparkling water, 1 egg, and a pinch of salt: mix the ingredients in a bowl just enough, without making it too smooth. Clean the artichokes by removing the hardest outer bracts and the inner chaff and slice them thinly. Dip the artichoke chips in the batter and fry in the peanut oil at 330 to 350°F. Drain and dry well. Cut the cod fillet into slices about ⅓ inch thick. Flour them, dip in the batter, and bread them with panko. Fry until golden

brown, drain, and salt. At the same time, heat the slices of bread on the griddle. Make the sandwich by spreading mayonnaise on the slices of bread, arranging first the cod and asparagus salad dressed with olive oil, white pepper, and a pinch of salt. Complete with the lemon rind. Close the sandwich, serving it on a plate accompanied by Amaro Zethus mostarda and artichoke chips.

ACKNOWLEDGMENTS

IT HAS BEEN A LONG ADVENTURE, OF WHICH IT WAS HARD TO SEE the end at times, but it ended up being beautiful and satisfying whenever a chapter came to an end.

Behind this book there are years of research, carried out with a team of collaborators without whom the Amaro Obsession project would not exist. First of all, I feel I have to thank Martina Proietti, my traveling companion, working partner, the perfect graft in my life, with whom I shared ideas, topics, and chapters of this work. Thanks also to Giammarco Blasi, aka Blasko, who has invested so much time and commitment to this project.

I would like to thank my life partner, Erica, and my mom, who have put up with me and supported me. Despite the arrival of hundreds of bottles of amari every day, they protested in

silence while giving up their space just for the sake of this book of mine. I love you.

Thanks to every passionate producer who has believed in this work since day one.

Thanks to all the chefs who have lent themselves to the collaboration, consenting to our invasion in their wonderful kitchens.

Finally, I thank those who did not support us, remaining mute to our requests: They have been a stimulus for us to continue the great work aimed at enhancing a spirit too often forgotten by us Italians and that will soon receive its deserved recognition in Europe and in the world.

RESOURCES

Bibliography

M. Alberini. Breve storia di Michele Savonarola, seguita da un compendio del suo "Libreto de tutte le cosse se manzano." Editoriale Programma: Treviso, 1991.

G. Baiguera, U. Caselli. *Manuale del Barman.* Giunti Editore: Firenze, 2016.

G. Bulgarelli, S. *Flamigni. Guida practica alla piante officinali. Osservare, riconoscere, e utilizzare le più diffuse piante medicinali italiane ed europee,* Ulrico Hoepli Editore: Milano.

S. Califano. *Storia dell'Alchimia. Misticismo ed esoterismo all'origine della chimica moderna.* Store Firenze University Press: Firenze, 2015.

G. Cremonini *Il Liquore. Itinerario tecnico descrittivo per conoscere I liquor.* La Galiverna: Battaglia Terme,1986.

L. Gerosa. *L'alba delle droghe. Contesti, culture, rituali.* Castelvecchi: Roma, 1997.

C. Hildebrand. *La grammatica delle spezie.* Gribaudo: Milano, 2018.

R. Jacobus Forbes. *Short History of the Art of Distillation: From the Beginnings Up to the Death of Cellier Blumenthal.* E.J. Brill: 1970.

V. Marzi, Giuseppe De Mastro. *Piante Officinali, Coltivazione, trattamenti di post-raccolta, contenuti di principi attivi, impieghi in vari settori industriali ed erboristici.* Mario Adda Editore: Bari, 2008.

J. McDaniel Brown, A. Renard Miller. *La guida Mixellany ai Vermut e altri aperitive.* Readrink: Bisceglie (BA), 2014.

———. *Viaggio di spirito: La storia del bere Vol. 1.* Readrink: Bisceglie (BA), 2015.

———. *Viaggio di spirito: La storia del bere Vol. 2.* Readrink: Bisceglie (BA), 2016.

G. Signore. *Storia della Farmacia.* Edizioni Edra: Milano, 2013.

G. Sinoué. *La via per Isfahan.* Neri Pozza: Vicenza, 1989.

Web References

www.accademiaitalianastoriafarmacia.org

www.assenzioitalia.it

www.bisd303.org

www.danielesegnini.it

www.federica.unina.it

grupsderecerca.uab.cat/arnau/

www.inherba.it

iniziazioneantica.altervista.org

www.lascuolamedicasalernitana.beniculturali.it

www.marenostrumrapallo.it

www.my-personaltrainer.it

www.tecnoalimenti.altervista.org

www.treccani.it

www.tuscanypeople.com

www.venividivici.us

www.whiskyitaly.it

INDEXES

Amari by Name

Amari by Region

General Index

Page numbers in *italics* refer to illustrations.

senna leaves: Amaro Svedese, 105
sensory analysis, 75, 82
Serge of Yugoslavia, 94
setmin, 87
Seu, Pier Daniele, 238
Seu Pizza Illuminati, 238
Severino, Justin, 196
sfumato, 105
Sherry Butt, 200
Shi, Stella, 232
shurhuq, 177
Siano family, 156
Sibyl, 138
Siegal, T. J., 213
Siegert, Johann, 189
Signore Di Diano, 158
Silybum marianum, 41
silymarin, 41
Simaroubaceae, quassia amara, 49
sirocco, 177
Slavonian oak barrels: Alpestre, 80;
    Alpestre Special Reserve 1983,
    80; Amaro Braulio, 97; Amaro
    del Boss, 171; Amaro Erbes
    Gran Riserva, 142; Vecchio
    Amaro del Capo Riserva del
    Centenario, 167
smallpox, 195
snake bites, 44
Soldatini, Marcello, 90
soldier's herb. *See* yarrow
Sopranos, The, 196
Sorbo, Enzo, 157
sow thistle: L'Amaro di Baragiano, 163
Sparvieri family, 152
speziale, 103
spritz, ix
Sri Lanka: cinnamon, 53; green
    cardamom, 53
"stable meadows," 120
St. Agrestis, 192
St. Anthony's Liquor, Ferdinando, 74
St. Hubertus, 95
St. John's wort: Amaro Casoni
    Heritage, 126
St. Peter's Wort, 65
Straub, Jacques, 210
Straub's Manual of Mixed Drinks
    (Straub), 210
Strega, 1970s crisis, viii
sugar: amaro classifications, 9; chicory,
    42; cinnamon, 53; import of, xi;
    julab, 19; *Manuale del Barman*,
    2; Renaissance, 25; vermouth, 12
Sur la lecture (Proust), 72
Sweden: amaro etymology, 9; Amaro
    Tonico con Erbe Svedesi, 143;
    glogg, 53; Gotland's Bittar, 186;
    green cardamom, 53; quassia,
    49; sacred tincture, 93
Sweet Polly, 213
Sweetbreads of Calves' Throat,
    Lampascioni, and Amaro
    Imperatore, 225
Syzygium aromaticum, 54

T
Tahiti vanilla, 62
Taneda, 34, 99
tansy: Alpestre, 80; Amaro Cerberus,
    133; Amaro San Carlo, 89;
    Amaro Venti, 100
tarássein, 51
Taraxacum officinale, 51
Tasmanian devil, 86
tasting rules, 75
tea leaves: Amarcardo Black,
    168; Amaro d'Abruzzo 77,
    147; Barruell, 144–45;
    Jannamaro, 151; karkadè,
    57; L'Amaro di Baragiano,
    163; Marseille Amaro, 191–
    92; red, 57, 144–45;
    wild fennel, 56
Tegtmeyer, Cindy, 189
temperature: amaro tasting,
    74; analytical tasting, 75;
    maceration, 6
Tesauro, Jason, xii
theriac, 24; Amaro Svedese, 105
thieves, Marseille Amaro, 191
thistle, xi, 10. *See also* milk thistle
thujone, 38
Tillino family, 93
Tomasi, Tomaso, 106
Tommy's Margarita, 214
Tommy's Restaurant, 214
tonic: amari definition, 34; bitter
    tastes, xii; cinchona elixir, 12;
    condurango, 44; dandelion,
    51; elecampane, 45; Elixir
    di China, 12; gentian, 45;
    gentianella, 46; Medical School
    of Salerno, xi; nepitella, 68;
    nutmeg, 58; quassia amara,
    49; rosemary, 61; verbena, 52;
    wormwood, 38
tonka bean: Amaro Cerberus, 133;
    Amaro Francescano, 134; Amaro
    Guelfo, 98; Amaro Salento, 161;
    Amaro Tenace, 115
Tonutti, Ivano, 91
Toro family, 149
Toso, Francesco Dal, 110
toute-épice, 61
Traditional Piedmontese Agri-food
    Products, 91
transhumance, 138
Trappist: Amaro Tre Fontane, 144;
    Antico Liquorificio Trappisti
    delle Tre Fontane, 141
Tre Fontane beer, 141
trifoglio fibrino, 52
trifoliata, 52
Trojan War, 34
Trombino, Ivano, 166
truffle: Amaro al Tartufo Pagnani,
    141; amaro classifications, 10;
    Amaro Vallenera al Tartugo
    Nero di Norcia, 135
Truffle Fashioned, 209

trumpet gentian: Tintura Stomatica,
    108
Turmbachhof farm, 105
turmeric, 44, *44*; Amaro Svedese, 105;
    China Martini, 92

U
Udine friars, 119
ÙE Acquavite d'Uva, 121
ugly radicchio, 42
Ugolino, 84
Ulrich, Domenico, 82
ultrasound extraction, 8
umami, xii
Umberto I, 170
Umberto II of Savoy, 94
unnimaffissu, 178
Usai, Daniele, 229

V
Valentini family, 107
valerian: Amaro Cortina, 111; Amaro
    Pugliese, 161; Elisir Novasalus,
    106
Vallet, Henri, 190
vanilla, 62
Vanilla planifolia, 62
Varnelli family, 137, 138
Vena, Pasquale, 163, 164
Venezuela: Bolivar, 189; quassia
    amara, 49
Venice, xi, 26, 68
Venus: myrtle, 58; verbena, 52
verbena, 52; Alta Verde, 102
Verbenaceae, 52
Verbena officinalis, 52
vermifuge: boldo, 38; gentian, 45
vermouth, 12; Bordiga 1888, 92;
    Compagnia dei Caraibi,
    87; Gamondi Spirits di
    Toso, 85; Glep Beverages,
    86; Golden Mai Tai, The,
    206; Justin Severino, 196;
    La Canellese, 89; Luigi
    Fassio, 87; Nunquam, 130;
    Roman chamomile, 40; Turin
    Vermouth, 81, 94; Vermouth
    Vandalo, 86; White Vermouth
    of Prato, 130; wormwood,
    38
Vignale family, 125
Vigo, Francis, 193
violets, 19
Virgin Mary, 41
vis, 135
Visconti, Attilio, 131
Vissani, Gianfranco, 220
vitamin C: chinotto, 65; hibiscus
    flowers, 57
vitamins: chinotto, 65; hibiscus
    flowers, 57; jujube, 66; moringa,
    68; pomegranate, 177
Vittorio Emanuele II, 109

Considered one of the most talented Italian bartenders at the international level, **Matteo Zamberlan**, a.k.a. Matteo Zed, won 3rd place at the Bacardi Legacy Cocktail Competition in 2012, 2nd place at the Diplomático World Tournament in 2013, and then became the 2015 world champion for the Americas in the Belvedere Martini Challenge.

In 2013, intrigued by Japanese mixing, he had the opportunity to work in the employment of the great master Hidetsugu Ueno at Tokyo's highly acclaimed Bar High Five, where he learned to make the Japanese concept of hospitality his own. In the same year Matteo became a judge for the World's 50 Best Bars. He has worked with many national and foreign trade magazines including *Drinks International*, *Bartenders Magazine*, and *BarLife*. His cocktails were included in Gaz Regan's book, *101 Best New Cocktails*. In 2015, Matteo was named Best Italian bartender abroad by *Bargiornale*. He lived in New York for four years where he worked for the best clubs in the city, including Joe Bastianich's Del Posto, the highly acclaimed Zuma, Sean Muldoon and Jack McGarry's Blacktail, and Armani Ristorante on Fifth Avenue, serving as a consultant and operation manager in the Trattoria and Ammazzacaffè projects in Brooklyn with a bar program totally focused on amari. In Rome, he created the first European amaro bar, Il Marchese, and in 2017 founded amarobsession.com, the first website in the world to uncover and tell the story of the Italian amaro.